CURRICULUM IN EARLY CHILDHOOD EDUCATION

Curriculum in Early Childhood Education: Re-examined, Rediscovered, Renewed provides a critical examination of the sources, aims, and features of early childhood curricula. Providing a theoretical and philosophical foundation for examining teaching and learning, this book will provoke discussion and analysis among all readers. How has theory been used to understand, develop, and critique curriculum? Whose perspectives are dominant and whose are ignored? How is diversity addressed? What values are explicit and implicit?

The book first contextualizes the historical and research base of early childhood curriculum, and then turns to discussions of various schools of theory and philosophy that have served to support curriculum development in early childhood education. An examination of current curriculum frameworks is offered, from both the US and abroad, including discussion of the Project Approach, Creative Curriculum, *Te Whāriki*, and Reggio Emilia. Finally, the book closes with chapters that enlarge the topic to curriculum-being-enacted through play and that summarize key issues while pointing out future directions for the field. Offering a broad foundation for examining curriculum in early childhood, readers will emerge with a stronger understanding of how theories and philosophies intersect with curriculum development.

Nancy File is Associate Professor in Early Childhood Education at the University of Wisconsin-Milwaukee.

Jennifer J. Mueller is Associate Professor in Early Childhood Education at the University of Wisconsin-Milwaukee.

Debora Basler Wisneski is Associate Professor in Early Childhood Education at the University of Wisconsin-Milwaukee.

CURRICULUM IN EARLY CHILDHOOD EDUCATION

Re-examined, Rediscovered, Renewed

Edited by
Nancy File, Jennifer J. Mueller, and
Debora Basler Wisneski

Routledge
Taylor & Francis Group

NEW YORK AND LONDON

First published 2012
by Routledge
711 Third Avenue, New York, NY 10017

Simultaneously published in the UK
by Routledge
2 Park Square, Milton Park, Abingdon, Oxon OX14 4RN

Routledge is an imprint of the Taylor & Francis Group, an informa business

© 2012 Taylor & Francis

The right of Nancy File, Jennifer J. Mueller, and Debora Basler Wisneski to be identified as authors of the editorial material, and of the authors for their individual chapters, has been asserted in accordance with sections 77 and 78 of the Copyright, Designs and Patents Act 1988.

Library of Congress Cataloging in Publication Data
Curriculum in early childhood education : re-examined, rediscovered, renewed / Nancy File, Jennifer J. Mueller, Debora Basler Wisneski, editors.
p. cm.
Includes bibliographical references and index.
1. Early childhood education – Curricula. 2. Curriculum planning. I. File, Nancy. II. Mueller, Jennifer J. III. Wisneski, Debora Basler.
LB1139.4.C874 2011
372.19 – dc22
2011010685

ISBN13: 978-0-415-88110-4 (hbk)
ISBN13: 978-0-415-88111-1 (pbk)
ISBN13: 978-0-203-80436-0 (ebk)

Typeset in Bembo
by Taylor and Francis Books

CONTENTS

CONTRIBUTORS

Mindy Blaise is an Associate Professor in the Department of Early Childhood Education at the Hong Kong Institute of Education. Her research interests include troubling and remaking early childhood teaching and research. With Professor Marilyn Fleer and colleagues from Monash University, Mindy has designed and delivered an innovative professional learning program, Contemporary Child Development, aimed at challenging practitioners to remake early childhood curriculum and teaching "otherwise." Her recent book *Teaching Across the Early Years* (co-written with Joce Nuttall) draws from critical theory and sets out to trouble the taken-for-granted assumptions and practices of early years teaching. She is currently conducting a sensory ethnography in Hong Kong and drawing from posthumanism for developing new insights on and understandings of dealing and living with difference.

Kathryn R. Branscomb is a Senior Research Analyst at Applied Survey Research (ASR) in San Jose, California, where she specializes in early care and education research. Prior to her work at ASR, Dr. Branscomb was an Assistant Professor of Early Childhood Education at the University of Oklahoma, where she taught coursework in infant/toddler care and development. She has applied experience as an infant classroom teacher and developmental assessment coordinator and conducts research in the areas of infant care, teacher preparation, and family support.

Cary A. Buzzelli is Professor of Early Childhood Education at Indiana University, Bloomington. He teaches courses in early childhood education and early childhood special education. His research focuses on the moral dimensions of teaching. With Bill Johnston, he co-authored the book *The Moral Dimensions of Teaching: Language, Power, and Culture in Classroom Interaction*. They also have published several articles on this topic. Dr. Buzzelli is currently engaged in a research project examining the moral dimensions of the teaching of economics in primary classrooms. This is a joint project with his wife, who is an economist. He spent a sabbatical semester in New Zealand, during which his two sons spent a term in a New Zealand primary school.

Betsy J. Cahill is the J. Paul Taylor Endowed Professor of Early Childhood Teacher Education at New Mexico State University. Dr. Cahill's research areas include the construction of gender and sexuality of young children, and the professional development of teachers.

Katherine Delaney is currently a doctoral student in the Curriculum and Instruction program at the University of Wisconsin-Madison. Prior to this she taught as a Lecturer in the Early Childhood Education program at the University of Wisconsin-Milwaukee. For several years, Ms. Delaney taught three- and four-year-old children in both university and urban preschool settings. Her research interests include pre-kindergarten policy, curriculum and enactment, urban education and culturally relevant pedagogy, and the use of funds of knowledge in curriculum development and implementation for young children.

Nancy File is an Associate Professor at the University of Wisconsin-Milwaukee in the Early Childhood Education program. Dr. File's research interests focus on teacher–child interaction and early childhood curriculum. She is interested as well in teacher education issues and questions, in a theoretical sense as well as on the ground in her teaching of preservice and inservice teachers. She taught mixed-age groups of preschoolers for nine years, mostly in campus-based child development laboratory programs.

Tammy L. Gibson received her MA in Curriculum and Instruction in 2006, and is currently a doctoral student of early childhood and critical pedagogy at New Mexico State University. Her interests are in feminism and gender issues within early childhood education. Ms. Gibson has taught at Dona Ana Community College and is co-director and lead teacher at the Learning Tree Preschool in Las Cruces, New Mexico. Ms. Gibson has taught early childhood for 11 years.

Carla B. Goble is the George Kaiser Family Foundation Endowed Professor of Child Development and Coordinator of the Child Development Academic Program at Tulsa Community College. Dr. Goble's other professional experiences include Child and Parenting Specialist with the Guidance Division of the Oklahoma State Department of Health and early childhood classroom teacher in the public schools and child care community. In 2003, she received the Oklahoma Friends of Education Outstanding Contributions to Early Childhood Education Award. She is also a graduate fellow of Zero to Three's Leaders for the 21st Century Fellowship Program.

Elizabeth Graue is a Professor in the Department of Curriculum and Instruction at the University of Wisconsin-Madison and Associate Director at the Wisconsin Center for Education Research. An early childhood educator and research methodologist by training, her research focuses on policy and practice in the early elementary grades. Dr. Graue's latest work focuses on measures of quality in elementary schools and on professional development for public preK teachers that weaves together developmentally responsive early mathematics and reciprocal funds of knowledge.

J. Amos Hatch is Professor of Theory and Practice in Teacher Education at the University of Tennessee. He is a qualitative researcher who has published numerous studies in the areas of young children's social relationships, teacher philosophies and practices, and urban teacher education. Dr. Hatch has written or edited a number of books, including most recently *Critical Pedagogy and Teacher Education in the Neoliberal Era* (co-edited with Susan Groenke). He was co-executive editor (with Richard Wisniewski) of *Qualitative Studies in Education* for four years and is currently co-editor (with Susan Benner) of the *Journal of Early Childhood Teacher Education*.

Lucinda G. Heimer is an Assistant Professor of Early Childhood Education at Wheelock College. Her research agenda includes a continued focus on larger systemic influences using critical, sociological, and post-structural perspectives in the hopes that insight and continual adjustment of policy and curriculum can be made to better meet the needs, abilities, and talents of all children. Implicit in this agenda is the desire to understand connections between preK and K-12 educators and policy professionals. She has taught many undergraduate and graduate courses, and she has supervised students in multiple urban school districts in preK, K, and first and second grade settings. Prior to joining Wheelock College, Dr. Heimer worked in educational institutions in both public and private sectors. Along with 10 years of higher education teaching experience, she has taught in preschool and elementary school classrooms. In addition, she has directed preschool programs in a university lab school and a parent cooperative preschool. Her most humbling and poignant work occurred as she worked with children and families on American Indian reservations in both New Mexico and Northern Wisconsin.

Judy Harris Helm assists schools and early childhood programs in integrating research and new methods through her consulting and training company Best Practices, Inc. Dr. Helm began her career teaching first grade, then taught, directed, and designed early childhood and primary programs as well as training teachers at the community college, undergraduate, and graduate levels. Included among the seven books she has authored, co-authored, or edited are *Young Investigators: The Project Approach in the Early Years*; *The Power of Projects*; *Windows on Learning*; *Teaching Your Child to Love Learning: A Guide to Doing Projects at Home*; and *Teaching Parents to Do Projects at Home*. She is currently principal design consultant for two new birth through eighth grade 21st Century Community Learning Centers, which will feature project work and engaged learning.

Diane M. Horm is currently the George Kaiser Family Foundation Endowed Chair of Early Childhood Education and Founding Director of the Early Childhood Education Institute (ECEI) at the University of Oklahoma at Tulsa. Through the ECEI, Dr. Horm is leading several applied research initiatives, including program evaluation research in collaboration with Oklahoma's State Pilot Program to Expand and Enhance Infant/Toddler Programming and Tulsa's Educare programs. Prior to her 2006 appointment at the University of Oklahoma she held faculty and administrative positions at the University of Rhode Island (URI), including Associate Dean of the College of Human Sciences, Professor of Human Development and Family Studies, and Director of the URI Child Development Centers. Horm was a visiting scholar at the U.S. Department of Education's National Institute on Early Childhood Development and Education and is a graduate fellow of Zero to Three's Leaders for the 21st Century Fellowship Program.

Sara Michael-Luna is an Assistant Professor of Early Childhood Education at Queens College, CUNY. She studies early childhood language and literacy in multilingual children. Dr. Michael-Luna has published empirical work examining how multilingual children and teachers understand racial, cultural, and linguistic assumptions in curriculum and pedagogy. She is currently examining the role curriculum and pedagogy play in emergent bilinguals' pre-literacy development and how multilingual early childhood teachers and teacher candidates understand the different ideologies present in their field placement curriculum and pedagogy.

Jennifer J. Mueller is an Associate Professor in the Early Childhood Education program at the University of Wisconsin-Milwaukee. She was a primary public school teacher for several years before entering the academy. She teaches courses supporting preservice and inservice teachers to critically reflect on how the larger sociocultural contexts of their work shape their approaches to teaching and learning in diverse and urban classrooms. Her research follows this line and focuses on issues of teacher identity and how constructions of race, socioeconomic status, gender, and sexuality frame how teachers take up teacher preparation and education. She has published articles and book chapters on these topics. She was the recipient of a UWM Distinguished Undergraduate Teaching Award.

Stuart Reifel is a Professor in the Early Childhood Education program at the University of Texas at Austin, where he holds the Cissy McDaniel Parker endowed fellowship. His interest in early childhood classrooms is based on his own nursery school and kindergarten teaching experiences, which brought him to research play. Over the years Dr. Reifel has looked at block construction, social relationships, and teacher thinking about play, with a major interest in the theories that help us understand them. His proudest achievement is the work his students do.

Jenny R. Ritchie holds the position of Associate Professor in Early Childhood Teacher Education at Te Whare Wānanga o Wairaka—Unitec Institute of Technology, Auckland, New Zealand. Her teaching and research have focused on supporting early childhood educators and teacher educators to enhance their praxis in terms of enacting an awareness of cultural, environmental, and social justice issues. She has recently led three consecutive two-year studies funded by the New Zealand Teaching and Learning Research Initiative, focusing on implementing early childhood pedagogies reflecting these commitments.

Sharon Ryan is Associate Professor of Early Childhood Education at Rutgers, the State University of New Jersey. She has worked in the early childhood field as a preschool teacher, consultant, curriculum advisor, and special educator. Dr. Ryan uses a range of qualitative and mixed methods designs to research early childhood curriculum and policy, teacher education, and the potential of critical theories for rethinking early childhood practices. She has published a number of articles, book chapters, and reports in these areas.

Mariana Souto-Manning is Associate Professor of Early Childhood Education in the Department of Curriculum and Teaching at Teachers College, Columbia University. From a critical perspective, Dr. Souto-Manning examines the sociocultural and historical foundations of early schooling, language development, and literacy practices. She studies how children, families, and teachers from diverse backgrounds shape and are shaped by discursive practices. Her work can be found in journals such as *Early Child Development and Care*, *Journal of Early Childhood Research*, *Journal of Early Childhood Literacy*, *Journal of Research in Childhood Education*, *Research in the Teaching of English*, and *Teachers College Record*. Her most recent books are: *Freire, Teaching, and Learning: Culture Circles across Contexts*, and *Teachers Act Up!: Creating Multicultural Learning Communities through Theatre* (co-authored with Cahnmann-Taylor). She has received several early career and innovation in research awards.

Andrew J. Stremmel is Professor and Department Head in Teaching, Learning, and Leadership in the College of Education and Human Sciences at South Dakota State University. He is former Director of the Child Development Laboratory School at Virginia Polytechnic Institute & State University, where he was a faculty member for 15 years. Dr. Stremmel's research interests are in the area of early childhood teacher education, in particular teacher action research, and Reggio Emilia-inspired, inquiry-based approaches to early childhood teacher education and curriculum. He has co-edited two books, *Affirming Diversity through Democratic Conversations* and *Teaching and Learning: Collaborative Exploration of the Reggio Emilia Approach*. He also has co-authored the book *Teaching as Inquiry: Rethinking*

Curriculum in Early Childhood Education, which is the first comprehensive early childhood education text provoked and inspired by the Reggio Emilia Approach.

Debora Basler Wisneski is an Associate Professor at the University of Wisconsin-Milwaukee. She teaches courses in early childhood curriculum, early literacy, and play. Her research interests include qualitative collaborative research with teachers and children, exploring particularly the areas of classroom community building and making meaning of play. Dr. Wisneski was a classroom teacher in childcare, preschool, and kindergarten settings before entering academia. She has been published in the *European Early Childhood Education Research Journal*, the *Early Childhood Education Journal*, and the journal *Early Child Development and Care*. Wisneski is a member of the American Educational Research Association, the Association for the Study of Play, and the US Coalition for Play. She is currently President of the Association for Childhood Education International and proud mother of her two favorite players, Henry and William.

PREFACE

Our plans for this volume came from many conversations together as we revitalized our early childhood education-focused master's degree program. We are situated within a large metropolitan area, and many of our undergraduate alumni remain close by after they finish their degrees. On the one hand, an administrative push for program growth led us to consider drawing these alumni back for more coursework. On the other hand, we believed strongly that ongoing professional development and support for teachers were vital to their work in the classroom. We focused our graduate program and coursework revitalization on teachers still within their first several years of teaching. These are teachers who have survived the hectic pace of the first years of induction, and they are still honing their craft. In addition, we believe that as they navigate the waters of the early-career teacher, new questions will continue to arise.

We planned new coursework framed always around our own sensibility about what teachers need to do their jobs. We all spent several years in the classroom ourselves, and we are dedicated to helping others grow to become effective practitioners. Thus, we designed one course as an advanced examination of early childhood curriculum. It is from the issues and ideas we have discussed in this course that we found the idea to collect readings into one source that could serve as the backbone for expanding discussions into the history, nature, endeavors, and problems of curriculum.

Our thesis is that advanced examinations of curriculum should focus on, first, the underpinnings of what is done in the name of curriculum in the field. We want to provoke an examination of the links between theory and philosophy, educational aims and values, and curriculum planning and enactment. Therefore, we have focused one section of the volume on links between theorizing about curriculum and developing curriculum, examined from various vantage points. Second, we

share a belief that closer examinations of curriculum require more critical examinations of our field. In this volume we have asked contributors to examine claims,
identify more clearly what is not explicit, and ask questions. We did not want to
produce a volume that describes "how to do" curriculum. Rather, we want
to invite a multi-faceted examination of what we've been doing in the name of
curriculum and how we can question anew and think differently about it.

We intentionally drew from a wide range of contributors. It is the case that the
voices of critical theorists in early childhood have often provided the basis for
questioning and thinking differently. Though, Moss (2007) helps us to remember
the ease with which we can take our paradigmatic values for granted and deem
them "better," and that this negatively affects the efficacy of important dialogue. It
is important, since we all share a vested interest in the field and in children, to
explore the relationships across and amongst views, beliefs, and ideas. We found the
work of all of our authors to be thoughtful and to inspire deeper examination of
curriculum decision-making.

We did not provide a common definition of curriculum to the contributors, nor
did we create one among ourselves. We have, instead, left this task to the authors.
We also leave it to you, the reader. Is curriculum the set of materials arriving in the
boxed kit? The material in the teachers' manual? A set of aims and content? A set of
principles accompanied by exemplars? Something both explicit and hidden?
A contextualized set of lived experiences that unfolds individually within each
classroom? Each of these definitions sets up something unique to be examined, and
each has some area of traction within the field. The multiplicity of understandings
constructed around the concept of curriculum indicates the complexity of the
teaching–learning process.

We acknowledge upfront that this volume is necessarily limited. Teaching is
about much more than planning and enacting curriculum. Planned curricula and
implemented curricula are different beasts. Curricula are enacted within a complex
web of classrooms, institutions, families, neighborhoods, communities, states, and
countries. We want to make clear that these realities are crucial to understand, and
that this volume necessarily limits the viewpoint in order to be manageable.

Finally, we have focused the volume on the United States context. While limiting, this also creates a more manageable piece to examine. Two chapters pose
somewhat of an exception to this focus. First, we have included a chapter examining the Reggio Emilia framework. The author, Andrew Stremmel, has focused
upon applications within the United States. Also, we asked a colleague in New
Zealand, Jenny Ritchie, to write about the national curriculum for young children,
Te Whāriki. She has paired with Cary Buzzelli to extend their thinking about aspects
of this curriculum to the United States context.

As we write this, we are aware of unique events within our own context and
how they shape teachers and teaching. Our home state of Wisconsin is embroiled in
a nationally broadcast showdown between the newly elected governor and legisla-
tors regarding a bill intended to address short-term budget deficits over the next

several months. The showdown has come, not so much from proposed cuts to the benefits received by public employees, which have been largely conceded as necessary, but from proposals aimed at drastically changing public employee unions, stripping them of almost all bargaining rights. In the highly charged political atmosphere, public employees, and very often teachers as the prime exemplar, have often been belittled and blamed, with many asserting that the state's current economic woes lie at their feet. One of our graduate students, a public school teacher, spoke just yesterday of how difficult it has been to sustain morale in this climate.

We know of the important work done by teachers. We are distressed at how often that work goes unrecognized, or is changed in the story to become unrecognizable as what we see happening in classrooms. Therefore, we affirm that teachers have important stories to tell and voices to be heard as we continue to examine what curriculum has been and what we hope it could be.

That said, we acknowledge a whole host of teachers in our own lives, who have pushed us to learn and provided a perspective we found helped to make us who we are today. Our teachers have been those who have formally occupied that role, as well as those who have informally served as mentors and co-learners with us, often because they are our professional colleagues.

Individually, Nancy thanks her extended family for living the value that education is important, and her parents in particular for encouraging a life beyond the small town in which they lived. As well, she thanks Jim, Mallory, and Peri for giving her the support needed for this and other professional endeavors. Jennifer thanks her family, of course. She also is indebted to her students, many of whom are now teachers themselves, for always pushing her thinking, causing her to question, and making her a better scholar. Debora thanks her extended family, who have always encouraged her, the Friday Girls and SAW for their supportive friendship, and Aron for everything.

Finally, we must thank this volume's contributors. It was extremely gratifying to know throughout the process that others, like us, thought this was a good idea. We have had lively conversations among ourselves while reading the chapters together, and we hope that you will also find that they trigger thought and debate.

Reference

Moss, P. (2007). Meetings across the paradigmatic divide. *Educational Philosophy and Theory*, 39, pp. 229–45.

Part I
Introduction

In this section our aim is to consider the context within which early childhood curriculum has been constructed and studied. Obviously, this topic alone could fill an entire volume. We are, therefore, necessarily brief in drawing attention to selected themes that we think help to set the tone for the sections that follow. Good sources abound which take up these topics in further detail, and these are noted in the reference sections of both chapters that follow.

In Chapter 1, Debora Wisneski takes up the topic of our field's history around curriculum. Her approach is critical, as she relates stories that are not a part of our collective narrative. Operating from an understanding that history shapes the present and impacts the field's identity, she offers alterative perspectives on who we as early childhood professionals are, and, thus, who we might be.

The role of Chapter 2 is to provide a review of research-based ways of knowing about curriculum. Nancy File explores a range of stances toward scholarly inquiry, including quantitative and qualitative approaches and reflective work published by teacher-researchers. Recognizing the overwhelming importance given to questions of "what works" in curriculum research, she also critiques the sources of those questions and the adequacy of positivist/post–positivist approaches for providing the answers being sought.

In this section we illustrate one of our aims for this volume, that it introduce questions and examine the claims and canon of the early childhood field. We believe that work on curriculum requires that we identify what is both explicit and implicit within the field and submit these topics to ongoing dialogue.

1

"SILENT VOICES OF KNOWING" IN THE HISTORY OF EARLY CHILDHOOD EDUCATION AND CURRICULUM

Debora Basler Wisneski

Introduction

When I was an undergraduate student at the University of Missouri-Columbia, I threw myself into my newly adopted professional field of early childhood education (ECE) by becoming a member of the Association for Childhood Education International (ACEI) under the guidance and mentorship of Dr. Stevie Hoffman. Around my junior year of undergraduate studies, I was elected to ACEI's executive board as a student representative. Intent on being well informed about the organization and my new responsibilities, I combed all the volumes of *Childhood Education* and historical documents of the International Kindergarten Union found in the library. These mapped the professional conversations and actions of the organization's earliest leaders, such as Patty Smith Hill and Susan Blow. At the same time, I found myself at conference meetings surrounded by experienced teachers witnessing to one another of the beauty, joy, and heartache of teaching and learning with their students. What I discovered through the readings and ACEI members were stories of women committed to serving young children and passionate about providing the most dignified education and care to all young children. I learned quite a bit about curriculum and instruction through the traditional designated coursework prescribed by my university. Yet it was the stories that Stevie and her colleagues told of their years of teaching young children and the stories of these early leaders that may have influenced me the most. Piaget and Dewey may have held the highest honors in leading the way for practitioners through theory, but it was the stories of the teachers' lives and their statements of wisdom that shaped me into the teacher I became (and am still becoming).

I was reminded of Stevie and many other early childhood educator stories when I was teaching an "Introduction to Early Childhood Education" course this past semester. Our class was critically examining the family tree typically presented in textbooks of early childhood, beginning with Plato and Aristotle, jumping to Comenius, Pestalozzi, and Froebel, on to Dewey and Piaget. One young woman posed the following question: "What about all the teachers who actually taught children and implemented these theories? While these ideas about education sound good, I would really like to know what the teachers thought. What do real teachers think about curriculum?"

These questions have been quite common throughout my years of working with preservice teachers. I imagine that many new teachers are looking for examples of mentor teachers for inspiration and guidance. As Lascarides and Hinitz (2000) have suggested, our history helps define who we are as educators in the field of early childhood education. The stories shared about the educators who have preceded us can demonstrate how ideas about curriculum have evolved and provide the context for understanding the theories and practices related to curriculum. However, when we look at how the history of early childhood education is presented in texts and the dominant discourse, we see limited examples of teachers as innovators of curriculum. Thus, our view of the field and of curriculum remains limited for early childhood teachers.

In this chapter I briefly highlight how our written history of early childhood education often leaves the stories of teachers' lives and contributions to curriculum unexamined. Then I share stories of teachers and others who are not usually presented in our condensed versions of history but who have influenced early childhood education and curriculum and whose lives have the potential to continue to influence how early childhood educators address curriculum. Much like Ayers (1992), I still believe "recovering the voice of the teacher—usually a woman, increasingly a person of color, often a member of the working poor—is an essential part of reconceptualizing the field of early childhood education" (p. 266). As the students in my class are fully aware, if anyone knows curriculum intimately and most deeply it must be the teacher. Yet, my undergraduate students also know full well that the teacher is often marginalized in the current American discourse of curriculum. As another student stated in a writing assignment:

> I'm not trying to make enemies of school administrators and those who create legislation like NCLB [No Child Left Behind]. It is doubtful that these people are out to sabotage education and despise teachers and their opinions. *However, the trend in education in the 21st century does not take into account the teacher's perspective* of how children learn and what they can achieve in the classroom.
>
> (student assignment, emphasis the author's)

In relation to curriculum, Ayers described an image of teachers in the early 1990s that has only become more solidified in the current culture of school reform and accountability. He stated:

Teachers are expected to "cover" the curriculum, to complete a textbook, to move children through a prescribed course of study. Teachers are reduced to assembly-line workers, clerks, and worse—they are expected to do their jobs, to ask no questions, to follow orders, to passively convey the stuff of learning to inert and inanimate youngsters.

(Ayers, 1992, p. 258)

Currently, in the US, teachers' voices are the "voices of silent knowing" that can help problematize and expand what we know about early childhood curriculum (Cannella, 2002). In searching for stories of teachers' voices within American history, I attempt to follow the questions Cannella (2002) suggests we ask, using a Foucaultian postmodern perspective, such as: What knowledges (of teachers) have been excluded or disqualified? Whose truths (about curriculum and teachers) have been hidden? What groups gained control over others through dominant discourses? By exploring these voices, perhaps early childhood educators may re-discover a part of their history that helps them re-think and re-shape their identities as teachers and curriculum planners, designers, and innovators.

A Condensed and Incomplete History: A Brief Review of ECE Texts and Textbooks

In 1987 Lascarides and Hinitz (2000) surveyed undergraduates in early childhood education to discover how much history was a part of their teacher training. They discovered that early childhood preservice teachers were rarely offered a separate course in the history of early childhood education and the history that they received was partial and not well defined. The researchers' concern was that future early childhood teachers lacked the historical knowledge of the field that was necessary to develop a professional identity. While professional organizations may occasionally sponsor a "history" session at annual conferences or graduate programs may provide a course examining early childhood education history, the topic is most commonly approached in undergraduate introduction course textbooks (e.g. Driscoll & Nagel, 2008; Feeney et al., 2010; Bredekamp, 2011; Morrison, 2011). Unfortunately, textbooks provide a condensed and mainstream view of the field which potentially limits the knowledge of our history. Generally, our history is presented within three areas: (1) major historic figures—the heroes and heroines, such as Caroline Pratt and John Dewey; (2) popular curricular models or theories, such as Maria Montessori or Jean Piaget; and (3) political, public, or governmental programs, such as Head Start. Some historic topics may address all three areas, such as Froebel as the "father of kindergarten" who designed a curriculum using "gifts and occupations" which eventually grew into the kindergarten movement in the US. The result of the way in which this information is presented may result, I believe, in misperceptions of how early childhood educators have developed and interacted with curriculum. As presented, it seems we have a few leaders such as Montessori, Dewey, or Piaget presented as the creators and keepers of curricular ideas, and that these ideas and/or curricula are disseminated outward to teachers, who are positioned as the purveyors or implementers of these curricula.

Furthermore, this presentation of our history gives the impression that the only leaders of curriculum theory or practice originated solely from white Western European individuals. Additionally, this leaves someone new to the field (or not so new) with the impression that these white Western European ways are the only ways to address curriculum and that only white people have done anything remarkable in the field of early childhood education. The same becomes evident when reviewing Lascarides and Hinitz's text (2000), when chapters are designated mostly to white individuals who influenced early childhood education and any chapters devoted to people of other races position the people as a minority group with only a few leaders, but mostly as a group that needs to be served by the white majority group. Some recent early childhood textbooks have begun to include minority leaders in the history of early childhood education. Bredekamp's latest edition (2011) does provide a small section acknowledging the contribution of African American women through the National Association of Colored Women, who in the early 1900s established black kindergartens in the south. However, with such a brief presentation we do not know how they enacted the curriculum; nor do we know more about the lives of these women that could provide a context for understanding their work in kindergarten curriculum.

So what other stories could be told about early childhood education and curriculum that might not have been told or have remained silenced? What counter-narratives may exist that can expand our knowledge? The following are brief examples of less familiar stories that are not often shared with undergraduate early childhood educators (as noted by their absence in standard introductory texts regarding ECE), but that offer intriguing images of those who have influenced early childhood education and curriculum.

Women in ECE: Reformers, Suffragists, and Radicals

The current image of the early childhood education teacher as passive conveyor of knowledge is quite the opposite of the teacher's role in early education and curriculum development in the US historically. Many of the founding mothers of early childhood education were hardly the genteel matrons huddled with small children, offering quiet songs and warm cookies. Rather, these women were deeply involved with the civil rights issues of their times and were advocates for the rights of all. One example of such a teacher is Ella Victoria Dobbs (1866–1952). The following synopsis of her life in early childhood education was drawn from the text *Dauntless Women in Childhood Education 1865–1931* (Snyder, 1972). (Further reading for more details of the lives of Dobbs and other reformers is recommended.)

Ella Victoria Dobbs began her career as an elementary school teacher in the US Midwest during the late 1800s. As she developed her teaching skills, she also became interested in and studied the manual arts, a form of teaching industrial manual work that was popular in high schools and colleges during the Industrial Revolution. She recognized that as children used their hands to make artistic and functional pieces through manual work they learned a great deal about character and content knowledge across disciplines. After studying with John Dewey and Arthur Dow at Columbia Teachers College, she became a Professor at the University of Missouri-Columbia and organized groups of teachers to experiment with different forms of "handwork" with children. The "handwork" eventually would resemble art and constructive play with materials such as clay, metal, textiles, and wood. Dobbs further explored children's hands-on work as curriculum by employing a scientific method of research with practicing teachers, who implemented the hands-on curriculum and documented the children's learning. These teachers would then adapt and create new methods of using materials with young children and Dobbs refined her thoughts on curriculum, believing that self-directed activity was critical to children's learning. The work of the children and teachers became so well regarded that Dewey himself visited the Missouri schools and sent his students to observe. What was unique about Dobbs' efforts was not just the type of curriculum she was espousing, but the manner in which she guided new teachers in classroom research (Snyder, 1972).

Dobbs not only was an innovator of curriculum and instruction, she also was a leader within the profession. In 1910, she founded the women's honor society, Pi Lambda Theta, responding to the fact that at the time women were not allowed in honor societies at universities. She was a founding member of the National Council of Primary Education and guided the group to merge with the International Kindergarten Union to create the Association for Childhood Education, striving for the increased use of self-directed activities for young children, more freedom of methods for teachers, and better collaboration between kindergarten teachers and primary grade teachers (Snyder, 1972).

Dobbs' interest in supporting teachers went beyond the field of early childhood education. She was heavily involved in the women's suffrage movement. Dobbs was a delegate to the last National American Woman Suffrage Association conference, and once the right to vote was won by women she helped begin the work of educating women about their rights through a new organization—the League of Women Voters. She helped open a Citizen School in Columbia, Missouri, and shared her commitment to active participation in citizenship with teachers. She recognized the necessity for teachers' voices to be heard in political matters to support classrooms, and urged teachers to educate the public about the matters of methodology and educational progress (Snyder, 1972). Snyder summarizes Dobbs' influence on early childhood education as follows:

> Ella Victoria Dobbs was outstanding for her broader interpretation of the role of teacher. First, the teacher should be an experimenter, one who by his scientific approach to the problems of education could himself contribute to

the greater knowledge of children and improved methods of teaching. Second, the teacher is a citizen—including women teachers—and must exercise the responsibilities of citizenship, attacking all forces inimical to a good life and identifying with those constructively working for a better society.

(Snyder, 1972, pp. 319–20)

Dobbs' teacher story offers much to be considered regarding thoughts and practices on curriculum. I wonder what an aspiring teacher might learn from having this image of an educator who constructs and experiments with curriculum with other teachers and children. What could it mean to new teachers to see an image of a teacher drawing deeply on content from the disciplines of study? What could it mean to see the image of a teacher as politically aware and active, striving for equality beyond the classroom walls? How can we better understand the idea of self-activity and self-direction in the context of the life of a teacher who had struggled for her own self-direction in citizenship, hampered by her placement in society based on her gender? The study of Dobbs' contribution to early childhood curriculum and the suffragist movement provides members of our field an opportunity to discuss the interrelatedness of educators' convictions, knowledge of content, and thus understanding of curriculum.

Upon further exploration of other leaders in early childhood education, it's clear that Dobbs was not the only early childhood educator who worked for civil rights in the US. Many early childhood educators were peace activists and civil rights activists, like Jane Addams and Florence Kelley. Furthermore, early childhood educators who were political and social activists were not only affluent or of Western European descent. Nor did these activist educators limit their influence within the field of early childhood education. One interesting example of an early childhood teacher of color who played a strong role in U.S. history is Shirley Chisholm. Most noted as the first African American woman to be elected to Congress in 1968 and the first to run for President in a major party of the US in 1972, Chisholm was a nursery school teacher at the beginning of her professional career. In 1946, after graduating from college, she began as a teacher's aide at the Mt. Calvary Child Care Center in Harlem and worked there for seven years. While working there she earned her Master's degree in early childhood education at Columbia University. Referring to teaching, she stated, "I was sure this was going to be my life's work" (Chisholm, 2010, p. 45). It was as a nursery school teacher that she began attending city council meetings and democratic club meetings to address the issues of her community. From this beginning she became a great advocate for the rights of minorities and women in American politics. While we may not know exactly how Shirley Chisholm addressed curriculum in her nursery school classroom, by reviewing her life story we may re-imagine our idea of an early childhood educator's role in society and thus re-imagine how we would address curriculum from that new perspective. Shirley Chisholm also provides us with an example of an

African American teacher—an image that is often limited in traditional early childhood history texts.

Minority Representation and Leadership in ECE: The Really Hidden History of Head Start

In the field of early childhood education and curriculum, rarely is leadership from minority communities presented as affecting education and curriculum. However, that is not to say that minority communities have had little impact in the field. One example is the influence of the Texas "Little Schools of 400," a preschool program first started by the League of United Latin American Citizens (LULAC) which became the inspiration for the federal Head Start program.

Many groups have been acknowledged as predecessors leading to the development of Head Start, such as the nursery school and infant school movements and various experimental programs at research institutions (Osborn, 1991; Zigler & Styfco, 2010). The story of LULAC and the "Little Schools" is not typically mentioned as part of Head Start's history in mainstream early childhood texts. However, according to historians of Mexican American education history (Barrera, 2006) and the history of the LULAC organization (Yarsinske, 2004) the Mexican American community of Texas inspired Lyndon B. Johnson to consider the power of early education in helping children in poverty.

Generally, research in Mexican American educational history has often portrayed Mexican Americans only as victims of discrimination and racism in schools and not as activists who helped establish their own education programs or institutions. However, from the perspective of the Texas Mexican community, Mexican Americans fought discrimination through establishing their own educational programs. In the case of Texas Mexicans in the late 1800s and early 1900s, young Mexican American children were systematically segregated from the public schools established by the white English-speaking community based on the children's lack of knowledge of the English language. The Mexican American community attempted to create quality schools for their Spanish-speaking children through private and religious sponsors. Yet more and more Spanish-speaking Mexican American children were entering the traditional English-speaking public schools, and there was concern for their underachievement in these settings. Felix Tijerina, the LULAC national president from 1956 to 1960, had the idea that Texas Mexican children would fare better in the public schools if they knew at least 400 English words by kindergarten age, an idea supported by some Hispanic academics at the time. So he created a system of "Little Schools of 400" for preschoolers based on this premise. In 1957 Tijerina found the resources to begin a pilot program with three children and hired Isabel Verver, a high school student with natural teaching abilities. The general program was to teach the children 400 basic words in English through a drill and practice method. Local school superintendents did not support the efforts since there were programs similar to this already in the English-speaking schools. Eventually, though, the "Little Schools" began to become popular within the Texas Mexican community. The "Little Schools" program was not without criticisms from the Texas Mexican community. Many feared that the schools were still segregating Texas Mexican children and forcing Americanization upon them. There was also debate about the "Little Schools" and their purpose among Mexican American educators. According to Barrera (2006), George I. Sanchez, a prominent professor at the University of Texas-Austin, criticized the "Little Schools" for supporting the idea that the main solution for the underachievement of Texas Mexican children was the teaching of English and ignoring the need to support their cultural heritage and Spanish language. Tijerina became an advisor to the Texas Education Agency and attempted to influence the newly established public preschools to adopt practices to support Spanish-speaking children. As the "Little Schools" and the preschools were established for Texas Mexican children, the former teacher-turned-Texas-governor Lyndon B. Johnson and his wife Ladybird Johnson met with LULAC and visited the schools. When Johnson became President of the United States he led the War on Poverty by creating a committee to plan a system of preschools for young children in poverty that became known as the Head Start program in the 1960s. While Johnson did not call upon LULAC and the teachers of the "Little Schools" to participate in the planning, the LULAC community to this day recognizes their contributions to the federal program (Yarsinske, 2004). In fact Judge Alfred Hernandez, another former president of LULAC, who passed away in 2010, attended the signing of the bill that authorized Head Start at the invitation of President Johnson. His obituary reads:

> In his work with LULAC, he was instrumental in establishing the "Little School of the 400", which was the basis for the Head Start Program, championed by "Lady Bird" Johnson, and signed into law by President Lyndon B. Johnson. He was invited to the signing of the bill by President Johnson, and dined at the White House.
>
> *(retrieved from http://www.legacy.com/obituaries/houstonchronicle/ obituary.aspx?n=alfred-j-hernandez&pid=145147073&fhid=10997)*

The history of LULAC, the "Little Schools," and Head Start can provide us lessons for today regarding early childhood education. The story helps demonstrate how the field of early childhood education shares a history with bilingual education. Perhaps our understanding of early childhood bilingual curriculum would be enhanced if we explored this relationship more deeply. This is critical when, according to current U.S. Census data, approximately 16% of the entire U.S. population is of Latino origin (http://quickfacts.census.gov/qfd/states/00000.html). Administrators of early childhood programs across the United States have reported concerns in meeting the needs of Latino families due to the limited number of bilingual or Latina/o teachers, a general lack of preparation of teachers to work with multicultural communities, and a lack of communication regarding services (Buysse et al., 2005). Recently Valdez and Franquiz (2010) have suggested that early childhood educators can better serve our young Hispanic students by focusing on developing a nuanced understanding of dual language learning that responds to distinct community differences within the larger group of Latinos in the US. They also have advocated for teachers to work as professional development communities to support their learning of language development and form coalitions with community groups and families. If early childhood teachers take heed of these recommendations, exploring more of the history of the Texas "Little Schools" may help early childhood teachers expand their knowledge of the Latino community's efforts in supporting bilingual curriculum.

A Teacher's Articulation of Neo-Humanist Philosophy through Early Childhood Curriculum

Stories of teachers and community groups who have an impact on curriculum in early childhood education should not be relegated to the distant past either. Indeed, there are teachers today who are making a difference in developing and implementing new curriculum outside the traditional discourse of the field. One such early childhood teacher is Niiti Gannon. Niiti was raised in Chicago, Illinois, but when she was 21 years old she went to India to be trained as a yogic nun in the service organization Ananda Marga. She explains her life path as follows:

> So when I was a young adult during the anti-Vietnam [War] era, I was restless to find out what was deeper and more meaningful than materialistic pursuits. At this time, I was introduced to meditation and loved it. I decided not to finish my studies to become a primary school teacher—which I was doing at the time—but rather to become a meditation teacher as there are too few meditation teachers in the world; especially woman meditation teachers.
>
> *(Niiti Gannon, personal communication, December 2010)*

Once Niiti received her training as a junior yogic nun, she learned to teach meditation and lived in several countries in the Far East. Eventually her job was to build schools for young children following the philosophy of neo-humanism as purported by Ananda Marga's founder, Prabhat Rainjan Sarkar. Sarkar wrote many books explaining the philosophy and how it related to education; however, there was no clear curriculum designed for early childhood at the time. Neo-humanism, according to Sarkar, is a yogic perception that all existence, living and non-living, is interconnected and an ethical system that requires one to become aware of the interconnectedness and to serve others (Ananda Rama Ac., 2000). Niiti, under her yogi name Anandanivedita, wrote a book called *Teach Me to Fly: Insights into Early Childhood Neo-Humanistic Education* (1999), chronicling her understandings of this philosophy and how it played out in curriculum and instruction of young children.

Niiti specifically explained how play, storytelling, the arts, and yoga can be used to teach children from a neo-humanist perspective, and how more familiar learning theories and teaching practices, such as Vygotskian theory, intersect with neo-humanist education. She also wrote children's literature to explain neo-humanist ideals to young children and designed curriculum books for her fellow teachers to use. Niiti's development of the curriculum for early childhood demonstrates the characteristics that neo-humanists expect teachers to possess: strength of character, righteousness, sense of social service, leadership capacity, advocacy, and the right to form policy.

Most current early childhood curriculum models profess to address the developmental needs of the "whole child," usually referencing the social, emotional, physical, and cognitive domains. What is often absent is the spiritual domain, even though the spiritual aspect of learning and growth were part the history of early childhood curriculum, as seen in Froebel's philosophy for kindergarten curriculum (Froebel, 2005) and Montessori's philosophy of education (Montessori, 1972), as well. Niiti's work in developing a neo-humanist curriculum reminds us that if we are to explore new ways of addressing curriculum we must go beyond developmental cognitive theories and truly open up the discussion to all domains of growth in children's lives. In addition to expanding our ideas about early childhood curriculum to the spiritual realm, Niiti is another example of how an early childhood teacher can take an active leadership role in theorizing and creating curriculum.

Conclusion

Our history teaches us who we are and who we can become. When reviewing the history of early childhood education and curriculum, it behooves us to explore the story of teachers. Teachers' lives provide the context in which curriculum is enacted on a daily basis, but also the context in which innovation and exploration of curriculum have occurred. The lives of teachers as curriculum innovators allow our conversation on and study of curriculum to expand. When we pay attention to teachers who are exploring ideas and philosophies outside of the mainstream hegemonic discourse of early childhood education (such as Ella Victoria Dobbs or Niiti Gannon) we find new ways of approaching how children learn and what they should learn. When we pay attention to teachers and social groups such as those within LULAC we see how early childhood education has a shared history and understanding to draw from, like bilingual education. We are given an example of how groups and individuals advocate for children through curriculum in different ways. Also, we are able to reframe our history not as one completely dominated by Western European ideas or by a majority culture but as a history that is inclusive to many peoples. This inclusion is important. First, as contributions from many cultures and ethnicities are presented as part of our history, more women and men from minority groups will see an image of themselves in the field and feel investment in a profession that is currently heavily dominated by white members. And second, when diverse ideas of early childhood curriculum are presented, we see a complex and thoughtful understanding of curriculum full of contentious issues in the lives of teachers and children rather than a monolithic determined "best practices" approach. When we pay attention to the stories of teachers' lives as part of our curricular history we are able to see how curriculum is part of the political and social historic context.

References

Ananda Rama Ac., Avtk. (Ed.) (2000). *Neo-humanist education: Documentation of neo-humanist education propounded by Prabhat Rainjan Sarkar.* Mainz, Germany: Ananda Marga Gurukula Publications.

Anandanivedita, Avk. (1999). *Teach me to fly: Insights into early childhood neo-humanistic education.* West Bengal, India: Gurukula Publications.

Ayers, W. (1992). Disturbances from the field: Recovering the voice of the early childhood teacher. In S. Kessler & B.B. Swadener (Eds.), *Reconceptualizing the early childhood curriculum: Beginning the dialogue* (pp. 256–66). New York: Teachers College Press.

Barrera, A. (2006). The "Little Schools" of Texas, 1897–1965: Educating Mexican American children. *American Education History Journal,* 33(2), 35–45.

Bredekamp, S. (2011). *Effective practices in early childhood education: Building a foundation.* New York: Pearson.

Buysse, V., Castro, D., West, T., & Skinner, M. (2005). Addressing the needs of Latino children: A national survey of state administrators of early childhood programs. *Early Childhood Research Quarterly,* 20(2), 146–63.

Cannella, G.S. (2002). *Deconstructing early childhood education: Social justice and revolution.* New York: Peter Lang.

Chisholm, S. (2010). *Unbought and unbossed: Expanded 40th edition.* Takerootmedia.com.

Driscoll, A. & Nagel, N.G. (2008). *Early childhood education, birth–8: The world of children, families, and educators.* New York: Pearson.

Feeney, S., Moravcik, E., Nolte, S., & Christensen, D. (2010). *Who am I in the lives of children? An introduction to early childhood education.* New York: Pearson.

Froebel, F. (2005). *The education of man.* Mineola, NY: Dover Publications Inc.

Lascarides, V.C. & Hinitz, B.F. (2000). *History of early childhood education.* New York: Falmer Press.

Montessori, M. (1972). *Education and peace.* Chicago, IL: Henry Regnery Company.

Morrison, G.S. (2011). *Fundamentals of early childhood education.* New York: Pearson.

Osborn, D.K. (1991). *Early childhood education in historical perspective.* Athens, GA: Education Associates.

Snyder, A. (1972). *Dauntless women in childhood education 1856–1931.* Washington, DC: Association for Childhood Education International.

Valdez, V. & Franquiz, M. (2010). Latinas in early childhood education: Issues, practices, and future directions. In E.G. Murillo (Ed.), *Handbook of Latinos and education: Research, theory, and practice.* New York: Routledge.

Yarsinske, A.W. (2004). *All for one and one for all: A celebration of 75 years of the League of United Latin American Citizens.* Virginia Beach, VA: The Donning Company Publishers.

Zigler, E. & Styfco, S. (2010). *The hidden history of Head Start.* New York: Oxford University Press.

2

CURRICULUM AND RESEARCH

What Are the Gaps We Ought to Mind?

Nancy File

Introduction

In this chapter I discuss trends and issues in research efforts focused on early child-hood curriculum in the United States. After decades of this work, I contend that it is still prudent for the field to heed the infamous caution from the London Underground system to "mind the gap." In the case of the Underground, the gap is used to denote the space between the platform and the car. A check of a thesaurus indicates that "space" is one family of related words for gap, but others include "hole" and "disparity."

Initially I examine research from two perspectives for study, noting gaps in general. The first perspective is questions framed as "what works," inquiry I will refer to as "*if*," and the second is questions of "*how*" curriculum works. Next, I make use of three synonyms for "gap." First, I discuss gap as "space," specifically using the thesaurus suggestion of "lull." I briefly trace the historical trends in research conducted on early childhood curriculum-related questions. Second, I employ gap as connoting "disparity" to reflect upon the thesaurus suggestion of "mismatch" in relation to research questions, concerns, and methods. Finally, I utilize the word "breach" from the thesaurus family of "hole" to explore the underlying drivers of research efforts. This review is necessarily brief; I am not able to fully discuss the possible range of research findings. Instead, I focus on highlighting trends and variations.

As noted by Powell (1987), efforts to conduct research on curriculum have been marked by "the confounding of content, activities, and materials with teaching techniques" (p. 194). In other words, while content and instruction may be separable at the theoretical level, it is more difficult to recognize these boundaries as research is conducted to understand curriculum. The definition of "curriculum" has been undertaken implicitly by researchers. For many, it represents a package of content and methods, as authored by an entity. However, qualitative researchers are more likely to regard curriculum as lived experiences in the teaching/learning process.

How Sufficient is Our Research Knowledge?

In general, the concept of gap can be employed to consider the question of how well "what we know" about curriculum matches "what we need to know." Different approaches can be taken to this problem, including questions related to curriculum effectiveness and curriculum processes.

Does Curriculum Work?

A question that has formed the base for much of the research has been that of effectiveness: Does a curriculum accomplish its purposes? Studies of early childhood curriculum effectiveness initially flourished in the 1960s as researchers implemented preschool interventions intended to prepare children for school. The Consortium for Longitudinal Studies was formed when several research teams pooled their efforts to examine long-term program effects. Based upon these data, Royce, Darlington, and Murray (1983) concluded, "It appears that a variety of curricula are equally effective in preparing children for school and that any of the tested curricula is better than no preschool program at all" (p. 442). Powell (1987) later countered this pronouncement with an assertion from a review of a wider-ranging literature that the type of preschool curriculum "does matter" (p. 205). He concluded that the research base provided cautious suggestions and, ultimately, further questions.

In the first decade of the millennium, preschool curriculum effectiveness was the purpose of the Preschool Curriculum Evaluation Research (PCER) initiative. Children's outcomes were examined across 14 preschool curricula in comparison to local classrooms implementing practice as usual for samples of, predominantly, children living in poverty. Overall, there were few findings that demonstrated the intervention curricula resulted in significantly different academic outcomes at either preschool or end-of-kindergarten. Based upon examining the patterns of findings across child assessment data (which included measures of reading, language, phonological awareness, and math), the report offered the conclusion that only two of the curricula were more effective than the control for outcomes over the preschool year (Preschool Curriculum Evaluation Research Consortium, 2008). An impact on math measures was found for a researcher-developed math curriculum, supplemented by DLM Early Childhood Express math software. Impacts across early literacy and language measures were found for a relatively prescriptive curriculum package, DLM Early Childhood Express with Open Court Reading. This particular curriculum continued to show effectiveness on similar academic measures at the end of kindergarten. Positive effects at the end of kindergarten on academic outcomes were noted also for a researcher-developed language curriculum (language effects) and for a relatively scripted curriculum developed by Success for All (reading effects). Overall, the lack of positive effects across most of the curricula at both times of assessment is noticeable (Preschool Curriculum Evaluation Research Consortium, 2008).

Concurrently with the implementation of PCER, the question of "does a curriculum work" was taken up via the "What Works Clearinghouse," an initiative of the U.S. Department of Education. Groups of researchers assess the available evidence for a curriculum, determining if studies meet conditions set for methodological rigor and then considering the findings. In examining the early childhood curriculum reviews, it does not take long to reach two conclusions. First, there is a dearth of research that meets the conditions set for consideration of the data. Randomized trials are regarded as the gold standard for demonstrating the causal relationship inherent in "what works" questions. Second, there are few conclusions established thus far regarding a curriculum found to "work."

A variation of this basic question has been for researchers to examine the effectiveness of a curriculum relative to differences among children—what works for whom—with a tendency to focus on child characteristics that are common demographic measures. The investigators from independent projects who made up the Consortium for Longitudinal Studies pooled their analyses to examine family structure (presence or not of a father), maternal education, child's sex, and child's "ethnic background" (which we would currently refer to as race, as samples were largely African American). In the pooled analyses, which admittedly may have masked differential effects of curricula in conditions where multiple curricula were being implemented, there were no significant effects of these variables in regression analyses predicting child outcomes such as IQ scores, achievement test scores, placement in special education, and grade retention (Lazar & Darlington, 1982).

On the other hand, individual-site project investigators who pursued curriculum comparison studies did report differential effects relative to these demographic variables. Miller and Bizzell (1983) reported that in middle school, boys who had been enrolled in non-didactic preschool models scored higher on reading and math achievement tests than boys who had enrolled in didactic models. These differences were larger and more consistent than the differences found in the subsample of girls, as well as being in a different direction (Miller & Bizzell, 1983).

A different approach to analyses was taken by the Preschool Curriculum Evaluation Research initiative. In the report released about cross-site analyses, child demographic variables, including race/ethnicity, sex, and maternal education, were treated as co-variates. Potential interactions of these variables with curricula were not examined (Preschool Curriculum Evaluation Research Consortium, 2008).

The research efforts discussed thus far were focused on broadly written curricula that direct the entire array of experiences offered to children in the classroom. Other researchers have examined curricula that are fairly targeted (such as literacy or math only). For example, Sophian (2004) reported significant results with a modest effect size for a Head Start-implemented early mathematics curriculum she described as "substantially richer conceptually than most preschool mathematics curricula" (p. 73).

Another feature of some studies is the use of outcome measures other than the standardized assessments utilized in the previously discussed research (these typically include the Peabody Picture-Vocabulary Test, measures of early literacy focused on phonological awareness and portions of the Woodcock–Johnson battery in much of the current research). For example, Klein et al. (2008) used an extensive researcher-developed assessment of children's mathematical knowledge to assess their curriculum. Justice and her colleagues examined children's natural language samples to evaluate implementation of the Language-Focused Curriculum with preschoolers (Justice et al., 2008). Research projects such as these extend the potential for examining *if* curriculum works.

However, despite these efforts to examine curriculum effectiveness, we are left with inconclusive answers to what appears to be a fairly straightforward question—what works? This reflects a significant gap indeed. But is the question entirely straightforward? Why are the answers we have long sought so elusive? I take up these questions again later in the chapter (pp. 22–23).

How Does Curriculum Work?

The research interests explored in this section are focused on the workings of curriculum. What might make curriculum effective or not? What processes operating within a curriculum are important? What do children experience within curriculum? Some researchers pair these questions with outcome assessments, similar to studies discussed in the preceding section, but descriptive measures and qualitative methods also come into use.

In an early investigation, Stallings (1975) examined first- and third-grade classrooms utilizing a range of curriculum models in Project Follow Through (intended to extend the benefits of Head Start approaches for low-income children). A large number of variables that captured teaching processes in the classrooms were included in the analyses, and they illustrate some of the complexity of curriculum and teaching. For example, Stallings noted that higher reading and math scores were associated with small group instruction in first grade but large group instruction in third grade. Systematic instructional patterns, with the introduction of information, followed by questioning and immediate feedback, were also associated with higher reading and math scores. On the other hand, Stallings concluded that children scored higher on a problem-solving measure when they were in classrooms with more flexibility, marked by things such as a variety of materials and activities and some child choice in grouping and seating during the day. The extensive report from Stallings reflects how dense an examination of the workings of curriculum can be.

More recently, Early and her colleagues (2010) detailed the experiences of children in preschool programs across several states. While they did not utilize the concept of curriculum in describing their work, they coded via observation the types of experience variations that occur within the curriculum. Overall they found that on average children spent slightly more time in teacher-assigned activities (37%) than in meals and routines (34%) and than in free choice activities (29%). Perhaps not surprisingly, various language and literacy activities (17%—categories were non-exclusive) were coded as comprising the content of children's activities more frequently than science (11%) or math (8%), but only slightly more than social studies and art (15% each). Extensive time was spent in what could only be coded as "no learning activity" (44%). This code was used when none of the other categories pertained during even a portion of the observation cycle; other choices included activity codes such as reading, letter/sounds, math, arts, oral language, social studies, and gross and fine motor. This raised concerns for the researchers, who noted that even during meals and routines engagement in informal learning activities could occur.

In regard to children's lived experiences with curriculum, some of the same demographic variables discussed in the previous section have been examined. Miller et al. (1985) conducted detailed observations of children's experiences in eight Head Start classrooms where teachers were conducting the same curriculum under carefully controlled conditions (for example similar materials, room arrangements, and curricular themes). They found that during language lessons, more individual instruction was given to boys who were off-task, in comparison to girls, who were more often reprimanded when off-task. Boys who volunteered more often and offered opinions more often were given a higher ratio of positive-to-negative validation by their teachers. Conversely, girls who volunteered more often and asked more questions were given a higher ratio of negative-to-positive reinforcement by their teachers.

The Early et al. (2010) study included an examination of classroom differences relative to race and income. In classrooms where children were relatively better off financially, there was more free choice time and less time spent as "no coded learning activity." When classrooms enrolled more African American children, there was more time spent in teacher-assigned settings, as well as in meals/routines. Classrooms with more Latino/a children were found to have higher proportions of time spent in teacher-assigned activities and more time spent in language/literacy activities.

The Early et al. (2010) study demonstrated differences in children's experiences relative to race and social class across a national sample. Looking at just one "mid-sized" city, McGill-Franzen et al. (2002) described considerable systematic differences in the curricula and pedagogy relative to literacy learning among five preschool programs operating under different auspices. Their descriptive case studies included three programs serving largely African American children from low-income families (Head Start, public school prekindergarten, and charitable/state-funded child care, all with income-eligibility standards) and two programs serving children from middle-class and/or well-educated families (university child care and religion-affiliated preschool). They found remarkable differences in resources for literacy favoring the latter two programs, as well as differences in enacted curriculum. In the three publicly funded programs, literacy experiences focused on less challenging books and activities, with little attention to writing, and the authors described the curricula as "less culturally relevant" and "impoverished" (McGill-Franzen et al., 2002, p. 460). Interestingly, this study shows its age, as the public school pre-kindergarten is described as purposefully non-academic in nature. The teachers are described as believing "that they are not supposed to teach children the letters of the alphabet or any printing, color names, or other similar kinds of things" (McGill-Franzen et al., 2002, p. 459). These goals may no longer be consistent with current emphases on early literacy learning.

These studies indicate that there may be systematic differences in the experiences children have in classrooms. In some cases differences are the result of curricular emphases, but in others they appear to be related to the differences among teachers as they enact curriculum. In addition, these differences may be related to interactions between teaching style and characteristics of the children. By taking an approach more detailed than labeling children's experiences via the curriculum package being utilized, these researchers have illustrated the complexity of the workings of curriculum.

An even closer examination of the experiences of individual children within the curriculum is provided by qualitative researchers. Teacher-researchers have particular power underlying their examinations of curriculum. For example, Gallas (1995) detailed in book form the connections between her approach to science curriculum, conducting "science talks," and children's construction of thinking. The analysis of classroom discourse provided unique insights into the complexity of curriculum in action, illustrating the theories children developed and questions emanating from their sense of wonder at the world. Ballenger (1999) reflected upon her approaches to teaching alphabet knowledge in relation to the ways children made use of their alphabetic knowledge to think about their own identities and their relationships with others. Mardell (1999) explained units he developed with preschoolers that led to deep explorations of topics others might have found unusual, including exploring music via an initial focus on the Beatles and an astronomy unit. Finally, the contributions of Paley are unparalleled in this area. For example, her description of a curriculum built around Leo Lionni's children's books reflects both the potential intellectual challenges for children and a profound understanding of children (Paley, 1998). With their base in classrooms, these teachers' narratives provide an understanding of the *how* of curriculum that is unique in its contribution to our knowledge. Yet, the work remains apart from the canon of the field defined as the research literature because it is localized (thus not generalizable) and non-peer-reviewed in its publication.

In summary, questions regarding *how* curriculum works have generally received less attention than questions of *if* a curriculum works. The gaps here between what we know and what we need to know are great. The quantitative observational research has typically involved complex coding schemes with answers that are elusive and recognizably partial. Qualitative research has only illuminated the tip of the iceberg that is curriculum enactment.

When and where are the ties among curriculum goals, how curriculum is taught and experienced, and what children actually learn most effectively connected? When research fails to show outcomes relative to a curriculum, is it possible to untangle whether this means the content was perhaps trivial, inappropriate, or poorly conceived, or the teaching strategies ineffective? What evidence can we gain from further quantitative inquiry of *if* questions? What insights are to be obtained from the detailed analysis of the qualitative researcher?

In terms of intent, questions of *how* appear to be considerably more complex than questions of *if*. Questions of *if* require willing participants to enact curriculum, and time as curriculum is enacted and we wait for outcomes. Questions of *how* require intensive resources, necessitating adequate and meaningful time invested in unpacking and/or understanding the teaching–learning process as it occurs.

Exploring Gap as Lull

One of the thesaurus synonyms for gap is "space." What may first come to mind is space in the physical sense, but one of the next-layer suggestions for space is "lull," gaps as manifested over time. Powell (1987) noted that curriculum research directed to *if* questions was central in early childhood in the 1960s and 1970s, as the intervention programs discussed earlier were conducted and the children followed over time. He further explained that large-scale research efforts diminished after this, due in part to the early conclusions, also discussed earlier, that curricular variations were relatively unimportant to child outcomes. Also, the increases in child care usage in the 1970s presented new venues and questions for research (Powell, 1987). At the time of his writing, the late 1980s, Powell did note that the emergence of public school prekindergarten programs had renewed interest in studying curriculum.

The public school prekindergarten movement has continued to grow in influence, and certainly to this day remains a force in research agendas. More recently, the emphasis on accountability and the resultant focus on achievement gaps has reinforced attention to effective teaching and learning in early childhood (Copple & Bredekamp, 2009). The climate for research set by the U.S. Department of Education for the last decade has been focused on "questions of what works best for whom under what circumstances ... that are best answered by randomized trials of interventions and approaches brought to scale" (Whitehurst, 2003, p. 12).

This trend reflects both change and continuity across the lull in research activity. What has not changed is an emphasis on preparing young children deemed vulnerable to school failure for a different path. As well, the underlying research impetus—finding what works—has remained constant. The venues for research have changed, from the federal Head Start program and researcher-implemented intervention programs, to the current emphasis on state-supported prekindergarten in addition to Head Start. However, the resurgence of these emphases is occurring at a different point in our sociocultural context. As described by Hatch (2007), during the lull in research focused on *if* questions, the work done by qualitative researchers had gained in acceptance and stature in the early childhood field. As many early childhood researchers either have training within applied developmental psychology or regard it as a root discipline, the emphasis on quantitative research is logical. However, as Hatch pointed out, qualitative researchers managed in the 1990s and into the new millennium to find venues for the presentation of their work, and postmodern perspectives were voiced. Hatch's sense of loss in terms of the capacity for multiple approaches to fully illuminate questions of interest is clear in his essay, in which he claimed that the stance toward renewing the primacy of positivist research traditions constitutes a return to modernity. He concluded by exhorting, "We must not capitulate to those who would go back to modern conceptualizations of what constitutes acceptable research" (Hatch, 2007, p. 20). Clearly, over the lull in research focused on *if* questions, the research context in early childhood had changed. Many researchers interested in questions of *how* advocate using new paradigms to understand teaching and learning.

While research questions focused on child care quality did fill some of the lull in curriculum research, this lull also produced another approach to curricular issues. In contrast to moving to understand the outcomes relevant to a particular curriculum, during the period from the late 1980s to the late 1990s, curricular research questions were refashioned by the position on Developmentally Appropriate Practice (DAP) from the National Association for the Education of Young Children (Bredekamp, 1987). Thus, the prevailing questions focused on the outcomes of classroom practices (a conflation of curriculum content and teaching strategies in most measures) that were considered to be more or less developmentally appropriate. A large part of this body of research was reviewed by Van Horn and his colleagues (Van Horn et al., 2005). Findings ranged across studies, from some favoring the effects of DAP on academic outcomes at the preschool level to studies in kindergarten evidencing mixed results, with children in high-DAP classrooms performing better on general cognitive measures, while their peers in classrooms emphasizing basic skills (termed developmentally inappropriate, or DIP) performed better on reading achievement. Van Horn et al. concluded that the results were mixed regarding academic and cognitive outcomes and more consistently favorable toward DAP for social outcomes, particularly in relation to measures of children's stress. However, they raised caution regarding almost the entire body of research by noting that only one study in their review had utilized models that accounted for the nesting of children in classrooms, such as hierarchical linear modeling or structural equation modeling. The use of analytic strategies that fail to account for this nesting factor can lead to an over-estimation of effects. Many of the studies reviewed by Van Horn et al. were published simultaneously with the earliest uses of these more sophisticated analytic strategies. The DAP line of inquiry subsequently experienced its own lull as multi-level models became more predominantly used, with a petering out of publications after the millennium.

The lulls that establish gaps in the research reflect shifting research interests in the field, at times raising curriculum to the forefront and other times finding this topic pushed to the background or redefined. Interest in the academic outcomes of curriculum has remained a constant, although in the first wave of studies IQ predominated as a measure, to be replaced later by measures of specific abilities related to literacy, language, and mathematics. Yet, in spite of more focused outcome assessments and greater analytic sophistication, as noted earlier, the answers to *if* questions remain weakly established.

Exploring Gap as Mismatch

The thesaurus provides another family of synonyms for gap, headed by divergence. Here a next-layer word is "mismatch." In this section I explore the gap between our research questions and the tools of scientific research employed to answer *if* questions in terms of a mismatch. I explore why such a seemingly straightforward question as "what works?" is so difficult to answer.

In a final report from his position as director of the Institute for Education Sciences, Whitehurst often compared *if* research questions in education to pharmaceutical research. He demonstrated complete faith in the methods of science, claiming in the conclusion, "Although rigorous evaluations that do not find effects are often viewed as failures, they should not be. It is the program being evaluated that failed, not the evaluation that disclosed that fact" (Institute of Education Sciences, 2008, p. 20). But is educational research that similar to pharmaceutical research? Is it the same in both fields to find out "what works"? Is the problem ineffective curricula, ineffective research methods, or something else?

There are certainly similarities in practice between educational *if* questions and pharmaceutical research. As described by Whitehurst (Institute of Education Sciences, 2008), in both fields initial work toward *if* questions is pursued by smaller-scale efforts toward exploration and development, followed by larger-scale randomized trials. This is the model espoused by the federal government of the first decade of the 21st century. Technically, the research processes have developed as being similar in nature, based upon empiricism.

But I contend there are important differences between the fields that relate to the lack of findings in education. Education questions have inherent complexities that pharmaceutical questions do not. In pharmaceutical research, dosage is carefully managed via quality control mechanisms in the production phase, albeit medication may be metabolized differently across individuals. In education research, curriculum is delivered via teachers, each of whom has a personal interface with the work. Even with tightly scripted curricula, teachers may diverge from script, and they certainly differ amongst each other on personal style. Teachers may deliver curricula differently, children may experience the same curriculum differently, and there may be interaction effects. For example, Pence et al. (2008) found variations in teacher fidelity to the curriculum both across time and across different aspects of the curriculum model they were evaluating. Recall, also, the findings discussed earlier about children's classroom experiences differing in relation to their sex even while learning via the same curriculum (Miller et al., 1985). Our nascent knowledge in how children experience curriculum is thus far based on variables related to demographic definitions of their identities. This leaves much more beneath the surface, as each child is an individual with a personal history, interests, experiences, personality, and so forth. There is much left to learn about individual processes involved in the activities of teaching and learning. Can the positivist/post-positivist approach to *if* questions capture these complexities?

Second, in understanding these endeavors, we must consider whether our outcome measures are adequate to the task. *If* questions have been studied via standardized assessments of children. If they are matched appropriately to the curriculum, one expects positive results if the curriculum is indeed effective. However, the question of that match is fraught with difficulty. Do we have valid assessments of all aspects of learning? To what degree, and specifically where, does any particular standardized assessment narrow our conceptions of children's learning and experiences, as contended by Graue (1998)? What values and cultural ways of knowing have impacted the development of assessments, making this a definitively non-neutral process? Graue argued that standardized assessments act to create impressions that development—or learning—is a singular process with universal paths. In sum, are the tools we have to assess effectiveness sufficient to understand learning among groups of diverse individuals?

Finally, *if* questions must be examined in exceedingly complex and messy contexts and systems. Children are nested within classrooms, which are nested within schools or agencies, which are nested within communities, and so on. Even with multi-level modeling, this complexity quickly outstrips the available tools. The potential impacts to our understanding are important. For instance, Baker and her colleagues (Baker et al., 2010) found that teacher implementation of an intervention curriculum was significantly related to center-level variables. Among their findings they noted that teachers who rated their work environments as more collegial, supportive, and fair implemented more activities in the intervention.

In sum, it is perhaps impossible to design a rigorous evaluation of curriculum that does not fail in some ways to account for what is involved in the highly contextualized processes of education. Our lack of answers may not be attributable to poor science, but instead to the inadequacies of our assumptions, models, and tools in relation to questions that are only simple on the surface. We must consider whether the answers we believe can be found are illusory or, indeed, would prove ultimately helpful in the form in which they can be addressed. Where can research most effectively inform practice?

Exploring Gap as Breach

Finally, another synonym for gap is hole, among which one of the next-layer words is "breach." I now employ the concept of breach to explore what I view as rifts in early childhood research.

In the 1960s, when interest in curriculum research initially surged, a common perspective held that a significant number of children were "culturally deprived," lacking language and reading skills, motivation, and positive attitudes toward education and schools (Riessman, 1962). This deficit perspective has long influenced early childhood practitioners and researchers. More recently, recasting has moved the perspective to one of differences arising from the contexts in which children are reared (Justice et al., 2008). Regardless, a primary driver behind curriculum research has been to learn how to move children living in poverty closer to the developmental profiles of children who are not. The rift here is in regard to curriculum goals. There are unspoken assumptions that children from the middle and upper classes reach these goals without much emphasis on curriculum and instruction while children living in poverty must be helped via effective curriculum. Goals have been reified on the basis of different developmental paths, which in turn have been reified by the tools used to chart development. The role that researchers have taken in these processes deserves to be critically examined. Who, after all, defines the ends of the curriculum toward which researchers have focused their assessments? The rifts here exist between children and their families, schools and curriculum, and the power inherent in our society of those who operate within the scientific realm.

Another rift exists between the *if* and *how* questions. They remain separate in part because the quantitative paradigm is the only available method for answering the former. Questions of *how* allow the possibility of alternative paradigms and a greater focus on local context. Furthermore, we still need to find places for the scholarship contributed from those who employ critical approaches to examine the meanings of curriculum (for example Cannella, 1997). Crossing the rifts found among vastly different epistemologies and methods remains a challenge. In the case of these rifts, the gap exists between approaches to how we know what we know, as well as defining what we need to know.

Conclusion

There are gaps between what we know about early childhood curriculum, what we need to know, and how we choose to know. Our knowledge base consists of some answers, although they may be contested on various grounds. Certainly, the research has pointed toward myriad further questions. I believe it important to examine carefully if some lines of research, such as effectiveness studies, hold less promise, given the logistical realities of research, than is claimed by some. I hope as well that emphasis on questions of *how* leads us to a richer understanding of the complex processes of teaching and learning in early childhood classrooms. By minding the gaps, we can begin to find ways to fill them.

References

Baker, C.N., Kupersmidt, J.B., Voegler-Lee, M.E., Arnold, D.H., & Willoughby, M.T. (2010). Predicting teacher participation in a classroom-based, integrated preventive intervention for preschoolers. *Early Childhood Research Quarterly*, 25, 270–83.

Ballenger, C. (1999). *Teaching other people's children: Literacy and learning in a bilingual classroom*. New York: Teachers College Press.

Bredekamp, S.E. (Ed.). (1987). *Developmentally appropriate practice in early childhood programs serving children from birth through age 8*. Washington, DC: National Association for the Education of Young Children.

Cannella, G.S. (1997). *Deconstructing early childhood education: Social justice & revolution*. New York: Peter Lang.

Consortium for Longitudinal Studies. (1983). *As the twig is bent ... Lasting effects of preschool programs*. Hillsdale, NJ: Lawrence Erlbaum.

Copple, C. & Bredekamp, S. (2009). *Developmentally appropriate practice in early childhood programs* (3rd ed.). Washington, DC: National Association for the Education of Young Children.

Early, D.M., Iruka, I.U., Ritchie, S., Barbarin, O.A., Winn, D.C., Crawford, G.M., et al. (2010). How do pre-kindergarteners spend their time? Gender, ethnicity, and income as predictors of experiences in pre-kindergarten classrooms. *Early Childhood Research Quarterly*, 25, 177–93.

Gallas, K. (1995). *Talking their way into science: Hearing children's questions and theories, responding with curriculum*. New York: Teachers College Press.

Graue, M.E. (1998). Through a small window: Knowing children and research through standardized tests. In B. Spodek, O.N. Saracho, & A.D. Pellegrini (Eds.), *Issues in early childhood educational research*, pp. 30–48. New York: Teachers College Press.

Hatch, J.A. (2007). Back to modernity? Early childhood qualitative research in the 21st century. In J.A. Hatch (Ed.) *Early childhood qualitative research*, pp. 7–22. New York: Routledge.

Institute of Education Sciences, U.S. Department of Education. (2008). Rigor and relevance redux: Director's biennial report to Congress (IES 2009–6010). Washington, DC. Retrieved February 17, 2010 from http://ies.ed.gov/director/pdf/20096010.pdf.

Justice, L.M., Mashburn, A., Pence, K.L., & Wiggins, A. (2008). Experimental evaluation of a preschool language curriculum: Influence on children's expressive language skills. *Journal of Speech, Language, and Hearing Research*, 51, 983–1001.

Klein, A., Starkey, P., Clements, D., Sarama, J., & Iyer, R. (2008). Effects of a pre-Kindergarten mathematics intervention: A randomized experiment. *Journal of Research on Educational Effectiveness*, 1, 155–78.

Lazar, I. & Darlington, R. (1982). Lasting effects of early education: A report from the consortium for longitudinal studies. *Monographs of the Society for Research in Child Development*, 47(2–3, Serial No. 195).

McGill-Franzen, A., Lanford, C., & Adams, E. (2002). Learning to be literate: A comparison of five urban early childhood programs. *Journal of Educational Psychology*, 94, 443–64.

Mardell, B. (1999). *From basketball to the Beatles: In search of compelling early childhood curriculum*. Portsmouth, NH: Heinemann.

Miller, L.B. & Bizzell, R.P. (1983). Long-term effects of four preschool programs: Sixth, seventh, and eighth grades. *Child Development*, 54, 727–41.

Miller, L.B., Bugbee, M.R., & Hybertson, D.W. (1985). Dimensions of preschool: The effects of individual experience. In I.E. Sigel (Ed.), *Advances in applied developmental psychology* (vol. 1, pp. 25–90). Norwood, NJ: Ablex.

Paley, V.G. (1998). *The girl with the brown crayon.* Cambridge, MA: Harvard University Press.

Pence, K.L., Justice, L.M., & Wiggins, A.K. (2008). Preschool teachers' fidelity in implementing a comprehensive language-rich curriculum. *Language, Speech, and Hearing Services in Schools,* 39, 329–41.

Powell, D. R. (1987). Comparing preschool curricula and practices: The state of the research. In S.L. Kagan & E.F. Zigler (Eds.), *Early schooling: The national debate* (pp. 190–211). New Haven, CT: Yale University Press.

Preschool Curriculum Evaluation Research Consortium. (2008). *Effects of preschool curriculum programs on school readiness* (NCER 2008–9). Washington, DC: National Center for Education Research, Institute of Education Sciences, U.S. Department of Education. Washington, DC: U.S. Government Printing Office.

Riessman, F. (1962). *The culturally deprived child.* New York: Harper & Row.

Royce, J.M., Darlington, R.B., & Murray, H.W. (1983). Pooled analyses: Findings across studies. In Consortium for Longitudinal Studies (Ed.), *As the twig is bent … Lasting effects of preschool programs* (pp. 411–59). Hillsdale, NJ: Lawrence Erlbaum.

Sophian, C. (2004). Mathematics for the future: Developing a Head Start curriculum to support mathematics learning. *Early Childhood Research Quarterly,* 19, 59–81.

Stallings, J. (1975). Implementation and child effects of teaching practices in Follow Through classrooms. *Monographs of the Society for Research in Child Development,* 40(7–8, Serial No. 163).

Van Horn, M.L., Karlin, E.O., Ramey, S.L., Aldridge, J., & Snyder, S.W. (2005). Effects of developmentally appropriate practices on children's development: A review of research and discussion of methodological and analytic issues. *The Elementary School Journal,* 105, 325–51.

Whitehurst, G.J. (2003). The Institute of Education Sciences: New wine, new bottles. Paper presented at the annual conference of the American Educational Research Association, April, 2003. (ERIC Document ED 478 983).

Part II
Influences on Curriculum

Our purpose in this section of the volume is to examine the theories and philosophies that have been applied to early childhood curriculum. We sought to provide both a description of the types of theorizing that have been conducted and a discussion of more specific curricular practices derived from those theoretical orientations. In focusing on the relationships between theory and practice, we wanted to highlight conundrums and gaps, in addition to describing work that has been done.

We begin with developmental theory, as this has been the most ubiquitous influence on early childhood practice. In Chapter 3 Nancy File discusses how developmental theory has become embedded into early childhood practice. She explains the reasoning of those who believe it is an appropriate base for practice and how that logic has become even more strongly reinforced through the most recent edition of the developmentally appropriate practice position statement from the National Association for the Education of Young Children. She also presents the concerns and critiques of many who have argued against the primacy of child development in early childhood, ending with questions for ongoing consideration about this contested relationship.

When it came time to identify an author for the chapter meant to focus on curricular applications of developmental theory, we found ourselves in a quandary. Should we include a chapter from an author wedded to the value of this theory for curriculum practice when we ourselves question the relationship? Could such an author tackle the critique that we hope to provide in this volume to stimulate future thinking? In the end, we asked Amos Hatch to contribute a chapter, knowing that he has many reservations about this relationship. And, he immediately presents this case in Chapter 4. His contribution is, in part, a story of his own teaching and the evolution he has experienced in taking on new perspectives throughout his career. Hatch manages to explore the connections between child development and early childhood curriculum by considering this a complex relationship with more- and less-warranted links.

Next, in Chapter 5, we present work done from the field of curriculum studies and more recent work by curriculum theorists. Jennifer Mueller explores a brief history of this field, which has also more recently included an emphasis on the political nature of curriculum. The frame she utilizes is to understand curriculum as a process rather than a product, with theory and practice being mutually constitutive. Finally, Mueller discusses more explicit connections between curriculum studies and early childhood via the work of the reconceptualists and as developed by collaborative work between theorists and teachers.

Following, Chapter 6 by Judy Harris Helm focuses on the use of projects in early childhood curriculum. There is literature available describing the latest interpretations of the project approach; Helm focuses instead on a deeper explanation of the connections between this approach to curriculum and John Dewey's work. Helm's chapter provides an example of the theory and practice relationship.

Finally, we move to critical approaches, the most recent influences on work in early childhood curriculum. In Chapter 7 Mindy Blaise and Sharon Ryan review how critical theories have been used to push the field past its taken-for-granted notions. Focused on the goal of transformations of practice, they also introduce recent theorizing, with its potential to pull the field toward even deeper examinations of our approaches to curriculum. Blaise and Ryan position critical theories as central to ongoing work in the field.

It is not unusual to hear our graduate students question just what a critical approach to curriculum looks like in practice. In the final chapter of this section, Chapter 8, Betsy Cahill and Tammy Gibson tackle this question. Drawing upon their own experiences as a consultant and a teacher, and their story of a local prekindergarten teacher, Cahill and Gibson provide examples of curriculum decision-making in action, based upon critical approaches. Their approach situates critical curriculum as varied actions, from small events in the classroom, to changes in teachers' priorities or approaches to their work.

In sum, the work of this section is to explore, through description and critique, the various theories utilized to conceptualize and shape early childhood curriculum. While each chapter exploring the links to enacted curriculum represents but one iteration of the possibilities available, each does illustrate how the relationship between practice and theory can be realized.

3

THE RELATIONSHIP BETWEEN CHILD DEVELOPMENT AND EARLY CHILDHOOD CURRICULUM

Nancy File

[I]t has been our experience that child development knowledge provides much clearer guidance for programming decisions than do other, more value-laden philosophies.

(Bredekamp, 1991, p. 203)

The question of what kind of useful knowledge developmental psychology produces is by no means completely settled.

(White, 2000, p. 284)

Developmental theories, particularly Piagetian stage theories, have become weapons of mass seduction in ECE across the globe, valorizing Piagetian developmental perspectives and, by default, mitigating against overt teaching and instruction.

(Grieshaber, 2008, p. 508)

Introduction

These quotations illustrate a range of opinion regarding the applicability of theory and research in child development for the work of early childhood practitioners. It is this relationship, and the varied stances toward it, that grounds my essay. I briefly explore the influence of child development on the early childhood field. Then, I discuss the varied perspectives, both supportive and unconvinced, that have been taken on the relevance of the former for the latter. My focus is on curriculum specifically; therefore the degree to which early childhood practitioners should know child development in order to understand and relate to children, for example, is beyond the scope of the essay. The question here is how knowledge of child development might be applied to making curriculum decisions. I close with questions for the field.

Exploring the Relationship of Child Development and Curriculum

Early childhood has roots in several fields. While child care was initially associated with child welfare and kindergarten spanned child development and/or education as a "home," nursery school programs for preschoolers were inextricably tied to the child study movement of the 20th century (Bloch, 1991; see this article for a more thorough history). Thus, from the beginning, practice in nursery schools was tied to the findings and goals of child development researchers. And, it is the relationship of child development to the field that has stood the test of time. Zimiles (1986) portrayed the essential nature of this relationship when he maintained that, "early childhood education was one of the first arenas in which a very important idea was being played out—that normal psychological development could be fortified and enhanced by designing an optimal environment for children" (p. 190).

Recalling familiar figures in child development (e.g. Gesell, Skinner, Erikson, Piaget, and Vygotsky), Spodek and Saracho (1999) traced the reflection of maturational, behavioral, psychodynamic, and constructivist theories on curriculum design. There has been change over time in the dominant perspectives from child development applied by early childhood practitioners. The influences of maturational, behavioral, and psychodynamic theorists have waned over time (Aldridge et al., 1997). The behavioral foothold was never strong in early childhood. Maturational and psychodynamic theories are rarely tied explicitly to the field these days. More recently, Vygotskian theory, and work by others within his tradition, has gained dominance in the discourse, while Piaget's influence has remained strong. Certainly, for the last 40 years, Piaget's name has been the predominant perspective in early childhood (Walsh, 1991).

The current importance of child development for curriculum in early childhood is exemplified in many places. For instance, practices for infants and toddlers are largely synonymous with our understanding of their early development. Lally, highly influential in infant/toddler curriculum, wrote in reference to what he termed the infant's "inborn curriculum":

> Most babies, except for those born with constitutional limitations, are genetically wired to seek out the skills and relationships that will help them survive and prosper in their early months and years. For teachers to assign their own learning agenda to the infants is inappropriate.
>
> *(Lally, 2009, p. 52)*

The authors of Creative Curriculum, a widely used, comprehensive birth through preschool curriculum that promotes its alignment with Head Start child outcomes and state learning standards, attribute its foundation squarely to child development theory and research (Teaching Strategies, 2010). Perhaps, however, the relationship between child development and early childhood curriculum is most cogently reflected in the use of "developmentally appropriate practice" (DAP) as the guiding principles of the National Association for the Education of Young Children (NAEYC), which has extensive influence on policy and practice (Bredekamp & Copple, 1997; Copple & Bredekamp, 2009). DAP principles have been widely distributed, and using the perspective of framing practice to be appropriate to children's development is dominant in the field.

At the same time, claims have been made that sources of curriculum other than developmental theory should be considered. Bloch (1991, p. 95) argued that an "undue reliance" on developmental theory came with associated costs for the field, including a focus on individual development that has deflected professional attention from structural inequities in society and schooling. Taking a different tack, Walsh (1991) contended that the perspectives on developmental theory within the early childhood field were too limited and, at times, based upon dubious conceptual understanding. Spodek and Saracho (1999) discussed the need to consider the cultural tools represented in the academic disciplines when making decisions about what and how to teach. Reflecting more recent trends, Graue (2008) traced the growing influence of standards in curriculum practice, which reflects the authority of disciplinary content fields. Indicative of the joint influences of developmental theory and discipline-based standards, in a special issue of *Early Childhood Research Quarterly* devoted to early learning in mathematics and science, several authors referenced developmental theory as well as content learning standards within their fields as they described their curricula (Starkey et al., 2004; Sophian, 2004; French, 2004).

In summary, although debate about the relationship between child development and early childhood has occurred, the historical connections between child development and early childhood curriculum endure to this day. Why has the relationship proven so robust? Goffin (1996) provides some insight into the persistence of this relationship when she described how developmental theory has enabled early childhood to enhance its professional stature. Furthermore, Goffin maintained that advocacy for early childhood has been boosted by the proposition that high quality early childhood practice facilitates children's development and learning. In the following sections I examine the perspectives of those who have embraced the relationship between child development and curriculum and those who have critiqued it.

The Child Development Position

In this section I review the positions of those who have maintained that developmental theory is rightfully placed as the dominant perspective for informing early childhood curriculum. In addition, I trace recent refinements of the DAP position statement.

In a recent essay, Ritchie, Maxwell, and Bredekamp (2009) proposed several favorable consequences that result from the application of child development research to early childhood practice. These include projected benefits to decisions about teaching strategies, but, importantly, also a focus on deep understanding of primary concepts in the curriculum, and better understanding of foundational learning processes. In addition, they proposed that "If we were to apply what we know from developmental psychology, teachers would have a solid understanding of ... the content of the curriculum in numeracy, literacy, language, and socio-emotional competence" (Ritchie et al., 2009, p. 25). They maintained that a focus on development and the body of knowledge from developmental science should be central to early childhood, and, notably, that child development research provides a knowledge base for understanding curriculum content.

NAEYC has held a dominant position in promoting the ties between child development and curriculum. In a position statement on curriculum, assessment, and program evaluation issued by the organization, practitioners were advised that curriculum should be "organized around the principles of child development and learning" (NAEYC, 2003, p. 7). Still, practitioners were directed to validate the subject matter included in a comprehensive curriculum with the professional standards issued by the disciplines. In other words, the position statement acknowledged that curriculum must be informed by the knowledge within disciplinary fields, such as mathematics and science. Unfortunately, there is little guidance available within this document about integrating these various sources of information to plan and enact curriculum.

While the influence of child development on early childhood curriculum has been traditionally strong, the relationship was codified with the publication of the *Developmentally Appropriate Practice* (DAP) guidelines from NAEYC. I will focus on the first revision of the original publication and the third edition of DAP, as these represent the modifications made after comment upon and critique of the initial position statement. In both of these later editions the essential prescription remains the same, however; DAP is based upon knowledge of general age-related characteristics of children and specific knowledge of individuals, situated within particular social and cultural contexts (Bredekamp & Copple, 1997; Copple & Bredekamp, 2009). From the start, child development, with both its normative view and its presentation of developmental variation, takes the lead. Context first gained a place in the revised edition, following the initial critique (Bredekamp & Copple, 1997).

There are similarities between the two revisions, as well as ways in which the third edition presents changes from the first revision. Both editions referenced the conventional theorists, including Erickson, Bronfenbrenner, Piaget, and Vygotsky, in broad strokes. Although Piaget and Vygotsky described different positions regarding the relationship between development and learning (File, 1995; Walsh, 1991), both editions take the stance that these theories can be unproblematically applied in concert, suspending any deeper reflection on the ramifications of these theoretical differences for teaching. Finally, the authority of child development for early childhood practice is reflected in the explication of 12 principles of development and learning that are intended to serve as core guidance for decision-making; note, however, that the principles are somewhat different between the revised and third editions (Bredekamp & Copple, 1997; Copple & Bredekamp, 2009).

In other ways, these two editions of DAP are different from each other and reflect continual refinement of the child development–curriculum relationship. In the revised edition we find that curriculum content is "determined by many factors, including the subject matter of the disciplines, social or cultural values, and parental input" (Bredekamp & Copple, 1997, p. 20). Even so, "teachers use their knowledge of child development and learning to identify the range of activities, materials, and learning experiences that are appropriate for a group or individual child" (p. 17). Recall, as described above, that in the 2003 position statement on curriculum, assessment, and program evaluation, both child development and professional standards from within the disciplines were recommended for curriculum decision-makers (NAEYC, 2003). Yet, by the time of the DAP third edition, "standards overload" was deemed "overwhelming," perhaps resulting in "potentially problematic teaching practices" (Copple & Bredekamp, 2009, p. 4). In the third edition, educational goals are informed by knowledge of child development and learning, with early learning standards being brought to bear carefully in the process. These standards represent the influence of programs or larger entities (e.g. states), as well as a written curriculum (also often developed externally), according to the DAP position statement. Specifically, in this edition, recent child development research is stressed, with the assertion that this research base is "helping to identify certain skills, abilities, knowledge, and approaches to learning that enable children to succeed in school and beyond" (p. 42). Gone is the reference from the revised edition, described above, to the influences of the disciplines, values, and family input on curriculum. Only empirical knowledge from child development, and its codification into early learning standards, is given voice and authority.

In the revised edition, it was noted that there were "relatively orderly sequences" in typical development (Bredekamp & Copple, 1997, p.10). This claim was supported by reference to the grand theories, such as Piaget's and Erikson's work, as well as big-picture summaries of development. In the third edition, these grand theories were coupled with smaller-scale theorizing, undertaken to study sequences in children's learning in specific areas, the example in the text being mathematics (Copple & Bredekamp, 2009). Research that has identified early predictors of children's later development was heavily utilized in this edition to inform guidelines for practice. The notion of utilizing "the developmental paths that children typically follow and the typical sequences in which skills and concepts develop" (p. 21) for planning and enacting curriculum is vital to this most recent edition.

In conclusion, the traditional relationships between child development and early childhood were elucidated and codified by the DAP position statements. Throughout its iterations, DAP pushed practitioners to embrace the idea that practice should relate to current understandings of child development. The DAP statements have been revised in response to critique, shifting contexts, and recent research. For instance, the third edition was situated within concern about achievement gaps, and it acknowledged the need for programs to achieve meaningful goals in children's learning (Copple & Bredekamp, 2009). However, the ties with child development remained as strong as ever, with child development being framed as universal and singular. There is little room for philosophy and values in this outlook, as well as knowledge from the content disciplines:

> Best practice is based on knowledge—not on assumptions—of how children learn and develop. The research base yields major principles in human development and learning. ... Those principles, along with evidence about curriculum and teaching effectiveness, form a solid basis for decision making in early care and education.
>
> *(Copple & Bredekamp, 2009, p. xii)*

> Developmentally appropriate practice as defined in this position statement is not based on what we think might be true or what we want to believe about young children.
>
> *(Copple & Bredekamp, 2009, p. 10)*

Critiques of the Relationship Between Child Development and Early Childhood

Critiques of the powerful position of child development theory and research for early childhood curriculum decisions have been varied. They have coalesced around some common themes that include concerns with how the knowledge base of child development has been applied to teaching and critiques of child development from postmodern stances. Still, the delineation I use in this section is not as clean as it sounds, and it provides a framework for discussion's sake only, rather than a reflection of how individuals may align themselves. I review examples from each theme below.

Concerns with Applying Child Development to Curriculum

Even those who have been supportive of early childhood's reliance on child development have acknowledged that this body of knowledge is not sufficient for informing practice (Bredekamp, 1991). One issue that has been raised is how much influence curriculum theory should have in the mix (Kessler, 1991). The specific contributions of curriculum theory and postmodern perspectives to early childhood curriculum practice will be discussed in other chapters, so I will not elaborate upon them here. Instead, I focus on the nature of the critiques of developmental theory and research.

One site of critique has been the slow response of the early childhood field to advances in child development research and theorizing. In the words of Lee and Johnson (2007), "the field has maintained an allegiance to outdated and limited developmental theories that require updating and broadening" (p. 233). In this case Lee and Johnson argued for an incorporation of systems perspectives that fully explore the relationship between development and cultural context. Previously I discussed the shifting ascendency over time of the major theoretical schools in child development. In considering Lee and Johnson's critique, I suggest we also reflect on the degree to which the ideologies developed within the fading traditions may continue to shape thinking from more closeted places, wherein we may not fully acknowledge those influences at work. For example, Graue, Kroeger, and Brown (2003) described teaching practices largely framed around normative views of kindergarteners, with some children deemed not ready for formal schooling and so given more time to develop via delayed school entry or retention in kindergarten. The existence of these responses to the variability in what children bring to the table is, on the surface, at odds with current theoretical perspectives. It is much more aligned with maturational theory, currently considered outdated in the mainstream. To what degree have maturational perspectives, and other voices from the past, continued to operate implicitly in our thinking? In sum, one source of critique begins with dissatisfaction with the prevailing theories and how they shape practice, whether or not they are directly named.

Child development research and theorizing is sometimes tied clearly to applications in practice by the scholars who generate the work, and at other times this is not the interest of the scholar. For some who critique the field, it is a scholar's lack of clear guidelines or applications to curriculum that is the rub; for example, Piaget's work has been ubiquitous in the field, yet he did not write extensively about curriculum (Egan, 1983; Grieshaber, 2008). This point is especially true of the grand theories that have served as the traditional backbone of the field. In this line of critique, the leap from development to practice is too great. In the words of Egan (1983), "converting psychology's *is* into an educational *ought*, especially when that 'is' does not describe a constraint of nature, is not only logically illegitimate, but it is educationally destructive" (p. 115). In other words, the bridge from child development to curriculum is precarious for some.

Some individuals have focused their criticism upon the consequences of relying upon developmental theory to guide practice. Haberman (1988) cautioned that "Our ability to explain and predict behavior, therefore, is not only enhanced by the power of the particular theory we have accepted, but decreased by the fact that we are ignoring other theories which compete or merely differ" (p. 36). He went on to express concern that the acceptance of predictability and regularity that accompanies these theoretical explanations belies his belief that "more about child development and behavior remains unexplained and will continue to be unexplainable" (p. 37). In essence, the question becomes, what are the limits of the power of this science? Responses range from Haberman's skepticism to the viewpoint from Ritchie et al.

(2009), discussed earlier. Recall that they asserted that what we know from "developmental psychology" can provide teachers a "solid understanding of ... the content of the curriculum in numeracy, literacy, language, and socioemotional competence" (p. 25). It is striking that such a tall order is proposed from the child development field to inform specific decisions for curriculum planning and enactment. What is conspicuously absent is reference to the academic disciplines for informing teachers about content, for example the conceptual structures and tools of inquiry of each field. Is it necessary to understand mathematics as a discipline in order to determine what and how to teach, or are the research findings from developmental psychology about young children learning it sufficient? Or are both important? That question is not explicitly addressed in the essay by Ritchie and her colleagues. Where are the limits of developmental theory, and if there are limits, what other fields must inform early childhood curriculum?

Some individuals have pointed out particular ways in which child development may not serve the early childhood field adequately. Grieshaber (2008) wrote that the dominance of developmental theories has "often [been] to the detriment of teaching by forcing teaching and teachers to take a back seat to children's development and learning" (p. 506). She critiqued teaching practices that are passive and reactive in nature, jeopardizing children's learning of accurate conceptual understandings about the world. Prior to the third edition of DAP being released, Barbarin and Miller (2009) discussed their concerns about the consequences of these practice guidelines. They speculated that focusing on development may result in teachers underestimating children's capabilities as they fail to recognize emerging skills. The result would be less challenging curricular experiences. They reasoned also that early childhood teachers who embrace DAP and are wary of standardized curriculum may take an "agnostic" perspective, responding to their perceptions of children's interests rather than clearly focusing on goals for what children should learn (Barbarin & Miller, 2009, p. 6). On the whole, however, Barbarin and Miller concluded that recent research in development has much to offer early childhood practice, particularly when synthesized with findings from educational research.

In the main, the critiques reviewed in this section are cautionary in nature; they reflect concerns with the specific child development knowledge being utilized or how the early childhood field can make use of it. They represent, by and large, calls to improve upon the contributions that the field can make to early childhood practice (although Grieshaber [2008] calls for greater paradigmatic shift).

The bridge between child development and early childhood is not unproblematic. Barbarin and Miller noted:

> If, for example, one looks at developmental journal articles on children's literacy or mathematical development, it is rare to find any description of the educational practices of the schools and preschools that children attend. It is also still rare in studies of teachers' thinking and teaching practices to find data

on how students interpret those practices or citations about the effects of the relevant literature on student thinking.

(Barbarin & Miller, 2009, p. 12)

Barbarin and Miller call for a greater synthesis between fields, with research that focuses on development, learning, and educational practices. They make the case for a strongly contextualized developmental science, setting a lead for those who wish to improve the connections between child development and early childhood.

Deep Concerns with the Science of Child Development

Another site of critique of the child development–early childhood relationship has been with the very nature of child development research and theory. While largely voiced by those working in postmodern traditions, the critique does extend beyond this group of scholars.

For some individuals, the task of fully understanding children is too complex for our research tools. Zimiles speaks to the issue thusly:

> When psychologists set out to measure psychological processes as part of a research effort, they are aware that they are bedeviled by a variety of undermining factors—the inherent complexity of the phenomena, the constraints of time and money, the deficiencies of their measurement procedures and the awkwardness of the measurement situation. But, upon completion of their research, they seem to be too easily satisfied in the belief that they had done the best that could have been done under the circumstances, and more important, they are too ready to regard their tenuous findings as authoritative.
>
> *(Zimiles, 2000b, p. 293)*

The postmodernists have critiqued the nature and constructions of child development. They have expressed concern that child development knowledge is generally not questioned as socially constructed, instead being assumed to be objective and rational (Cannella, 1997; Lubeck, 1996). As such, it limits our understanding of children, but certainly also of the impact of the "knower" on the "known" and how this has impacted the knowledge base. Furthermore, it serves to reify in practice what we have framed that we know about children and curriculum from research-based sources. As curriculum developers draw upon the developmental sequences identified by researchers, they ensure that particular questions continue to be asked, with findings that most often confirm expectations.

Additionally, critics argue that with its focus on universal sequences, child development has lacked sufficient focus on context and diversity, framing a particular discourse on what is considered normal (Lubeck, 1996; Bloch, 2000). As described by Cannella (1997), "allowing for individual variation, we describe what a two-year-old is like, the differences between three- and four-year-olds, what a class of kindergartners will be like" (p. 59). The result has been that approaches to curriculum are taken for granted, resulting in "views implying the existence of a single best and most efficient theory of learning and development or a universal tool to evaluate developmental outcomes or quality of services for children and families" (Lenz Taguchi, 2008, p. 271). For instance, in the third edition of DAP, it is recommended that teachers consider "the developmental paths that children *typically* follow and the *typical* sequences in which skills and concepts develop" (Copple & Bredekamp, 2009, p. 21, emphasis added) when making instructional decisions.

For postmodernist critics, the science of child development is too problematic to serve as the primary source of curriculum decisions because it is, in the words of one psychologist, "a paradigmatically modern discipline, arising at a time of commitment to narratives of truth, objectivity, science and reason" (Burman, 1994, p. 157). Indeed, Burman (2008) has contended that the dominant discourse in developmental psychology has been relatively untouched by postmodern approaches. What is offered from child development is rather singular still.

In conclusion, critical theorists have focused on problematizing assumptions, beliefs, and practices that have historically been relatively unexamined in the field. Moss questioned:

> How can we proliferate a multiplicity of discourses and avoid replacing one dominant discourse with another? There are no easy or certain answers because the dominant discourse draws strength from its denial of multiplicity and diversity. There is, according to this discourse, just one way of knowing, thinking, and practicing, the supreme task being to define and follow a particular way.
>
> *(Moss, 2006, p. 133)*

Questions

It is clear that there is both strong and committed belief in the relevance and importance of child development for early childhood curriculum, as well as a history of questioning this relationship that extends back at least two decades. If child development is not a sufficient base for our curriculum decision-making, what else is needed? The influence of the content disciplines is increasingly expressed via the plethora of standards, a focus also accompanied by its own issues and gaps (Graue, 2008). As we chart our future course, we may find it helpful to consider questions such as the following.

1 *Where are the limits of the knowledge base in child development?* The DAP statements have strongly advocated for what child development research and theory provide for early childhood. Where the child development knowledge base is

limited, or has limited application, has been examined primarily within the postmodern literature. There is certainly space for wider examination of this question, particularly among those who find the connection between the fields most important to maintain. Can those who espouse empiricist stances acknowledge weaknesses, gaps, limits, and dangers?

2 *What do these limits mean for our practice?* Within the DAP document, examples of developmentally appropriate practices are contrasted to other practices. Many of the contrasts to developmentally appropriate practice are inappropriate things to do with children of any age, regardless of developmental stature. For example, the third edition cautions practitioners to not treat children's backgrounds as deficits when planning curriculum and to avoid trivial curriculum content (Copple & Bredekamp, 2009). Remember that the case for DAP is premised upon "principles of child development and learning" (Copple & Bredekamp, 2009, p. 10). The presumption that these examples indicate practices existing in contrast to taking a developmental approach assumes that theory and research have pointed us in this direction. Is this the case, however? Is it disingenuous to trace admonitions such as these back to principles of child development? How can we more knowingly and transparently examine the influence of values, ideals, and morals on our curriculum practices? What are the costs of not recognizing the contributions of values, ideals, and morals as such?

3 *Are there sites where we can foster dialogue among those with different positioning on the question of the child development–early childhood relationship?* We must consider whether there are sufficient opportunities for those with a wide range of positions to talk together and debate, rather than continue the monologues typically conducted through largely separate professional publication systems. The positivist influence on child development is robust (Cannella, 1997; Burman, 1994). Postmodern theorists have called both for alternative ways of understanding children and for reconceptualizing practice in early childhood (Bloch, 2000). However, Hatch (2007) recently detailed movements to more severely limit the type of research accepted as sufficiently rigorous to inform practice. Meaningful, broad dialogue about what matters in science, and how this translates to practice, is more important than ever, and as difficult as ever.

4 *To what degree should curriculum respond to "what is" and "what should be" questions?* In the practices of child development researchers, which often lack full contextualization, questions of "what is" are easily tied to the task of child development researchers as they observe and explain children's growth and learning. These readily move into questions of "what will be." However, this is not the same as asking "what should be." Children's families and communities provide an understanding of desirable traits and skills, in part shaping the "what should be." Yet, their voices are largely silent in the professional discourse. Has the early childhood field's reliance on child development allowed us to build a sensibility that assumes science can be the sole or primary place to find these answers regarding the children we hope to raise?

References

Aldridge, J., Sexton, D., Goldman, R., Booker, B., & Werner, M. (1997). Examining contributions of child development theories to early childhood education. *College Student Journal*, 31, 453–59.

Barbarin, O.A. & Miller, K. (2009). Developmental science and early education: An introduction. In O.A. Barbarin & B.H. Wasik (Eds.), *Handbook of child development and early education: Research to practice* (pp. 3–13). New York: Guilford.

Bloch, M.N. (1991). Critical science and the history of child development's influence on early education research. *Early Education and Development*, 2, 95–108.

——(2000). Governing teachers, parents, and children through child development knowledge. *Human Development*, 43, 257–65.

Bredekamp, S. (1991). Redeveloping early childhood education: A response to Kessler. *Early Childhood Research Quarterly*, 6, 199–209.

Bredekamp, S. & Copple, C. (1997). *Developmentally appropriate practice in early childhood programs* (rev. ed.). Washington, DC: National Association for the Education of Young Children.

Burman, E. (1994). *Deconstructing developmental psychology*. London: Routledge.

——(2008). *Developments child, image, nation*. London: Routledge.

Cannella, G.S. (1997). *Deconstructing early childhood education: Social justice & revolution*. New York: Peter Lang.

Copple, C. & Bredekamp, S. (2009). *Developmentally appropriate practice in early childhood programs* (3rd ed.). Washington, DC: National Association for the Education of Young Children.

Egan, K. (1983). *Education and psychology: Plato, Piaget, and scientific psychology*. New York: Teachers College Press.

File, N. (1995). Applications of Vygotskian theory to early childhood education: Moving toward a new teaching–learning paradigm. *Advances in Early Education and Day Care*, 7, 295–317.

French, L. (2004). Science as the center of a coherent, integrated early childhood curriculum. *Early Childhood Research Quarterly*, 19, 138–49.

Goffin, S.G. (1996). Child development knowledge and early childhood teacher preparation: Assessing the relationship. *Early Childhood Research Quarterly*, 11, 117–33.

Graue, E. (2008). Teaching and learning in a post-DAP world. *Early Education and Development*, 19, 441–47.

Graue, M.E., Kroeger, J., & Brown, C. (2003). The gift of time: Enactments of developmental thought in early childhood practice. *Early Childhood Research & Practice*, 5(1). Retrieved from http://ecrp.uiuc.edu/v5n1/graue.html.

Grieshaber, S. (2008). Interrupting stereotypes: Teaching and the education of young children. *Early Education and Development*, 19, 505–18.

Haberman, M. (1988). What knowledge is of most worth to teachers of young children? *Early Child Development and Care*, 38, 33–41.

Hatch, J.A. (2007). Back to modernity? Early childhood qualitative research in the 21st century. In J.A. Hatch (Ed.), *Early childhood qualitative research* (pp. 7–22). New York: Routledge

Kessler, S. (1991). Alternative perspectives on early childhood education. *Early Childhood Research Quarterly*, 6, 183–197.

Lally, J.R. (2009). The science and psychology of infant–toddler care. *Zero to Three*, 30(2), 47–53.

Lee, K. & Johnson, A.S. (2007). Child development in cultural contexts: Implications of cultural psychology for early childhood teacher education. *Early Childhood Education Journal*, 35, 233–43.

Lenz Taguchi, H.L. (2008). An "ethics of resistance" challenges taken-for-granted ideas in Swedish early childhood education. *International Journal of Education Research*, 47, 270–82.

Lubeck, S. (1996). Deconstructing "child development knowledge" and "teacher preparation." *Early Childhood Research Quarterly*, 11, 147–67.

Moss, P. (2006). Early childhood institutions as loci of ethical and political practice. *International Journal of Educational Policy, Research, and Practice: Reconceptualizing Childhood Studies*, 7(1), 127–36.

NAEYC. (2003). *Early childhood curriculum, assessment, and program evaluation: Position statement with expanded resources.* Retrieved from http://www.naeyc.org/files/naeyc/file/positions/CAPEexpand.pdf.

Ritchie, S., Maxwell, K.L., & Bredekamp, S. (2009). Rethinking early schooling: Using developmental science to transform children's early school experiences. In O.A. Barbarin & B.H. Wasik (Eds.) *Handbook of child development and early education: Research to practice* (pp. 14–37). New York: Guilford.

Sophian, C. (2004). Mathematics for the future: Developing a Head Start curriculum to support mathematics learning. *Early Childhood Research Quarterly*, 19, 59–81.

Spodek, B. & Saracho, O.N. (1999). The relationship between theories of child development and the early childhood curriculum. *Early Child Development and Care*, 152, 1–15.

Starkey, P., Klein, A., & Wakeley, A. (2004). Enhancing young children's mathematical knowledge through a pre-kindergarten mathematics intervention. *Early Childhood Research Quarterly*, 19, 99–120.

Teaching Strategies. (2010). Research foundation: The Creative Curriculum. Retrieved from www.teachingstrategies.com/national/pdfs/RF_Creative_Curriculum.pdf.

Walsh, D.J. (1991). Extending the discourse on developmental appropriateness: A developmental perspective. *Early Education and Development*, 2, 109–19.

White, S.H. (2000). The social roles of child study. *Human Development*, 43, 284–88.

Zimiles, H. (1986). Rethinking the role of research: New issues and lingering doubts in an era of expanding preschool education. *Early Childhood Research Quarterly*, 1, 189–206.

——(2000a). On reassessing the relevance of the child development knowledge base to education. *Human Development*, 43, 235–45.

——(2000b). The vagaries of rigor. *Human Development*, 43, 289–94.

4

FROM THEORY TO CURRICULUM

Developmental Theory and Its Relationship to Curriculum and Instruction in Early Childhood Education

J. Amos Hatch

Introduction

I studied early childhood education in a college of education. My terminal diploma says that I have a Ph.D. in curriculum and instruction. The transcripts from all three of my degrees show that I had extensive coursework in child development and early childhood education, but I was also exposed to heavy doses of curriculum theory and design as well as lots of coursework in instructional theory and research. My path as an early childhood professor has taken me far away from my roots as a student of curriculum and instruction, but the notion that curriculum can be thought of as a separate and distinct discipline from instruction provides an interesting tool for considering the topic on which I have been invited to write: the application of developmental theory to early childhood curriculum.

Given the way developmental theory is usually construed in our field and my take on curriculum as the intellectual substance that should be taught in educational settings, I argue that the connections between developmental theory and curriculum are tenuous at best. To organize my case, I present a brief description of what I take to be the hegemony of developmental perspectives in theorizing and policy making in mainstream early childhood education. I then make distinctions between curriculum and instruction and point out how these distinctions are largely missing when child development theories dominate the discourses of early childhood. Describing the impact of developmental theory on early childhood instruction (as opposed to curriculum), I contrast the implications of applying precepts from Piaget to those from Vygotsky. I conclude with examples from math and science that demonstrate the advantages of distinguishing curriculum from instruction and highlight the disadvantages of the field's overreliance on Piagetian-influenced developmental theory.

Developmentally Appropriate Thinking

Developmentally appropriate practice (DAP) is a brand. It is *the* brand of the National Association for the Education of Young Children (NAEYC), and, as a brand, it has been adopted (sometimes co-opted) by countless programs, policies, and products in the US and around the globe. NAEYC has been thoughtful and strategic about marketing, protecting, and updating DAP—its most valuable commodity. In the second and third of three major DAP iterations so far (Bredekamp, 1987; Bredekamp & Copple, 1997; Copple & Bredekamp, 2009), NAEYC has adjusted adroitly to the complaints of its critics. The documents have changed in form and substance, but the reliance on developmental theory as the bedrock on which the DAP brand is built remains constant; it is after all, *developmentally* appropriate practice.

In a recent article (Hatch, 2010), I describe my search through a collection of current textbooks designed for early childhood college courses. My goal was to examine what future early childhood teachers are reading about teaching and learning in these texts. As might be expected, the efficacy of developmentally appropriate practice and the central importance of knowing child development theory were taken for granted throughout these contemporary textbooks. None of the texts I examined (all published in 2006 or later) had enough time to make reference to the 2009 DAP guidelines, but it is certain that their next editions will do so. It seems just as certain that child development theory will continue to dominate future versions of the DAP brand and strongly influence the materials, programs, and policies that drive the early childhood education mainstream. It would be unthinkable to disconnect DAP from NAEYC and impossible to construct a "developmentally appropriate practice" without its defining ingredient: developmental theory. But, what does this have to do with early childhood curriculum (and instruction)?

Distinguishing the What from the How in Early Childhood Education

Plenty of evidence suggests that mainstream early childhood educators are preoccupied with how children develop, how classrooms are organized, how adults interact with children, and how children interact with their surroundings. In fact, early childhood curriculum as described in the current literature, including all three DAP handbooks, is largely focused on how classrooms ought to be organized and run. Missing until recently is a careful consideration of what should be learned in these classrooms.

Curriculum in many early childhood contexts has been taken to mean setting up stimulating environments and following the lead of the child. Early childhood curriculum has emphasized child-centered approaches and child-initiated activity. In this discourse, curriculum is said to emerge from the interests and developmental capacities of children. The role of children is to act as explorers and discoverers, while teachers are to be guides and facilitators. The processes of the classroom become the focus of early education. In these settings, the intellectual substance to be learned has been little more than an afterthought.

In a book on teaching in kindergarten (Hatch, 2005), I offer a conception of curriculum and instruction that highlights the differences between the what and how of early childhood education. In this way of thinking, curriculum is focused squarely on the subject matter content that young children ought to be taught. The content comes from subject matter disciplines, including language arts, mathematics, science, social studies, health and physical education, and the arts. In contrast, instruction is conceptualized as the ways that teachers work with students to insure that the substance of the curriculum is learned. Curriculum is what is to be taught; instruction is how the curriculum is taught.

Contrary to what is provided in most texts about early childhood education, my book lays out a wide range of teaching strategies that teachers are encouraged to apply. The conceptualizations of curriculum and instruction are intentionally clean and neat. They are meant to help teachers and future teachers avoid confusing what they teach (curriculum) with how they teach it (instruction).

Others within the field have also moved in the direction of placing more emphasis on distinguishing between curriculum and instruction. Coming from different angles, Epstein's (2007) *The Intentional Teacher: Choosing the Best Strategies for Young Children's Learning* and *Teaching Young Children: Choices in Theory and Practice* by MacNaughton and Williams (2004) are prominent examples. Epstein (2007) published her book with NAEYC, utilizing the "intentional teaching" concept "to broaden our thinking about early curriculum content and related teaching strategies" (p. viii). My view is her book is valuable because Epstein takes seriously the notion that there is genuine curriculum content to be learned in early childhood classrooms. She acknowledges that curriculum comes from knowledge generated in the academic disciplines. The book does less well at broadening early childhood teachers' conceptions of teaching strategies because of its emphasis on the primacy of "child-guided" activities. However, the book's premise that it is important to include real intellectual substance in early childhood curriculum is a big step forward.

MacNaughton and Williams (2004) are Australian authors, and the focus of their book is on enriching early childhood educators' knowledge of alternative theories and expanding their repertoires of teaching strategies. They provide an extensive taxonomy of teaching strategies that include 15 general (e.g. demonstrating, grouping, questioning) and 10 specialized (e.g. deconstructing, empowering, philosophizing) teaching techniques. For each of the specialized teaching strategies, MacNaughton and Williams provide a theoretical overview to support teachers' understandings. The theorists they draw on in these sections include some who are not often found in early childhood curriculum texts, including Derrida (deconstructing), Freire (empowering), and Lipman (philosophizing). Although they acknowledge traditional notions related to the impact of developmental forces, MacNaughton and Williams honor the cognitive capacities of young children to process genuine curriculum content, and they provide instructional tools for teachers that mark clear boundaries between the what and how of early childhood teaching. Both books support my case that early childhood curriculum need not and should not be conflated with early childhood instruction.

Like MacNaughton and Williams (2004), I used my kindergarten book to identify sets of teaching strategies so that early childhood teachers could see that their roles as instructors go beyond setting up stimulating environments and waiting for opportunities to facilitate development (Hatch, 2005). Given real curriculum content and real children who need to learn that content, the teaching strategies are presented as options designed to improve teachers' chances of helping all children be successful learners. These strategies are arranged on a continuum that ranges from incidental to direct teaching, and include three kinds of thematic teaching (units, projects, and integrated theme studies) and seven types of tactical teaching (grouping, modeling and demonstrating, coaching, tutoring, discussing, practicing, and individualizing). No strategies are given more attention or status than any others. Teachers are called on to use the continuum to frame instructional decisions that maximize all children's chances of learning the material in the curriculum.

Like Epstein's (2007), my kindergarten book identifies curriculum content synthesized from academic disciplines (e.g. literacy, math, science, social studies, health, physical education, and the arts). Both books rely on recommendations from professional organizations in the various disciplines as content is selected for inclusion, and for both books the message is the same: real content is important in early childhood curriculum, and we have a good idea of what that content should be.

The kindergarten curriculum I describe is meant to be an example of what is possible; it is not intended to be *the* kindergarten curriculum. In my sample kindergarten curriculum, I stayed away from using the terms "objectives" and "standards," preferring "elements" to name the distinct pieces of content to be taught. That is because I want to provide early childhood teachers with a roadmap of what ought to be learned in kindergarten. It is not a capitulation to manic attempts to create arbitrary standards, then apply ill-suited measurements to assess them—what I have called accountability shovedown (Hatch, 2002). I want to promote teaching real content because doing so makes sense for young children. I do not want the identification of elements to be appropriated by those who would say that the mastery of these "objectives" or the accomplishment of these "standards" ought to become the criteria by which young children or their teachers are judged.

Developmental Theory and Early Childhood Curriculum and Instruction

I know that curriculum can be defined in many ways and that early childhood definitions based on developmental theory have their own logic once basic premises

are accepted; but I think those premises need to be challenged. Here, I am challenging the utility of developmental theory as a source for understanding the
"what" of early childhood curriculum. Curriculum content, the substance of early
childhood education, cannot logically be identified based on knowledge of child
development theory; that is, figuring out what subject matter knowledge should be
taught does not follow from understandings of what children are like at particular
ages and stages. This helps explain why descriptions of developmentally appropriate
early childhood curriculum are so often devoid of serious consideration of the
intellectual content children should be expected to learn (Kessler & Swadener,
1992; Stone, 1996).

If developmental theory has little to tell early childhood professionals about the
intellectual content that young children can and should be learning (i.e. the curriculum), what about its relationship to instruction? The short answer is that developmental theory can tell us a lot more about instruction than it can about
curriculum. However, it gets complicated very quickly because applying constructs
from different developmental theorists leads to classroom practices that look quite
different from one another. As a prime example, differences between the constructivist theories of Piaget and his followers (e.g. Piaget, 1968; Piaget & Inhelder,
1969; Furth, 1970) and the socio-cultural theoretical approach of Vygotsky and his
disciples (e.g. Vygotsky, 1978; Luria, 1976; Wertsch, 1985) lead to quite different
instructional stances.

As I have argued elsewhere (Hatch, 2010), the field likes to lump developmental
theories together and pretend that early childhood educators can comfortably meld
Piagetian and Vygotskian approaches in the classroom. However, the basic
assumptions of these two seminal developmental theorists with regard to the relationship between learning and development lead to conceptions of instruction that
are not easily reconciled. Piaget's position is that cognitive development needs to be
in place *before* learning can be meaningful and effective. One of Piaget's most
quoted axioms encapsulates this key feature of his theory: "Learning is subordinated
to development and not vice-versa" (Piaget, 1964, p. 17). The point is hammered
home by one of Piaget's most prominent interpreters: "Learning is inconceivable
without a theoretically prior interior structure" (Furth, 1970, p. 160).

Vygotsky has a different view of the relationship between learning and development. For him, learning *leads* development. Learning is conceived to be an inher-
ently social activity, and interactions between children and more capable others are
the vehicle for generating developmental progress. In his words, "learning awakens
a variety of internal developmental processes that are able to operate only when the
child is interacting with people in his environment" (Vygotsky, 1978, p. 90).

Yes, knowledge of developmental theories like those associated with Piaget and
Vygotsky can be used to inform instruction, but educators need to be much more
discerning about how they apply developmental theory in early childhood practice.
It is not a surprise that those who fail to see the need for content-rich curriculum in
early childhood classrooms are those who favor the application of Piagetian

principles. If they agree with Piaget that "when we teach too fast, we keep the child from inventing and discovering himself" (as quoted in Duckworth, 1964, p. 3), then activities that aim to teach certain curriculum content will not have a prominent place in their classrooms. What is a surprise is that they do not see (or at least acknowledge) the inherent contradiction between their approach and the application of Vygotskian theoretical principles. Vygotsky is always cited in DAP and other mainstream early childhood texts, but the application of his ideas related to the place of learning as the engine that drives development is virtually ignored.

If Vygotsky's notion that learning leads development were taken seriously, then "appropriate" classrooms would look and operate differently than those based primarily on Piagetian principles. Teacher and student roles would be constructed in new ways, and the curriculum and instruction experienced by students would be different than are prescribed in the current early childhood literature. If learning as opposed to development were the defining element in early childhood classroom experiences, then curriculum content would have a much more prominent place. If learning via social interaction with more capable others took the place of individual exploration and discovery, then *teaching* intellectual substance as opposed to *facilitating* individual development would be much more visible. Teachers would actually be applying knowledge of Vygotskian concepts such as the zone of proximal development (Vygotsky, 1978; Bodrova & Leong, 2007; Berk & Winsler, 1995) in their work. They would focus their instruction on scaffolding skills and concepts that are just beyond the students' level of independent functioning. They would be actively engaged in interactions with children that are strategically designed to send the message to students that what they can do with the teacher's support today, they will be able to do alone tomorrow. In sum, teachers would be planning activities and implementing instructional strategies that emphasize learning over development (see Hatch, 2010).

In this chapter, I am trying to make the case that developmental theory as it is being conceptualized in contemporary discourses has little to offer in terms of defining the substantive curriculum to be learned in early childhood classrooms. A central issue is that early childhood educators have conflated notions of curriculum and instruction, assuming that the "how" of setting up and facilitating early experiences takes precedence over the "what" that might be included in a carefully designed content-rich curriculum. While developmental theories are not useful in deciding what content ought to be included in early childhood curriculum, they do have profound implications for how instruction is conceptualized and enacted. Examining the differences between Piagetian and Vygotskian notions of the relationship between learning and development, and recognizing how Piaget's ideas have trumped Vygotsky's, provides insight into why curriculum and instruction have not been considered distinct entities in our field. If Piaget (as quoted in Duckworth, 1964, p. 3) is correct in asserting that "the goal of education is not to increase the amount of knowledge, but to create opportunities for a child to invent and discover," then a concern with including specified "knowledge" in the curriculum seems misplaced. In the next section of this chapter, I use specific examples from math and science to argue that unchallenged Piagetian precepts may be limiting how early childhood educators think about curriculum and instruction, and undermining opportunities for young children to learn and develop.

Math and Science Learning

In this section, I offer examples of how making clear distinctions between curriculum and instruction can improve young children's chances of learning important content in early childhood classrooms. I utilize recent research on young children's capacities to process math and science content and contrast that research with precepts from developmental theory that continue to dominate early childhood practice. Using examples of specific content, I also point out the potential inadequacies of math and science teaching based on outdated developmental axioms.

I have chosen to focus on math and science for three reasons. First, it seems clear that math and science instruction should be receiving more attention in early childhood because of the current emphasis on the STEM fields (science, technology, engineering, and mathematics) in K-12 and higher education (President's Council of Advisors on Science and Technology, 2010). Second, research on the capacities of young children to learn math and science content has demonstrated that assumptions at the base of traditional early childhood approaches have underestimated the cognitive capacities of young children (e.g. Bransford et al., 2000; Meadows, 2006). Third, based on reactions to research syntheses that showed the efficacy of actively teaching key reading skills and concepts (National Reading Panel, 2000; Neuman et al., 2000; Snow et al., 1998), significant progress toward systematically including literacy content in early childhood curricula has already been made.

It is worth noting at the outset of this discussion that the Piagetian orthodoxy that dominates mainstream early childhood thinking has been thoroughly critiqued by scholars from across many disciplines, including developmental psychologists. Cognitive scientists (e.g. Bransford et. al., 2000; Meadows, 2006) who study how children learn have discovered that young children are capable of mental processing that was considered impossible based on Piagetian notions of cognitive development. For example, these scientists have documented that young children can think about their own thinking, metacognitively monitor their own learning, and intentionally adjust their own mental processes to adapt to different learning situations. These findings directly challenge Piagetian understandings that children are capable of metacognitive thinking only after they have reached the formal operational stage of cognitive development (about age 12).

In addition, studies in disciplines such as cultural anthropology (Lave, 1988, 1993) and cultural psychology (Rogoff, 1990) have shown how learning happens in a variety of social and cultural contexts. Findings from these studies demonstrate that children do not learn new skills and information in isolation; learning happens in social interaction with adults or more capable others. Children are not expected to be "little scientists" who explore and experiment on their own in order to discover the cultural knowledge that they need. Learning happens best when they act in the role of "apprentice thinkers" who learn directly from "more skilled partners" (Rogoff, 1990, p. 15), a conceptualization that looks more like the application of Vygotskian than Piagetian constructivist theory.

Research into young children's mathematics learning demonstrates the inadequacy of expecting children to construct complex understandings based on free play, independent exploration, and discovery. Challenging Piagetian assumptions about how children acquire logico-mathematical knowledge, Ginsburg and colleagues (2006, p. 174) summarize:

- young children are competent in a wider range of mathematical abilities than Piaget's (1952) theory might lead one to believe;
- when given instruction, young children are ready to learn some rather complex mathematics;
- free play is not enough to promote early mathematical thinking.

Math content is not currently emphasized in early childhood curriculum or meaningfully addressed in typical early childhood teaching. Based on a comprehensive National Research Council review of research on mathematics teaching in early childhood settings, Cross, Woods, and Schweingruber conclude:

> Young children in early childhood classrooms do not spend much time engaged with mathematics content. The time that is spent engaged in mathematics is typically of low instructional quality and, more often than not, is conducted as part of whole class activities or embedded in center time or free play. Early childhood teachers rarely teach mathematics in small groups. They report that they are much more likely to use embedded mathematical strategies or do the calendar, which they consider to be teaching mathematics, rather than provide experiences with a primary focus on mathematics.
>
> *(Cross et al., 2009, p. 275)*

As a university instructor, I have been guilty of perpetuating the paucity of high quality mathematics teaching in early childhood settings. By way of example, for years I preached to students in my kindergarten methods classes that it was developmentally inappropriate to expect kindergartners to master the concept of missing addends (e.g. $2 + - = 5$). Citing an article by Kamii, Lewis, and Booker (1998) and their reference to Inhelder and Piaget (1964), I taught my students that children up to about age 7 should not be taught missing addends because they were not developmentally ready to reverse their thinking (they would likely respond by adding 2 and 5 and writing 7 in the blank). I used the Piagetian notion of reversibility (i.e. the ability to think in opposite directions simultaneously) to make a larger point about the futility and potential dangers of expecting young children to master mathematics content that they were not cognitively capable of understanding.

My approach now in the same classes is to encourage future kindergarten teachers to take students as far as the students can go in their math learning. I show preservice teachers a progression of math concepts and skills drawn from my book (Hatch, 2005) and from other sources (Clements et al., 2004; NCTM, 2000), and I provide a range of instructional strategies that make it possible for young children to acquire mathematics knowledge that has been thought to be beyond their capacities in the past. With regard to missing addends, young children can learn the deep structure of mathematical sentences so that they understand the fundamental algebraic axiom that both sides of an equation must be equal. When confronted with equations like $2 + \_ = 5$, their mental processing turns to making sure that elements on both sides of the equal sign are equivalent. Going beyond the limitations associated with children's cognitive development as described by Piaget and his interpreters means that young children can and should be learning more mathematics content in early childhood classrooms.

Similar issues apply in early childhood science curriculum and instruction. Genuine science content has even less prominence than mathematics in most early childhood curricula. Children are given opportunities to explore and discover, but systematic teaching of scientific concepts and processes is difficult to find. Again, the assumption that young children are not cognitively ready to comprehend abstract scientific principles and that they should be given opportunities to explore and construct scientific understandings on their own dominates mainstream thinking about early childhood science. But, as with mathematics, there is evidence that this kind of thinking shortchanges children's chances to form solid foundations in science. As Duschl, Schweingruber, and Shouse (2007) have noted, "Contrary to older views, young children are not concrete and simplistic thinkers. ... Children can use a wide range of reasoning processes that form the underpinnings of scientific thinking" (pp. 2–3). And others question the appropriateness of Piaget's view of "child as little scientist." Segal (1996, p. 152) points out that the content and processes of science are too complex to understand without instruction and support, noting that to discover science principles on his or her own, the child has to be not just a little scientist but "quite a brilliant theorist."

My approach to introducing preservice teachers to early childhood science teaching has also changed over the years. In the past, I emphasized setting up opportunities in kindergarten classrooms for children to explore objects and materials related to science concepts, for example learning centers that allowed children to experiment with physical properties like magnetism, gravity, and buoyancy. I passed along the same Piagetian logic I was taught in my own early childhood science preparation, logic exemplified in a widely used contemporary early childhood curriculum text's advice to prospective teachers:

> Science is, and should be, a natural part of a child's daily experience. It is not a separate subject to be reserved for specific experiences in the curriculum; it is present everywhere in the world around the children, and they are anxious to explore it, discover answers, and build new understandings.
>
> *(Eliason & Jenkins, 2008, p. 239)*

My approach to teaching about science teaching has changed. I take the same tack as I use with math and the other subject matter areas. I tell my students there is real science to be learned in kindergarten and it is their responsibility to actively teach science content and science processes. Instead of just setting up the science table with an assortment of objects (e.g. rocks) for children to manipulate, explore, and "play" with, I recommend (and have preservice teachers practice) designing activities that teach specific scientific processes (i.e. observation, classification, hypothesizing, investigation, interpretation, and communication) along with real content in the areas of life science, physics, and earth and space science (Hatch, 2005). For example, the scientific process of classification can be systematically taught in ways that help children use their senses to get reliable information from the world, identify similar and different attributes of objects, make distinctions between objects based on those attributes, form conceptual categories based on those distinctions, and start to understand that all knowledge can be organized into a hierarchy of superordinate, coordinate, subordinate categories. So children can be taught to observe and classify rocks by their attributes while they also learn the basics of rock taxonomy (e.g. sandstone and limestone are kinds of sedimentary rock).

It is clear to anyone who has spent time observing children's "science play" or talking to young children about their conceptions of science that their scientific understandings are limited and frequently distorted. We have dismissed these gaps and misunderstandings based on our assumptions about young children's limited developmental capacities, rationalizing that the processes of exploration and discovery are more important than acquiring accurate scientific understanding (Lind, 1999). But the contention that young children are cognitively incapable of processing real scientific content and learning real scientific processes does not hold up. The key is that scientific understandings are taught in ways that respect the intellectual capacities of young children and that teachers carefully scaffold connections between what is familiar and unfamiliar to their young students (Bransford et al., 2000; National Research Council, 2001).

Conclusions

In this chapter, I argued that developmental theory has almost nothing to say about curriculum, when curriculum is understood to be the content that young children are exposed to in early childhood classrooms. Noting the hegemonic influence of developmental theories on early childhood policy and practice (as exemplified in the branding of the DAP), I made the case that the dominance of developmental theory leads the field to blur differences between curriculum and instruction. I described frequently ignored differences between precepts at the core of Piagetian and Vygotskian theories related to the relationship between learning and development and pointed out implications of those differences for early childhood instruction. I concluded by presenting examples from the curriculum areas of math and science that show the disconnect between the field's emphasis on Piagetian developmental theories and current research on the learning capacities of young children. These examples demonstrate that the field needs to take a careful look at its overdependence on developmental theory and consider the advantages of making clear distinctions between what is considered to be curriculum and what is taken to be instruction in early childhood classrooms.

References

Berk, L.E. & Winsler, A. (1995). *Scaffolding children's learning: Vygotsky and early childhood education.* Washington, DC: National Association for the Education of Young Children.

Bodrova, E. & Leong, D.J. (2007). *Tools of the mind: The Vygotskian approach to early childhood education.* Upper Saddle River, NJ: Pearson.

Bransford, J.D., Brown, A.L., & Cocking, R.R. (Eds.). (2000). *How people learn: Brain, mind, experience, and school.* Washington, DC: National Academy Press.

Bredekamp, S. (Ed.). (1987). *Developmentally appropriate practice in early childhood programs.* Washington, DC: National Association for the Education of Young Children.

Bredekamp, S. & Copple, C. (Eds.). (1997). *Developmentally appropriate practice in early childhood programs* (rev. ed.). Washington, DC: National Association for the Education of Young Children.

Clements, D.H., Sarama, J., & DiBiase, A.M. (Eds.). (2004). *Engaging young children in mathematics: Standards for early childhood education.* Mahwah, NJ: Erlbaum.

Copple, C. & Bredekamp, S. (Eds.). (2009). *Developmentally appropriate practice in early childhood programs* (3rd ed.). Washington, DC: National Association for the Education of Young Children.

Cross, C.T., Woods, T.A., & Schweingruber, H. (Eds.). (2009). *Mathematics learning in early childhood: Paths toward excellence and equity.* Washington, DC: The National Academies Press.

Duckworth, E. (1964). Piaget rediscovered. In R.E. Ripple & V.N. Rockcastle (Eds.), *Piaget rediscovered: A report of the conference on cognitive studies and curriculum development* (pp. 1–5). Ithaca, NY: Cornell University School of Education.

Duschl, R.A., Schweingruber, H.A., & Shouse, A.W. (Eds.). (2007). *Taking science to school: Learning and teaching science in grades K-8.* Washington, DC: National Academies Press.

Eliason, C. & Jenkins, L. (2008). *A practical guide to early childhood curriculum* (8th ed.). Upper Saddle River, NJ: Pearson.

Epstein, A.S. (2007). *The intentional teacher: Choosing the best strategies for young children's learning.* Washington, DC: National Association for the Education of Young Children.

Furth, H.G. (1970). *Piaget for teachers.* Englewood Cliffs, NJ: Prentice-Hall.

Ginsburg, H.P., Kaplan, R.G., Cannon, J., Cordero, M.I., Eisenband, J.G., Galanter, M., & Morgenlander, M. (2006). Helping early childhood educators to teach mathematics. In M. Zaslow & I. Martinez-Beck (Eds.). *Critical issues in early childhood professional development* (pp. 171–202). Baltimore, MD: Paul H. Brookes.

Hatch, J.A. (2002). Accountability shovedown: Resisting the standards movement in early childhood education. *Phi Delta Kappan, 83,* 457–62.

——(2005). *Teaching in the new kindergarten.* Clifton Park, NY: Thomson Delmar Learning.

——(2010). Rethinking the relationship between learning and development: Teaching for learning in early childhood classrooms. *The Educational Forum*, 74, 258–68.

Inhelder, B. & Piaget, J. (1964). *The early growth of logic in the child.* New York: Harper & Row.

Kamii, C., Lewis, B.A., & Booker, B.M. (1998). Instead of teaching missing addends. *Teaching Children Mathematics*, 4, 458–61.

Kessler, S. & Swadener, B.B. (Eds.). (1992). *Reconceptualizing the early childhood curriculum: Beginning the dialogue.* New York: Teachers College Press.

Lave, J. (1988). *Cognition in practice: Mind, mathematics, and culture in everyday life.* New York: Cambridge University Press.

——(1993). The practice of learning. In S. Chaiklin & J. Lave (Eds.). *Understanding practice* (pp. 3–32). New York: Cambridge University Press.

Lind, K.K. (1999). Science in early childhood: Developing and acquiring fundamental concepts and skills. American Association for the Advancement of Science Project 2061. Retrieved from http://www.project2061.org/publications/earlychild/online/experience/lind.htm.

Luria, A.R. (1976). *Cognitive development: Its cultural and social foundations.* Cambridge, MA: Harvard University Press.

MacNaughton, G. & Williams, G. (2004). *Teaching young children: Choices in theory and practice.* Berkshire, UK: Open University Press.

Meadows, S. (2006). *The child as thinker: The development and acquisition of cognition in childhood.* New York: Routledge.

National Reading Panel. (2000). *Report of the National Reading Panel: Teaching children to read.* Washington, DC: National Institute of Child Health and Human Development.

National Research Council. (2001). *Eager to learn: Educating our preschoolers.* Washington, DC: National Academy Press.

NCTM. (2000). *Principles and standards for school mathematics.* Reston, VA: National Council of Teachers of Mathematics.

Neuman, S.B., Copple, C., & Bredekamp, S. (2000). *Learning to read and write: Developmentally appropriate practices for young children.* Washington, DC: National Association for the Education of Young Children.

Piaget, J. (1952). *The child's conception of number.* London: Routledge & Kegan Paul.

——(1964). Development and learning. In R.E. Ripple & V.N. Rockcastle (Eds.), *Piaget rediscovered: A report of the conference on cognitive studies and curriculum development* (pp. 7–20). Ithaca, NY: Cornell University School of Education.

——(1968). *Six psychological studies.* New York: Random House.

Piaget, J. & Inhelder, B. (1969). *The psychology of the child.* New York: Basic Books.

President's Council of Advisors on Science and Technology. (2010). *Prepare and inspire: K-12 education in science, technology, engineering, and math (STEM) for America's future.* Retrieved from http://www.whitehouse.gov/assets/documents/PCAST_H1N1_Report.pdf.

Rogoff, B. (1990). *Apprenticeship in thinking: Cognitive development in social context.* New York: Oxford University Press.

Segal, G. (1996). The modularity of theory of mind. In P. Carruthers & P. Smith (Eds.). *Theories of theories of mind* (pp. 141–57). Cambridge: Cambridge University Press.

Snow, C.E., Burns, M.S., & Griffin, P. (1998). *Preventing reading difficulties in young children.* Washington, DC: National Academy Press.

Stone, J.E. (1996). Developmentalism: An obscure but pervasive restriction on educational improvement. *Educational Policy Analysis Archives*, 4, 1–29.

Vygotsky, L.S. (1978). *Mind in society: The development of higher mental processes.* Cambridge, MA: Harvard University Press. (Original work published in 1930.)

Wertsch, J.V. (1985). *Vygotsky and the social formation of mind.* Cambridge, MA: Harvard University Press.

5

THE CURRICULUM THEORY LENS ON EARLY CHILDHOOD

Moving Thought into Action

Jennifer J. Mueller

Introduction

This chapter takes us to the field of curriculum studies and curriculum theory to add to our understanding of the larger context in which curriculum, and curriculum in early childhood education (ECE), has evolved. We attend to the larger debates and paradigms in education in the US over the last century to help us to understand how these contexts were also shaping early childhood.

Insight into where we have been and why is important in understanding our direction as a field. We have come upon what I argue are "what next?" and "how do we?" moments in consideration of curriculum in ECE. In particular in ECE, just as in curriculum studies as a field, there is struggle with the dynamism of theory and practice as they apply to the reality of day-to-day classroom work. As Kessler (1991a, 1991b, 1992) and others have proposed, reconsidering early childhood curriculum within the larger debate and discussions of curriculum theory may help us move out from this moment, and, as Cornbleth (1990) suggests, help us to "[realize] the potential of curriculum to contribute to a more meaningful and empowering education of young people" (p. 5).

Curriculum, Curriculum Studies, and Curriculum Theory: A Brief and Selective Overview

Defining curriculum is a tricky enterprise. If we think of curriculum as the stuff of what happens in schools there are many avenues to pursue in considering what that might mean. Curriculum often is the formal products and documents that guide what is to occur in classrooms. Pinar (2004) posits that curriculum actually is school, in total, as experienced by students and teachers.

Curriculum studies has evolved in two veins—one of curriculum development and the other of curriculum theorizing. If we understand curriculum to be the study of that which constitutes knowledge, questions that comprise a study of curriculum include: how we conceive of the nature of knowledge; how students (children) come to learn that knowledge; and which knowledge is of greatest value and importance. The shifting nature of the socio-cultural-historical contexts of our society and, thus, education and curriculum over more than a century provides evidence that the basic idea and conception of curriculum are not static, universal, or uncontested.

Curriculum studies as a field emerged at the turn of the 20th century as the country struggled to define the aims and goals of education (Kliebard, 2004) amidst a changing population and an ever-shifting social and cultural milieu. Kliebard describes the debates around the purposes and aims of education during the 20th century having been defined by four predominant interest groups. The humanists rested on the idea that education and curriculum ought to focus on the "development of reasoning power" (p. 9) and a steeping in Western-based subject areas. The developmentalists operated from the "assumption that the natural order of development in the child was the most significant and scientifically defensible basis for determining what should be taught" (p. 11) in schools. Adherents to a social efficiency model focused on the elimination of waste in the curriculum through "scientific management techniques" (p. 20), precise measurement, and differentiation of education according to students' perceived proclivities and ultimate "destinations." And, the social meliorists believed that education was the key to social progress, correction of social ills, and promulgation of social justice.

The Technocratic View

Overarching these debates was predominance of the scientific/rationalist/empiricist paradigm during most of the 20th century. This, according to Cornbleth (1990), shaped concepts of curriculum in all four factions. Out of this paradigm of thought emerged what Cornbleth calls the "technocratic" view of curriculum. In this view curriculum is construed as a product, separate from policy and from classroom use. Curriculum is also set apart from politics, giving it the appearance of neutrality and separation from the competing values and interests of any historical time. This view indicated that curriculum was scientifically, objectively, and rationally derived, was objectives focused, and thus could have knowable and attainable end results or outcomes. This was derived from an assumption that the "means–end" progression is a "direct path" where the "precision and control over the otherwise disorderly nature of curriculum and teaching" are paramount, thus conveying the image "of scientific efficiency, effectiveness, and progress" (p. 15).

This view of curriculum has arguably been one of the greatest influences on what we know as curriculum, and we can see the continued (and renewed) predominance of this approach in schools today. In laying out what he calls seven "curriculum episodes" (Scott, 2008, p. 18) of the past century, Scott makes the case for the predominance of the theory of social efficiency as the blueprint for school curriculum. Major scholars of the time, including Bobbitt, Charters, and Tyler in the 1920s and 1930s, argued for "precision, objectivity, and prediction" in curriculum development and proffered that we could determine exactly "what should be taught in schools and how educational knowledge should be structured" (p. 6). Out of this movement came the suggested importance of behavioral objectives where knowledge and skills could be broken down into their essential elements. The important skills were determined by the activities of experts in fields of study. Through the objective study of these experts, curricular goals could be derived. The skills were then translated into teaching strategies, and objective testing could determine if the learner had acquired the skills.

Alongside this movement, and thus also influenced by the technocratic model, was the faction of educational scholars who adhered to the doctrine of developmentalism, as noted above. Led by G. Stanley Hall, this group operated from the belief that one could catalog what happened in the minds of children, and a systematic and accurate cataloging would conclude what should be taught in schools (Kliebard, 2004). Buoyed by the scientific, empiricist paradigm, research entailed careful, systematic "observation and recording of children's behavior at various stages of development" (p. 11). The developmentalists believed that "the curriculum riddle could be solved with ever more accurate scientific data" (p. 24).

In addition, the larger debates of the time focused on whether or not all children could learn a select body of "important" knowledge or content, and, given a vast array of capabilities and "destinations," curriculum needed to be differentiated to meet the capacities of learners (which could be scientifically discovered). Here Hall contributed by suggesting the idea of "probable destination" where through careful study of child development the life outcome of a child could be determined, and then a curriculum devised to support that destination. And indeed, Kliebard (2004) suggests, "predicting future destination as the basis for adapting the curriculum to different segments of the school population became a major feature of curriculum planning" (p. 13).

Bloch, in several publications (1991, 1992, 2000), has carefully laid out the connections of current early childhood research and curriculum to the developmentalist faction. She notes (Bloch, 1991) that Hall's ideas began the child development movement that connected psychology to science and to child development, which coupled science with the study of pedagogy and curriculum in early childhood education.

Bloch explains that eventually a departure from Hall's version of child study was necessitated by better science—i.e. more scientific and objective ways of researching children to formulate a pattern of "normal" child development. And while strong ties between psychology and pedagogy shaped both elementary/secondary and early childhood, early childhood ran a somewhat separate course from that of elementary and secondary education. Bloch maintains that in elementary education, social reconstructionist theories did have more influence for theorists and educators to focus on school as a means of social reform. However, for early childhood Bloch suggests:

> Early education as a professional group was more heavily aligned with psychology, psychiatry, home economics, and child and family studies programs at the university level ... behavioral theories supported the importance of early ... personality development in children. The institutional presence of laboratory nursery schools ... emphasized teaching women about ... family arts, as well as about scientific knowledge about child development and child rearing. Child development professionals aligned themselves ... with psychology to engage in theoretical debates on individual development and family influences, as well as to appear to be a fairly "hard" science.
>
> *(Bloch, 1992, p. 103)*

Bloch (2000) further highlights that since the fields of child development and developmental psychology have been dominated by "quantitatively oriented psychological studies" (p. 258), thus so has the field of early childhood education.

Goffin (1996) points out that this scientism initially (and importantly) supported the professionalization of the field of early childhood. She notes that the faith put into the ability of "scientifically derived solutions" to solve social ills ran parallel with "an undervaluation of children as public responsibility." This required that early childhood take on an advocacy role, and the emergence of "predictable and achievable child development outcomes" supplied an "important lever for arguing the inadequacy of many existing early childhood education settings and for promoting the importance of better prepared and compensated personnel ... child development knowledge provide[d] a concrete frame of reference for improving classroom practice" (p. 125).

The Dawns of Change

Moving forward in our historical overview, Kliebard (2004) highlights the social meliorist faction of educational theory that emerged initially from the Great Depression, "from the undercurrent of discontent about the American economic and social system." Curriculum via this faction became the means through which "social injustice would be redressed" (p. 154). So we forward now to the mid- to latter parts of the 20th century, to a period of increased awareness and social unrest regarding inequitable distribution of opportunity across social groups—a time where sociology of education in particular began to more carefully document the actual experiences of children in schools, the impact that children and teachers had on the curriculum, and inequality of access to educational opportunities in schools (e.g. Gracey, 1972; Lubeck, 1985; Rist, 1970). And, while early critiques of this movement stemmed from an initial behaviorist bent and over-subscription to determinism (Kessler & Swadener, 1992) the sociology of the curriculum elucidated the existing dynamism between curriculum and children and teachers, revealing that the "process of schooling [was] ... complex, context-bound, interactive" (p. xxiv).

It was in this context that work of particular curriculum theorists (Huebner, MacDonald) laid "important groundwork for *reconceptualizing* the field" (Pinar et al., 1995) of curriculum theory that began in the 1960s and 1970s (and most will argue is still unfolding.) According to Pinar et al., the work of these theorists supported the field in questioning the basic assumptions of the mainstream. Malewski (2010) suggests that this set the stage for understanding the contextualized notion of curriculum where the consideration of curriculum via "democratic ideology, media representations, and issues of power and access" (p. 2) were revealed. As a result, the field experienced a dramatic shift in the concepts and questions it focused on, the methods it used, and the purposes of its work. This represented a move from a focus on curriculum development and curriculum as a transcendent product, to the idea of "understanding" (Pinar, 2004) curriculum as a sociological, contextualized *process* laden with issues of power, authority, phenomenology, and interpretation.

Early Childhood Follows

Returning now to early childhood, as the reconceptualist movement was unfolding in curriculum studies (the becoming of curriculum theory), early childhood programming was in a social meliorist movement engaged in addressing the war on poverty and issues of the "deprived" child. The continued push for professionalization in the field resulted in the publication of *Developmentally Appropriate Practice in Early Childhood Programs Serving Children from Birth through Age 8* (Bredekamp, 1987)—heretofore referred to as DAP. The emergence of DAP was in response to the fear of push down of the rationalist, behavioral objective-oriented curriculum of the elementary school (Copple & Bredekamp, 2009). During the latter part of the 20th century, as more and more public school systems took on younger and younger students as part of their purview, those in the field of early childhood spoke out against the "direct instruction academic oriented" (Bloch, 1991) view of teaching and learning that was characteristic of the elementary curriculum.

However, while rejecting the behavioral objective and academic orientation toward curriculum, the DAP document maintained the rationalist scientism given its home in developmental and child psychology. DAP represented a re-emergence of the developmentalist perspective with the child as the focus, though now with better science to support its claims. The DAP document (Copple & Bredekamp, 2009) firmly states that its position is "grounded ... in the research on child development and learning" (p. 1). Bredekamp, one of the authors and main proponents of the DAP movement in early childhood, suggests that:

It is reasonably safe to say that the developmentalist perspective of the document reflects the consensus position of the early childhood profession ... It
has been our experience that child development knowledge provides much
clearer guidance for programming decisions than do other, more value laden
philosophies.

(Bredekamp, 1991, pp. 202–3)

However, those "value laden philosophies" also emerged on the ECE
scene (beginning mainly in the late 1980s and early 1990s) as a reconceptualist
movement in early childhood that has closely mirrored the movement in curriculum theory. Drawing heavily from critical theory (including post-modern, feminist,
post-structuralist, post-colonial, and interpretivist orientations), the reconceptualists
have taken the position that it is crucial that we understand childhood, early
childhood education, classroom practice, and curriculum as inseparable from the
larger politicized, structural, and value-laden contexts in which the field exists.
Early childhood practice is not neutral or apolitical and, as Cannella and Bloch
(2006) point out, the work of the reconceptualists has "crossed disciplinary and
geographic boundaries [and] fostered hybrid ways" (p. 6) of understanding early
childhood theory and practice. They note that this movement highlights the role of
the state as an authority creating "children as societal objects and subjects of educational and care practices" (p. 7), and begs the deconstruction of this role. And
Kessler (1992) points out that the movement has elucidated the relationship
between knowledge and power important to our understanding of curriculum—
particularly since the movement helps us to reconstruct our ideas related to
knowledge and what is important to teach in educational settings. Kessler (1992, p. xxii)
urges the following reconsideration of the concept of knowledge to guide early
childhood practice:

- certain forms of knowledge have more status than other forms;
- knowledge is distributed unequally, such that students from higher-status families
  achieve more or receive more of the high-status knowledge;
- school knowledge is viewed as belonging to a particular group, and control of
  knowledge is seen as a means by which that group maintains its dominant
  position in society.

Certainly the effects can be seen in early childhood in the types of research
that have been engaged in since the movements emerged. In early childhood positivist, psychological research has certainly continued, particularly in consideration of
curriculum interventions, child outcomes in early childhood, and the support of the
economic benefits of early childhood education. However, there has been a
breakthrough in research on early childhood that fully engages the range of paradigm and viewpoint made available through the reconceptualization. For example,
File's chapter (Chapter 2) highlights different ways that research has approached the

study of curriculum. And Blaise and Ryan's chapter (Chapter 7) delineates how critical theory has shaped a research agenda within the field.

The reconceptualist movement in early childhood emerged largely as critique of the DAP document, and mainly via the critical theory lens. This large scale logging of critique, in fact, I argue, illustrates the DAP document's predominance in the field of early childhood. The DAP document remains the major definer of what is "good" early childhood practice (indicating that that can be defined) and how curriculum needs be derived out of a sophisticated understanding of child development theory and research.

Mainstream early childhood curriculum remains steeped in a paradigm that ultimately suggests that there is a "best" and "right" way for development to unfold. The reconceptualists point out that this necessarily leaves some groups of children out. Statements in the DAP document indicate this idea. For example, Copple and Bredekamp (2009) suggest that to minimize achievement gaps evident across social groups, one goal in early childhood classrooms should be to engage "proactive vocabulary development to bring young children whose vocabulary and oral language development is lagging ... closer to the developmental trajectory typical of children from educated, affluent families" (p. 7). This suggests that there is an optimal trajectory of development that is based on one cultural model.

The reconceptualist critique of DAP is illustrated when Dahlberg and Moss (2005) suggest that DAP continues its adherence to developmental psychology. And, via reconceptualist curriculum theory, the idea that curriculum can be "evidence based" and we can predetermine and adhere to a definitive notion of "positive outcomes" is problematic. They note that DAP provides a particular way of understanding children and thus "normalizes" them through its characterizations. The generalizations of DAP are considered universal and thus reliable, therefore governing children's development. They point out that

> the quasi-scientific status of developmental norms slips from description to prescription: from a mythic norm (mythic because no one actually fits it) to statements of how people should be: whether milestones, gender types, reading ages, cognitive strategies, stages or skills ... they become enshrined within an apparatus of collective measurement and evaluation that constructs its own world of abstract autonomous babies; of norms, deviation from which is typically only acknowledged in the form of deficit or problem.
>
> *(Dahlberg and Moss, 2005, p. 7)*

The technocratic and decontextualized form of curriculum as a product that can universally guide student learning and development in a preconceived, measurable, accountable manner prevails in education. This further suggests the continued predominance of knowledge viewed in a product-oriented manner that is based in dominant culture ways of knowing and being. However, as many scholars across disciplines (and indeed the DAP document itself) note, we need only look to the larger trends of underachievement and under-attainment in schools by children of color and children from low-income families to suggest that this view of knowledge and its resultant form of curriculum have not functioned to serve all children in schools. The reconceptualists argue that valuing alternative and localized views of knowledge, multiplicity of voice, incorporation of diverse ways of making meaning, and attendance to the legitimacy of a variety of cultural ways of knowing are necessary in order for curriculum to serve all children and families.

In the 2009 revision of DAP there is evidence that the issues raised by reconceptualist scholars have been acknowledged and given credence. The document begins by noting the need to attend to "critical issues in the current context" (Copple & Bredekamp, 2009, p. 1). These "issues" include the increase in children being served in early childhood settings whose heritage home-language is not English and in children living in poverty. In addition Copple & Bredekamp highlight the responsibility for early childhood curriculum to attend to the problem of achievement gaps across social/cultural groups, and the cultural mismatches between home and school settings that may precipitate these gaps. And, indeed, several reconceptualist scholars are cited as part of the "research base" of DAP—though their inclusion has not changed DAP's fundamental theoretical orientations.

So now we are at the point where, aware of the tensions of the field, I turn our attention to issues of practicality. Pinar et al. (1995) point out that the reconceptualist movement in curriculum theory has been largely ignored in mainstream curricular products—particularly textbooks. And, we could argue that the movement in early childhood has had little effect on directives for mainstream practice in the field. I suggest in the next section that to move requires concerted focus on the practice of teachers who enact the curriculum in action and process.

"How Do We Actually *Do* This?" (Or, How Does Curriculum Theory Move Us into "What Next?")

Given our foray through history in this chapter, I argue that the technocratic approach to curriculum, while predominant, has not served ultimately to meet the aims and goals of the educational interests of children. Arguably the fact that the reconceptualist movements arose gives credence to this view. Yet, curriculum theory as part of the reconceptualist movements has had seemingly little influence on practice in schools in such a way as to shift the tides in our educational dilemmas. Current political contexts will do little to support teachers to move in the directions suggested by the reconceptualists, and, in fact, will further entrench the technocratic model.

Farquhar and Fitzsimons (2007) posit that we have moved into a period of "intensified government involvement in educational institutions and increasing standardization of curricula" (p. 225). These authors further signify that early childhood education has been forced to conform to economic and market pressures to maintain its relevance and, indeed, its very existence. Moss points out:

early childhood education and care includes large swathes of under-resourced "childcare" services, often competing with each other in market conditions; combined with nursery education or kindergarten provision that is subject to increasingly strong regulation through prescriptive curricula, testing and inspection systems in order to ensure they produce children who are ready for school.

(Moss, 2007, p. 241)

DAP has necessarily (some argue appropriately) responded to this context. Copple and Bredekamp (2009) note DAP's responsibility in these times of standardization and accountability measures, particularly in light of No Child Left Behind (NCLB), to support preschool and kindergarten teachers to enact developmentally appropriate practice in ways that prepare teachers and children for this context. They note the DAP utilization of "accumulating evidence and innovations in practice [that] provide guidance as to the knowledge and abilities that teachers must work especially hard to foster in young children, as well as information on how teachers can do so" (p. 3). In times of uncertainty, the DAP model gives teachers support and a means to do what they can view as "good" for children.

Even in this political and economic context, inherent in the arguments of post-modern, reconceptualist scholars, both in curriculum theory and in early childhood, is the assumption (perhaps the hope) that the movement to a more complex, contextualized, inclusive, and diverse view of curriculum will improve the state of education. However, the enactment of this must occur in the details of daily life in classrooms, in the interactional space of curriculum, teachers, and children. And, critique of critical theory influences on curriculum studies suggests that they have been long on deconstruction and short on suggestions for new directions (Cannella & Bloch, 2006). Lenz Taguchi (2007) further notes that the deconstructive approach can be challenging for educators, given that the eclectic practices necessitated by the critical, inclusive, multi-voiced approach are by their very nature relativistic and ambiguous. She suggests that because they are not "sufficiently grounded in any one (universalist or better) theory" they "lack the normative qualities expected of a robust pedagogy" (p. 285).

If reconceptualist ideas about curriculum have not been taken up in mainstream curriculum documents, Cornbleth (1990) interestingly points out that it is often the case in practice that curriculum (of any sort) is not used as intended by curriculum developers, or ignored altogether by educators. Teachers and children hold pre-existing beliefs and engage in activity in classrooms before curriculum materials are applied. Thus those beliefs act on, with, and in what is intended in the curriculum and the curriculum is often adapted to those beliefs (Nuthall, 2005).

In the effort to move into "what next?" we must consider how these shifts in curriculum theory and early childhood can impact *classroom practice*. There is debate in curriculum theory currently as to whether or how its worth as a field should be defined in terms of its viability in practice (Malewski, 2010). I want to be careful not to position this line of thinking in the debate on what is often termed the "divide" between theory and practice. And I tend toward the more hybrid view purported by reconceptualist scholars that the theory/practice divide is a false dichotomy (or troublesome binary) that itself requires deconstruction, "dissolution and/or transgression" (Lenz Taguchi, 2007, p. 275).

And here, I position myself as an early childhood teacher educator, intensely focused on the very real and on-the-ground struggles of my students—both pre-service and inservice teachers. They are teaching young children in public schools where the call for fidelity to curriculum is the answer to achievement gaps and children are deemed as "behind" before they even get a start. They are teaching in childcare centers where they report that adherence to DAP in order to retain accreditation has created tunnel vision where procedure according to DAP outstrips a focus on the actual needs of children. We espouse in their teacher education coursework a reconstructionist-oriented view of curriculum as multi-voiced, inclusive, interdisciplinary, and process focused. Yet, in the day-to-day reality of their work with children they face the technocratic model of curriculum. While it provides them with guidance for practice, they see the daily reality that it does not necessarily or always support learning and growth for their children. In practice, the tension, for these teachers, weighs heavy. Almost every time we work together they desperately ask, "But how do we actually *do* this?" Perhaps the problem for them lies in the incongruence of trying to exert a necessarily ambiguous and tentative process into a structured, authoritative model.

We can look to research to provide some examples of localized practice, and theory and practice informing/becoming each other. There are examples of early childhood reconceptualist scholars working with specific groups of teachers toward more democratic, inclusive, and particular visions of curriculum and curriculum enactment with young children (e.g. Jipson, 1991; Lenz Taguchi, 2007; Lewis et al., 2006). In the variety of scenarios within this vein of research some similarities emerge. Curriculum, while it may begin from a standardized place, is posed as a site for de- and reconstruction taking into account the learning needs of the children, and exposing dominant discourses. Curriculum is posed as a community-based project where a variety of perspectives must be brought to bear and where outcomes emerge from the learning, rather than being predetermined. And finally, the voices of children and teachers along with the theorist or teacher educator work in concert to reflect the ongoing move toward learning and growth that is not static, rather ever-evolving.

Certainly this kind of work was reflected in Dewey's Laboratory School at the University of Chicago, where Dewey created a model of curriculum with/in practice in an attempt to mesh and reconcile the world of the child and "the social aims, meanings, values incarnate in the matured experience of the adult," with "the educative process" as "the due interaction of these forces" (Dewey, 1902, p. 8). The Laboratory School was organized so Dewey was able to, with his teachers, engage in pedagogical tinkering such that they could, in an ongoing fashion, "construct a curriculum that best facilitated that process" (Kliebard, 2004, p. 55). Kliebard reports that Dewey, along with his teachers, studied, reflected upon, and puzzled with practice so as to bring the child into the curriculum, wherever in the process that child began.

Additionally, we can see this kind of work reflected in the pedagogistas of Reggio Emilia. These consulting teachers work with the preschool teachers in an ongoing form of professional development, reflectivity, and curricular processing. This runs counter to the U.S. model of professional teacher support, where (if it exists at all) it is often a one-time smattering of information that the teacher is then expected, on his/her own, to approximate and incorporate into classroom practice. The process with the pedagogistas is an individualized relationship that is not constructed as a series of reproducible events. Rather they function as "critical, caring friends offering a permanent provocation to new thinking and practice who enter a long-term commitment" to be part of the work (Dahlberg & Moss, 2005, p. 187).

Conclusion

The above scenarios represent an ideal—something to move toward, and yet not necessarily within the reality of what many of our teachers experience. But that does not relieve my colleagues and me of the reality of *our* curricular decision-making and the tensions of preparing teachers within contextualized practice. We have to come face to face with the reality, both in a critical mode and in practice, that context is a very real feature of our teachers' work that cannot simply be overridden. We need to support their efforts at subversion of the official curriculum in the name of continually and over-again coming to understand what their children need as learners.

Perhaps this tension lies in what Moss (2007) characterizes as an unwillingness of the differing factions in early childhood to speak. He notes that communication across these divides is constrained because the modernists tend not to see paradigm, and the post-foundationalists "see little virtue in the paradigm of modernity" (p. 233). Malewski (2010) envisions the need for "proliferation" in curriculum studies, where the aim is not that "one cluster of theories overtakes another on the way toward 'one right way' approaches." Rather, he pleads for us to

> maintain a commitment to a field that celebrates the growth of its theories and stories—and to be seized by its vigor and intensity—and to assert our human inventiveness so as to personalize our theorizing regardless of how unsettling and unwieldy.
>
> (*Malewski, 2010, p. 23*)

We continue to explore the processes for working with our teachers via our relationships with them in preservice preparation, and then further interrogation of practice in graduate studies. It is important to keep an eye toward and be realistic about the larger contexts in which they are working in order that they can remain critical, reflective, questioning, and open to the possibilities of curriculum in motion. Curriculum theory helps us to do this.

References

Bloch, M. (1991). Critical science and the history of child development's influence on early education research. *Early Education and Development*, 2(2), 95–108.

——(1992). Critical perspectives on the historical relationship between child development and early childhood research. In S. Kessler & B.B. Swadener (Eds.), *Reconceptualizing the early childhood curriculum: Beginning the dialogue* (p. 3–20). New York: Teachers College Press.

——(2000). Governing teachers, parents, and children through child development knowledge. *Human Development*, 43(4), 257–65.

Bredekamp, S. (1987). *Developmentally appropriate practice in early childhood programs serving children from birth through age 8*. Washington, DC: National Association for the Education of Young Children.

——(1991). Redeveloping early childhood education: A response to Kessler. *Early Childhood Research Quarterly*, 6, 199–209.

Bredekamp, S. & Copple, C. (1997). *Developmentally appropriate practice in early childhood programs serving children from birth through age 8*. Washington, DC: National Association for the Education of Young Children.

Cannella, G. & Bloch, M. (2006). Social policy, education, and childhood in dangerous times: Revolutionary actions or global complicity. *International Journal of Educational Policy, Research, and Practice*, 7, 5–19.

Copple, C. & Bredekamp, S. (2009). *Developmentally appropriate practice in early childhood programs serving children from birth through age 8*. Washington, DC: National Association for the Education of Young Children.

Cornbleth, C. (1990). *Curriculum in context*. London: Falmer Press.

Dahlberg, G. & Moss, P. (2005). *Ethics and politics in early childhood education*. New York: RoutledgeFalmer.

Dewey, J. (1902). *The child and the curriculum*. Chicago, IL: University of Chicago Press.

Farquhar, S. & Fitzsimons, P. (2007). Philosophy of early childhood education. *Educational Philosophy and Theory*, 39(3), 225–28.

Goffin, S. (1996). Child development knowledge and early childhood teacher preparation: Assessing the relationship—A special collection. *Early Childhood Research Quarterly*, 11(2), 117–33.

Gracey, H. (1972). *Curriculum or craftsmanship: Elementary school teachers in a bureaucratic system*. Chicago, IL: University of Chicago Press.

Jipson, J. (1991). Developmentally appropriate practice: Culture, curriculum, connections. *Early Education and Development*, 2(2), 120–36.

Kessler, S. (1991a). Alternative perspectives on early childhood education. *Early Childhood Research Quarterly*, 6, 183–97.

——(1991b). Early childhood education as development: Critique of the metaphor. *Early Education and Development*, 2(2), 137–52.

——(1992). The social context of early childhood curriculum. In S. Kessler & B.B. Swadener (Eds.), *Reconceptualizing the early childhood curriculum: Beginning the dialogue* (pp. 21–42). New York: Teachers College Press.

Kessler, S. & Swadener, B.B. (1992). Reconceptualizing curriculum. In S. Kessler & B.B. Swadener (Eds), *Reconceptualizing the early childhood curriculum: Beginning the dialogue* (pp. xiii–xxviii). New York: Teachers College Press.

Kliebard, H. (2004). *The struggle for the American curriculum: 1893–1958* (3rd ed.). New York: RoutledgeFalmer.

Lenz Taguchi, H. (2007). Deconstructing and transgressing the theory–practice dichotomy in early childhood education. *Educational Philosophy and Theory*, 39, 275–90.

Lewis, T., MacFarlane, K., Nobel, K., & Stephenson, A. (2006). Crossing borders and blurring boundaries: Early childhood practice in a non-western setting. *International Journal of Early Childhood*, 38(2), 23–34.

Lubeck, S. (1985). *Sandbox society: Early education in Black and White America*. London: Falmer Press.

Malewski, E. (2010). Introduction: Proliferating curriculum. In E. Malewski (Ed.), *Curriculum studies handbook: The next moment* (pp. 1–39). New York: Routledge.

Moss, P. (2007). Meetings across the paradigmatic divide. *Educational Philosophy and Theory*, 39(3), 229–45.

Nuthall, G. (2005). The cultural myths and realities of classroom teaching and learning: A personal journey. *Teachers College Record*, 107(5), 895–934.

Pinar, W. (2004). *What is curriculum theory?* Mahwah, NJ: Lawrence Erlbaum Associates.

Pinar, W., Reynolds, W., Slattery, P., & Taubman, P. (1995). *Understanding curriculum*. New York: Peter Lang.

Rist, R. (1970). Student social class and teacher expectations: The self-fulfilling prophesy in teacher education. *Harvard Educational Review*, 40(3), 411–51.

Scott, D. (2008). *Critical essays on major curriculum theorists*. London: Routledge.

6

FROM THEORY TO CURRICULUM

The Project Approach

Judy Harris Helm

Introduction

The project approach is a curriculum framework with a legacy from the progressive movement in the US and the Plowden Report in Great Britain. This chapter defines the project approach and how it is currently practiced in classrooms in the United States. The history of the project approach and its roots in the University of Chicago Laboratory School and in the British Infant Schools of the 1960s are explained. Then the philosophy of John Dewey is used to highlight the links between theory/philosophy and practice.

Description of the Project Approach

A project is an in-depth investigation of a specific topic of high interest. Children are involved in closely observing and systematically examining and inquiring. Project work consists of three phases. In phase one, the topic is selected, teachers and children discuss what the children know, and the direction of the investigation is determined based on what they want to know. In phase two, students investigate the topic through field site visits and interaction with experts and find the answers to their questions. In the third phase, teachers and students reflect on what was learned and then complete the project with a culminating event or activities. Specific events in the project process are as follows:

- Phase 1: Beginning
  - identification of a potential topic initiated by children;
  - building of children's background knowledge;
  - narrowing the topic further; and
  - helping children create a list of questions to investigate.

- Phase 2: Investigation

  - collecting resources for investigating the topic (books, videos, artifacts);
  - using resources;
  - meeting with experts on the topic;
  - investigating through field site visits;
  - recording new questions; and
  - recording and representing what was learned.

- Phase 3: Culmination

  - reflecting by children on what they've learned;
  - listing by children of what they know now; and
  - sharing by children of what they have learned (making a book, giving a presentation, sharing with another class).

The key feature of project work is the investigation, which is a research effort deliberately focused on finding answers to questions about a topic posed by either the children, the teacher, or the teacher working with the children. The goal of project work is for the children to experience learning about a topic in which they have great interest and to experience directing their own learning—to seek answers to questions that are interesting to them. This is in contrast to other curriculum approaches in which knowledge is predetermined and children seek answers to questions posed by the teacher. Lilian Katz contrasted project work with systematic instruction in this way:

> *Systematic instruction*: (1) helps children *acquire* skills; (2) addresses *deficiencies* in children's learning; (3) stresses *extrinsic* motivation; and (4) allows teachers to direct the children's work, use their expertise, and specify the tasks that the children perform.

> *Project work*, in contrast: (1) provides children with opportunities to *apply* skills; (2) addresses children's *proficiencies;* (3) stresses *intrinsic* motivation; and (4) encourages children to determine what to work on and accepts them as experts about their needs.

> *(Katz, 1994, p. 1)*

These investigations are undertaken by the whole class or a group of children in a class. The project approach is not considered to be a whole or complete curriculum but instead an *approach* to achieving curriculum goals through student investigation. Project work often, however, contributes to the achievement of curriculum goals in many areas; teachers who use project work integrate curriculum goals into the project experiences. Teachers take advantage of the ability of project work to capture students' curiosity and motivate them to learn emerging academic skills, such as decoding, getting meaning from text, writing words, creating diagrams, and counting.

Classrooms where project work is a regular part of learning experiences have common features. There is a wealth of materials and artifacts related to the project topic; children are engaged in hands-on exploration; interaction with a variety of adults is evident; and children represent what they have learned in a variety of ways. Typically in early childhood classrooms using the project approach, not every child is participating in the project at the same time or doing the same type of work. Children are involved in other learning experiences unrelated to the project topic. Some children are painting at the easel, building with Lego, and completing puzzles, as project work occurs side by side with other developmentally appropriate activities.

History of Project Work

Considering the description of project work provided above, one can see how the project approach is consistent with the tradition of hands-on, child-directed, integrated learning of many early childhood programs. Most scholars who write about project work and its many forms (Edutopia, 2010; Helm & Katz, 2011; Katz & Chard, 2000; Markham et al., 2003) credit John Dewey's work at his experimental Laboratory School at the University of Chicago, 1896–1904, for articulating the concepts now known as the project approach. Projects were a major component of the progressive education movement.

In the United States, interest in project work surfaced again in the 1960s and 1970s, when early childhood teachers and administrators traveled to observe British Infant Schools in England where project work was an important part of the curriculum (Smith, 1997). In 1967, an influential report on Primary Education in England by the Central Advisory Council for Education, referred to as the Plowden Report, affirmed the importance of child-centered education and the flexibility, child decision-making, and integrated learning which are features of project work. As articulated in the Plowden Report:

> The idea of flexibility has found expression in a number of practices, all of them designed to make good use of the interest and curiosity of children, to minimise the notion of subject matter being rigidly compartmental, and to allow the teacher to adopt a consultative, guiding, stimulating role rather than a purely didactic one. The oldest of these methods is the "project." Some topic, such as "transport" is chosen, ideally by the children, but frequently by the teacher. The topic cuts across the boundaries of subjects and is treated as its nature requires without reference to subjects as such.
>
> *(Central Advisory Council for Education, 1967, pp. 198–99)*

This description of project work in the Plowden Report is similar to the description of project work as it is now implemented and described earlier in this chapter (pp. 67–69). The Report continued:

It begins with a topic which is of such inherent interest and variety as to make it possible and reasonable to make much of the work of the class revolve round it for a period of a week, a month or a term or even longer. Experience has shown that it is artificial to try to link most of the work of a class to one centre of interest. It has become more common to have several interests—topic is now the usual word—going at once. Much of the work may be individual, falling under broad subject headings. One topic for the time being can involve both group and class interest, and may splinter off into all kinds of individual work.

(Central Advisory Council for Education, 1967, p. 199)

It was in the British Infant Schools that Lilian Katz observed project work and began to think and write about it. Interest in the potential of project work was renewed in the US two decades after the Plowden Report with publication of the first edition of *Engaging Children's Minds: The Project Approach* (Katz & Chard, 1989). Interest in project work in early childhood was also stimulated by the impressive reports and displays of group projects conducted by children in the pre-primary schools of Reggio Emilia (Edwards et al., 1993, 1998; Gandini, 1993; New, 1990, 1991; Rankin, 1992). According to Gandini:

Projects provide the backbone of the children's and teachers' learning experiences. They are based on the strong conviction that learning by doing is of great importance and that to discuss in group and to revisit ideas and experiences is the premier way of gaining better understanding and learning.

(Gandini, 1997, p. 7)

There are many variations of project work, with most variations corresponding to the ages of students and developmental variations in their skills. Project work in a preschool classroom with children who are beginning to learn about the world of literacy looks significantly different than project work in a fifth-grade classroom where students are well along the way toward becoming literate. Today during project investigations older children use the internet for research, read and analyze original written materials, and create written reports (Boss & Krauss, 2007).

Within all of these variations, however, there are consistent characteristics which delineate projects from other hands-on, concrete approaches to curriculum. Thomas (2000) summarized five criteria that distinguish project-based learning: (1) projects are central, not peripheral to the curriculum; (2) projects are not enrichment or add-on but a major component of the experience; (3) projects are focused on questions which drive students to explore and learn knowledge of a discipline (or content area); (4) projects involve students in constructive investigation—that is, the project must involve the transformation and construction of new knowledge and new understandings; and (5) projects are student-driven, not "teacher-led, scripted or packaged" (p. 5). Projects are authentic; they feel like explorations of real-life experiences.

Variations of project work include project-based learning (Polman, 2000) and problem-based learning, often called PBL (Barrell, 2006). Another project method that centers investigations on the neighborhood and community near the school is called place-based education (Smith, 2002; Sobel, 2005). In all of these approaches to project work, learners are autonomous as they construct personally meaningful artifacts that are representations of their learning (Grant, 2002). Consistently throughout these curriculum approaches, projects are described as *integrated* curriculum because the teacher integrates desired knowledge and skills into the investigative process (Thomas, 2000). The project provides motivation for learning and an opportunity to practice academic skills such as reading, writing, and scientific thinking (Katz, 1994).

Theoretical Base of the Project Approach

The project approach has evolved with practice and has been influenced by a variety of theorists such as Dewey, Piaget, and Vygotsky. Project work as practiced in schools in the US today is most commonly linked to John Dewey. In the remaining sections of this chapter, the focus will be on John Dewey's theory of education because most authorities on the project approach attribute the root of project work to Dewey's philosophy. Katz and Chard (1989) and Glassman and Whayley (2000) attribute the project approach directly to John Dewey and the progressive education movement.

Dewey stated his beliefs in "My Pedagogic Creed" (1897), *Democracy and Education* (1916), *The School and Society* (1915), and *The Child and the Curriculum* (1902), in addition to the many lectures and other writings. Although his earlier writings did not discuss projects, they provide insight into the theoretical foundations behind the structure, strategies, and methods of the project approach. Later writings, specifically, *How We Think* (1910, 1933), provide details of project work.

Two tenets of Dewey's philosophy provide a foundational understanding for the project approach and can be directly connected to the project approach as defined earlier in this chapter (pp. 67–69). These include Dewey's conceptualizations of the primary aim of education and the nature of the young child. Dewey's writings also provide guidance for specific practices in the process of project work, including the role of the teacher, the selection of topics, the role of experts and field site visits, and the use of authentic artifacts in project work.

Foundational Understandings from Dewey

The Primary Aim of Education

Dewey described the development of the capacity for learning as the primary aim of education. He stated that "the aim of education is to enable individuals to continue their education—or that the object and reward of learning is continued capacity for growth" (Dewey, 1916, p. 105). Dewey contrasted his aim of education with the direct teaching of segregated content knowledge, which he believed led to a static education process with an unnatural separation between the activity the student engages in to reach the goal and the goal itself. Education, according to Dewey, should be viewed as dynamic and ongoing, with the enhancement of the capacity to learn as the primary force in a child's education.

Today, when teachers and parents describe project work, they often say that doing projects enables children to "learn how to learn." They believe that the experience of doing projects enables students to develop skills that assist them to be efficient learners and successful students in the future. In Katz's (1994) contrast between systematic instruction and project work cited earlier, the characteristics of intrinsic motivation, development of proficiencies, the application of skills, and the ability to determine what to work on could all be considered enhancement of children's capacity for future learning.

The ability to apply academic skills such as reading, writing, scientific investigation, and numeracy is an important feature of project work and key to building capacity for future learning. Some teachers in the field mistakenly describe project work as the opposite of "academic" learning. However, one of the justifications cited for doing project work (Dewey, 1933; Helm & Katz, 2011; Katz & Chard, 1989) is to provide a reason to learn academic skills and an opportunity to practice those academic skills in a meaningful way.

Nature of the Young Child

Dewey's (1899) description of the nature of the young child also provides a foundational understanding for project work. Dewey described what he called *the impulses of children* that are available for schooling. The four impulses (or instincts) he referred to are the social instinct, the instinct of making (also called the constructive impulse), the investigation instinct, and the expressive instinct (also called the art instinct).

The social instinct of children is shown in "conversation, personal intercourse and communication" (Dewey, 1899, p. 29). Children want to communicate with other adults and children. Young children are driven to connect their experiences, which are totally self-centered, to the experiences of others. This instinct to communicate is, according to Dewey, "perhaps the greatest of all educational resources" (p. 29), one to be used wisely.

Project work is situated within a community of learners who converse and communicate about what they are learning. Talking with and listening to children during the project process is important. Children's conversations reveal their interests, and their questions of each other reveal their thinking processes. Recording their thoughts and ideas, a feature of project work, encourages the development of communication skills. Writing is introduced as an extension of that communication skill.

The second of Dewey's instincts which provides a foundational understanding for doing project work is the constructive impulse—the impulse to make things. According to Dewey (1899), this instinct first finds expression in play, in movement, gesture, and make believe.

Today in project work with young children we see children creating play environments such as post offices or stores, developing plays about what they are studying, and building elaborate, often large, models or constructions such as a combine harvester or furnace. For very young children it is in the process of constructing and making things that we see them confront and overcome problems and become intrinsically motivated to find solutions and persevere in learning.

Dewey's third instinct which provides a foundational understanding for project work is the instinct to investigate, to find things out. According to Dewey (1899), the instinct of investigation grows out of the combination of the construction impulse with the conversational. Dewey contrasted this type of concrete investigation, the way young children learn, to conducting experiments, which leads to abstract learning such as chemical processes which have no meaning for young children. He stated, "The young child has not much interest for abstract inquiry" (p. 30).

In project work children learn through interaction with peers and hands-on investigation. They generate their own questions for investigation, discuss hypotheses with peers, use their notes and drawings as resources, and interview experts.

The fourth impulse which provides a foundational understanding for project work was described by Dewey as the art instinct, the expressive impulse. This impulse also grows out of the expressive and constructive instincts and the refinement and full manifestation of these instincts. Dewey (1899) described the process of art, "Make the construction adequate, make it full, free, and flexible, give it a social motive, something to tell, and you have a work of art" (p. 30). Regarding young children, however, he said, "the art instinct is connected mainly with the social instinct—the desire to tell, to represent" (p. 30).

Today in project work in classrooms with young children we see this in the way their paintings, drawings, and sculptures represent their relationship with what they are studying. These usually are specific representations and may involve storytelling about the process.

Guidance for the Project Approach Process

Katz and Chard (1989) and Helm and Katz (2011) provide a framework for project work in early childhood classrooms. This framework includes phases, strategies, and methods. As teachers learn to facilitate project work they must learn how to navigate these phases, respond to student interest, and support child investigation (Clark, 2006). Dewey's philosophical tenets again provide guidance. In later years Dewey, in his writing and lectures, specifically described activities known as projects where students were involved in activities that required thinking as well as doing (Tanner, 1997). This later work addressed the appropriate role of the teacher, choice of a topic, the use of experts and field site visits, and materials and equipment to be brought into the classroom.

Role of the Teacher

The role of the teacher in the project approach is to facilitate and guide the project process. In many aspects the teacher becomes a co-learner in the project, a member of the community of learners. According to Dewey:

> The teacher is not in the school to impose certain ideas or to form certain habits in the child, but is there as a member of the community to select the influences which shall affect the child and to assist him in properly responding to those influences.
>
> *(Dewey, 1897, p. 24)*

Dewey's philosophy of the role of the teacher and school has been mistakenly described as one in which the child's interest of the moment is humored and children pursue whatever strikes their fancy. In reality, Dewey's view of the role of the teacher is much more directive. He described the dilemma of following child interest and providing direction in this way:

> A question often asked is: If you begin with the child's ideas, impulses, and interests, all so crude, so random and scattering, so little refined or spiritualized, how is he going to get the necessary discipline, culture, and information? If there were no way open to us except to excite and indulge these impulses of the child, the question might well be asked. We should either have to ignore and repress the activities or else to humor them. But if we have organization of equipment and of materials, there is another path open to us. We can direct the child's activities, giving them exercise along certain lines, and can thus lead up to the goal which logically stands at the end of the paths followed.
>
> *(Dewey, 1915, p. 25)*

Although the teacher is part of the community of learners, the teacher is still in control of the learning experience. Dewey (1915) wrote that "Through direction, through organized use, they tend toward valuable results, instead of scattering or being left to merely impulsive expression" (p. 25).

The importance of having goals for project work and organizing and directing experiences to incorporate these goals, such as the anticipatory planning process described by Helm and Katz (2011), is consistent with Dewey's recommendations. The role of the teacher in contemporary project work is also to use knowledge about child development and the expectations for knowledge and skills of society to determine what aspects of the experience are most appropriate. Dewey (1933) provided similar specific advice for guiding projects. He wrote that activities should be adapted to the children's stage of development; they should have "the most ulterior promise as preparation for the social responsibilities of adult life" (p. 44); and they should be maximally influential in "forming habits of acute observation and consecutive inference" (p. 44).

This organization of the learning experience could not occur for Dewey (1915) in isolation of a connection between the teacher and the child. The role of the teacher is to have meaningful and frequent conversations with children, to listen carefully to their thoughts, questions, and concerns. The teacher must be a keen observer. Dewey wrote, "I believe that only through the continual and sympathetic observation of childhood's interests can the adult enter into the child's life and see what it is ready for, and upon what material it could work most readily and fruitfully" (p. 29).

Selection of Topics

Dewey's writing provides guidance on appropriate topics for project work. According to Dewey, the young child's education should provide authentic explorations related to the occupations of adults in a democratic society. Dewey made it clear that what children should be learning about and learning to do is authentic, meaningful work. Project topics must be meaningful. According to Dewey (1897), "The child's own instincts and powers furnish the material and give the starting point for all education" (p. 20). Specifically regarding the nature of very young children, Dewey noted:

> We all know how self-centered the little child is at the age of four or five. If any new subject is brought up, if he says anything at all, it is: "I have seen that," or "My papa or mamma told me about that." His horizon is not large; an experience must come immediately to him, if he is to be sufficiently interested enough to relate it to others and seek theirs in return.
>
> *(Dewey, 1915, p. 29)*

Appropriate topics for project work are topics that originate with the children's experience but link children to the real work of society and what it is that people do. An investigation of the pizza parlor down the street where the children and their families eat would be an appropriate project topic. In contrast, a topic such as Extinct Animals or the Costa Rican Rainforest, although worthwhile topics for exploration at some point in a child's life, do not connect with either the world of the young child or the work they see adults do. To ignore the children's interest in their own immediate world would be non-educative, according to Dewey:

Save as the efforts of the educator connect with some activity which the child is carrying on of his own initiative independent of the educator, education becomes reduced to a pressure from without. It may indeed give certain external results, but cannot truly be called educative.

(Dewey, 1897, p. 20)

Role of Experts and Field Site Visits

The involvement of adults in the investigations of young children is important. Current-day project investigations, especially those of very young children, bring them in contact with adults who are doing adult work. According to Dewey:

Little children have their own observations and thoughts mainly directed toward people—what they do, how they behave, what they are occupied with and what comes of it. ... Their interest is of a personal rather than of an objective or intellectual sort. Their minds seek wholes, varied through episode, enlivened with action and defined in salient features—there must be go, movement, the sense of use and operation.

(Dewey, 1915, p. 88)

As described in the project phases above, meeting with experts on the topic and investigating through field site visits are an integral part of project work. In the process of interviewing and interacting with adults, children learn how to ask questions, listen, and use information from others. An important job of the teacher in guiding project work is providing access to experts either within the classroom or at off-site locations.

Use of Authentic Artifacts

John Dewey's writing also provides guidance regarding materials and equipment offered during project work. The use of real objects and the investigation of authentic processes such as cooking were an important consideration for Dewey. Tanner (1997) concluded that the biggest difference between learning experiences prescribed by Dewey and those occurring in kindergartens of his day could be captured in the word "real." Dewey was concerned that kindergartens of his time, in the interest of being child centered, used materials that were artificial, that real things and real acts were not part of the child's world. Dewey instead thought that real things should make up the classroom; that imagination and imaginative play come through suggestions, reminiscences, and anticipations about the things the child uses. The more natural and straightforward these connections are, the more imaginative the child might be.

In current project approach practice, similar to Dewey's concerns, an emphasis is placed upon using real objects and artifacts. For example, in a Pizza Project, it is important that real pizza pans, oven paddles, and rolling pins be used rather than plastic replicas of pizzas or pots and pans made of brightly colored plastic (which even young children would determine is not ovenproof) or ones with eyes and faces on them.

Conclusion

The purpose of this chapter is to present the theoretical foundations of project work. Although John Dewey is not the only educational philosopher who has had an impact on projects as an approach to curriculum, he is cited extensively for his writing on project work. His philosophy has provided not only foundational understandings of project work, but also guidance for specific practices in the process of supporting project work. Some of these basic tenets have been described. They were relevant not only for the classrooms during Dewey's time, but also for project work in today's classrooms. Since Dewey's Laboratory School, project work has continued to evolve, reflecting changes in the education field. For example, teachers using the project approach now routinely plan ways to integrate standards and expectations (Helm, 2008). Documentation of project work has become more sophisticated, incorporating technologies which enable extensive study, reflection, and sharing (Project Zero and Reggio Children, 2001).

In closing, additional foundational understandings for project work and guidance can also be found in the writings of Bruner (1996), Vygotsky (1978), and Malaguzzi (Edwards et al., 1993). The reader may also want to examine these for a full understanding of the theoretical bases of the project approach.

References

Barrell, J. (2006). *Problem based learning: An inquiry approach.* Thousand Oaks, CA: Corwin Press.

Boss, S. & Krauss, J. (2007). *Reinventing project-based learning: Your field guide to real-world projects in the digital age.* Washington, DC: International Society for Technology in Education.

Bruner, J. (1996). *The culture of education.* Cambridge, MA: Harvard University Press.

Central Advisory Council for Education (England). (1967). *The Plowden Report: Children and their primary schools.* London: Her Majesty's Stationery Office.

Clark, A. (2006). Changing classroom practice to include the project approach. *Early Childhood Research and Practice,* 8(2). Retrieved December 13, 2010, from http://ecrp.uiuc.edu/v8n2/clark.html.

Dewey, J. (1897). My pedagogic creed. *The School Journal,* 54(3), 77–80.

——(1899). *The school and society: Being three lectures by John Dewey, Supplemented by a statement of the university elementary school.* Chicago, IL: University of Chicago Press.

——(1902). *The child and curriculum.* Chicago, IL: University of Chicago Press. Dover edition (2001). Mineola, NY: Dover Publications.

——(1910). *How we think.* Boston: Heath.

——(1915). *The school and society*. Chicago, IL: University of Chicago Press. Dover edition (2001). Mineola, NY: Dover Publications.

——(1916). *Democracy and education*. New York: Free Press.

——(1933). *How we think* (rev. ed). Lexington, MA: Heath.

Dodge, D.T., Colker, L., & Heroman, C. (2002). *Creative curriculum for early childhood* (4th ed.). Washington, DC: Teaching Strategies.

Edutopia. (2010). What works in education. Retrieved October 11, 2010, from http://www.edutopia.org/.

Edwards, C., Gandini, L., & Forman, G. (Eds.). (1993). *The hundred languages of children: The Reggio approach*. Stamford, CT: Ablex.

——(1998). *The hundred languages of children: The Reggio approach—advanced reflections* (2nd ed.). Stamford, CT: Ablex.

Gandini, L. (1993). Fundamentals of the Reggio Emilia approach to early childhood education. *Young Children, 49*(1), 4–8.

——(1997). Foundations of the Reggio Emilia approach. In J. Hendricks (Ed.), *First steps toward teaching the Reggio way* (pp. 14–25). Upper Saddle River, NJ: Prentice Hall.

Glassman, M. & Whayley, K. (2000). Dynamic aims: The use of long-term projects in early childhood classrooms in light of Dewey's educational philosophy. *Early Childhood Research and Practice, 2*(1). Retrieved October 14, 2010, from http://ecrp.uiuc.edu/v2n1/glassman.html.

Grant, M.M. (2002). Getting a grip on project-based learning: Theories, cases, and recommendations. *Meridian: A Middle Schools Computer Technologies Journal, 5*(1). Retrieved May 1, 2010, from http://www.ncsu.edu/meridian/win2002/514/index.html.

Harlan, J. (1984). *Science experiences for the early childhood years*. Columbus, OH: Merrill.

Helm, J.H. (2008). Got standards? Don't give up on engaged learning! *Young Children, 63*(4), 14–20.

Helm, J.H. & Katz, L.G. (2011). *Young investigators: The project approach in the early years* (2nd ed.). New York: Teachers College Press.

Katz, L.G. (1994). *The project approach*. Champaign, IL: ERIC Clearinghouse on Elementary and Early Childhood Education.

Katz, L.G. & Chard, S.C. (1989). *Engaging children's minds: The project approach*. Norwood, NJ: Ablex.

——(2000). *Engaging children's minds: The project approach* (2nd ed.). Stamford, CT: Ablex.

Markham, T., Larmer, J., & Ravitz, J. (2003). *Project-based learning handbook* (2nd ed.). Oakland, CA: Wilsted and Taylor.

New, R. (1990). Excellent early education: A city in Italy has it! *Young Children, 45*(6), 4–10.

——(1991). Early childhood teacher education in Italy: Reggio Emilia's master plan for "master" teachers. *Journal of Early Childhood Teacher Education, 12*, 3.

Polman, J. (2000). *Designing project-based learning science: Connecting learners through guided inquiry*. New York: Teachers College Press.

Project Zero and Reggio Children. (2001). *Making learning visible: Children as individual and group learners*. Reggio Emilia, Italy: Reggio Children.

Rankin, B. (1992). Inviting children's creativity: A story of Reggio Emilia, Italy. *Child Care Information Exchange, 85* (May–June), 30–35.

Rotherham, A.J. & Willingham, D. (2009) 21st century skills: The challenges ahead. *Educational Leadership, 67*(1), 16–21.

Smith, G. (2002). Place-based education: Learning to be where we are. *Phi Delta Kappan, 43*, 584–93.

Smith, L. (1997). "Open education" revisited: Promise and problems in American educational reform. *Teachers College Record, 99*(2), 371–415.

Sobel, D. (2005). *Place-based education: Connecting classrooms and communities*. Great Barrington, MA: Orion Society.

Tanner, L.N. (1997). *Dewey's laboratory school: Lessons for today.* New York: Teachers College Press.

Thomas, J.W. (2000). *A review of research on project-based learning.* San Rafael, CA: Autodesk Foundation. Retrieved from http://www.bobpearlman.org/BestPractices/PBL_Research.pdf.

Vygotsky, L.S. (1978). *Mind in society: The development of higher psychological processes.* Cambridge, MA: Harvard University Press.

7

USING CRITICAL THEORY TO TROUBLE THE EARLY CHILDHOOD CURRICULUM

Is It Enough?

Mindy Blaise and Sharon Ryan

Introduction

The early childhood curriculum is a complex field of interrelationships between teachers and children, content and pedagogy, and what takes place in early learning sites and larger social contexts. Given its complexity, theory is at the heart of the early childhood curriculum. As Pinar, Reynolds, Slattery, and Taubman (1996) argue, contemporary views of curriculum are about understanding the sociocultural and political dimensions of knowledge production, not the technical development and implementation of a course of study.

The field's earliest efforts at curriculum were rooted in philosophies concerning the relations between the young child and larger bodies of knowledge (Williams, 1992). In our attempts to be recognized and accepted as a profession, most of the 20th century has involved us using theories of child development and learning to advocate what content and pedagogy should constitute appropriate programs for young children. However, a number of scholars since the early 1990s (e.g. Grieshaber & Cannella, 2001; Kessler & Swadener, 1992; Yelland, 2010) have pushed back against psychological theory as the source of curriculum for young children. Many of these scholars have turned to critical theories drawn from philosophy, sociology, and cultural studies to examine the politics of the curriculum, particularly the assumed benign impacts of developmentally appropriate practice (e.g. Hatch et al., 2002; Lubeck 1998). For these critical theorists, the curriculum becomes a site where children and staff question relations of power and work together to transform society in local and contextualized ways (MacNaughton, 2005).

This chapter is an introduction to critical theories and their application to early childhood curriculum. We begin with a review of the work that has been con-ducted using critical theories to investigate and question taken-for-granted early childhood practices. In doing so we highlight what makes a theory critical and show how some theoretical orientations have been applied to the early childhood curriculum. The focus then shifts from a review to an examination of some of the most recent efforts to trouble and remake early childhood curriculum. We suggest that these newer forms of critical theorizing, in their efforts to dismantle the logic of dualisms inherent in Western thought (e.g. male/female, adult/child, theory/practice), help toward understanding how curriculum has the potential to be transformative. This chapter concludes by reasserting the importance of critical theory for contemporary early childhood practice.

Review of Critical Theorizing and Early Childhood Curriculum

Critical theory is a set of theoretical traditions that has its roots in the 19th century philosophies of Marx, the 20th century work of members of the Frankfurt school, and the writings of Habermas. These modern critical traditions (Popkewitz, 1999) have since been challenged by postmodern theorists whether they are post-structural, postcolonial, or some blending of frameworks such as feminist post-structural or queer theories. At the heart of any critical theorizing, however, is an effort to understand how power works in society through structures like schooling to perpetuate inequities. Using various conceptual tools to consider how power operates in education in relation to knowledge and authority, critical theories question taken-for-granted assumptions (or ideology) the field holds to be true about teaching, learning, childhood, and curriculum. In uncovering whose values and knowledge perpetuate particular truths about early childhood education, the assumption is that it then becomes possible to create more inclusive and just forms of curriculum.

Most of the critical work in early childhood has been conducted using postmodern theories. Postmodern simply means past modern, and postmodern theories "challenge the modernist focus on the macro and universal to the exclusion of the micro; they embrace ambiguity and uncertainty, and refuse modernist discourses that classify, control, and measure against what is considered the 'norm'" (Grieshaber & Ryan, 2006, p. 534). To understand how postmodern theories do these kinds of things, we begin this review with a description of post-structural theory and the influential work of Michel Foucault as his concepts of power, knowledge, and subjectivity have been applied in a large number of studies of early childhood curriculum. As postmodernists are concerned with those who are marginalized by curriculum making, we then turn to other postmodern work that draws on post-structural concepts and combines them with other theories to focus on issues of gender, sexuality, "race," and ethnicity.

Post-structuralism

Foucault's views of power, knowledge, and subjectivity have been drawn on by a range of critical scholars in early childhood education. For Foucault (1980), power is a process operating in our social world, rather than something possessed by individuals. Power operates within all relationships and is expressed through discourse. Therefore, Foucault (1980) argues for understanding power as something that circulates and at the same time operates to produce particular kinds of subjects. For Foucault and critical theorists who use his work, "individuals are the vehicles of power, not its points of application" (p. 98). From this perspective, it becomes important to understand how the strategies and techniques of power work, not simply who has or does not have power. Emphasis is placed on locating *how* power is producing different kinds of subjectivities and knowledge.

For Foucault (1980), knowledge and power are tied in relationship to one another and expressed in and through language. Power relations exist within fields of knowledge, which produce and exercise particular forms of power relations. As meaning is created through language, then it is neither fixed nor essential. Therefore there are no certain truths, only those we speak into action using particular knowledge to support our assertions. Language and discourse are the keys to how we create meaning as socially constructed individuals or subjects. Subjectivity is a term used to capture the complexities of how the self is not a separate and isolated entity, but instead how we recognize ourselves and are always entangled and intersect with others (Mansfield, 2000). As a social and political site of struggle, language becomes the site where knowledge and subjectivities are formed, reformed, and transformed.

Human beings interact in a range of discourse communities, each of which creates a politics of truth and determines what can be said and done by different subjects in that community. For example, in the discourse of schooling, teachers have more power because of their qualifications and positioning as experts compared to children and families when it comes to asserting what knowledge should constitute the curriculum. At the same time, because power circulates in relation to knowledge there are also spaces within the discourse of schooling where children and parents may be able to exercise more agency and power than teachers. Language therefore is the space where social meanings, such as what it means to be a child, girl, second language learner, etc., are open to challenges, redefinitions, and reinterpretations.

Educators using post-structuralism in their daily work engage in a critical questioning of their practice by asking themselves what discourses are at work here, whose knowledge is shaping the curriculum, who benefits and who loses if I use this knowledge, and what other knowledges and practices might I bring into play to create a more equitable curriculum for students? One educator who has written about this kind of critical questioning is Guigini, a teacher-researcher whose work is documented by MacNaughton (2005). After engaging with Foucault's ideas, Guigini began to explore what power and control were in her setting. She began this by revisiting past observations she had kept for 13 years. While rereading them she found that she described children's behavior as "socially unacceptable" and then planned for them to be "dealt with" (p. 52). She also noticed how a colleague and university supervisor affirmed her claims about a particular child's behavior and her practices. By rereading these observations with a post-structural eye, Guigini was able to see how these truth claims worked to normalize middle-class behaviors as socially acceptable. In doing so, Guigini recognized how developmentally appropriate practices were constructing some children as socially acceptable and others as unacceptable. By critically questioning her past practices, Guigini was able to see how she was narrowly constructing teaching, learning, and childhood as either "good" or "bad." She wrote that post-structural concepts of power and knowledge enabled her to "be creative and flexible in how meanings are constructed rather than constrained by the fixed and static meanings some psychological ways of thinking would have her believe" (p. 53).

Early childhood settings are saturated with power relations and knowledge production is continuously being (re)constructed. A large portion of post-structural research is interested in how early childhood curriculum regulates children's subjectivities. The following section reviews studies that have been inspired by post-structuralism for critically theorizing and troubling gender, (hetero)sexuality, "race," and ethnicity.

Troubling Gender

Using Foucault's concepts while foregrounding gender, a feminist post-structuralist perspective shifts away from understanding gender as biologically fixed, coherent, and stable, towards situating gender as a social, relational, and unstable construction that is always located within power relations. Additionally, children are assumed to be active agents in their gender identity work. As social actors, young children are no longer simply "learning" or "soaking up" the social meanings, values, and expectations of how to be a girl or a boy exclusively from their parents, teachers, peers, or the media. Rather, children themselves are producing and regulating gender by constantly "doing" and "redoing" femininities and masculinities that are available to them.

Since Davies's feminist post-structuralist gender research (Davies, 1989) with preschool children, a large body of research (see Grieshaber & Ryan, 2006, for a review) has been generated that draws on Foucault's conceptualizations of subjectivity to examine how children perform gender. Davies's research is significant because it demonstrated how post-structuralist understandings of knowledge, power, and subjectivity could be used to trouble commonsense understandings of gender with young children. After reading feminist stories to preschool children and then discussing with them what they thought, Davies (1989) found that children did not simply accept the notion that boys and girls can do or be anything (i.e. boys wearing dresses or girls choosing not to marry a prince). Instead, children's resistance to these feminist storylines meant the field needed to rethink their beliefs about how children take up gender as well as the kind of curriculum that was considered to be the most effective for challenging gender bias and stereotypes. Davies also observed children in these classrooms taking up gender in multiple ways, debunking the notion that gender is fixed and stable. Instead, her findings showed the fluidity of gender by disclosing the strategies children used for transgressing gender norms or the male/female binary despite the risk of being seen as not doing their gender right.

Troubling (Hetero)Sexuality

Scholars have been building on this important gender research by using insights from queer theory to continue troubling subjectivity, but now addressing (hetero) sexuality (i.e. Blaise, 2005, 2009, 2010a; Boldt, 1997; DePalma & Atkinson, 2009; Renold, 2005; Semann & DeJean, 2010; Taylor & Blaise, 2007; Taylor & Richardson, 2005). Drawing on the work of Foucault (1978) and Butler (1993, 1999), these scholars critique heteronormativity, or the expectation that everyone in society is heterosexual. Queer scholars are committed to rethinking the relationship between sex, gender, and sexuality, proposing a new appreciation of gender as performance, and suggesting that (hetero)sexuality is an effect of gender.

A large portion of the queer research in early childhood that troubles gender and (hetero)sexuality involves empirical studies of children's play. This research shows that children are knowledgeable about heterosexual gender norms and how they use these discourses to regulate the gendered social order in their classroom. Blaise's (2005) qualitative case study of gender combines feminist post-structuralism and queer theory to provide an in-depth look at how power is a dimension of gender and (hetero)sexuality and how these discourses play out in the kindergarten class-room. Case studies of Madison, Penny, and Alan explore the risks that children take to transgress heterosexual gender norms, as well as the investment they have in "playing it straight." Building on this work, Blaise (2009, 2010a) continues to conduct collaborative queer research with children and teachers about heterosexual gender norms. Her findings suggest the necessity for teachers to proactively engage with children's knowledge rather than closing down opportunities for discussions around what it means to be gendered in today's world. For instance, as an active participant observer, Blaise (2009) shows how group time in a kindergarten class-room was used to explore with children their understandings about what it means to be pretty, have boyfriends, be fashionable, and to be a part of gendered power relations. Queer perspectives were useful for understanding how children take an active part (re)constructing knowledge about gender and (hetero)sexuality, and for transforming what it means to be gendered so all children have a sense of belonging in their classrooms.

Troubling "Race" and Ethnicity

Postcolonialism and critical race theory are used in tandem by scholars and teachers interested in locating the politics of children's and adults' racialized identities

(MacNaughton & Davis, 2009). Postcolonialism connects the colonial past with the present (Ghandi, 1998), and provides conceptual tools, to understand the workings of colonialism. Colonial discourse is based on the processes of "othering" or the discriminatory practices that position particular cultures as primitive, less than, or "other." For example, Gupta (2006) and Viruru (2001) show how the British colonial past is ever present in the curriculum in early childhood classrooms in India and how Western values should not be used to judge what another culture considers to be quality early education. In conversations with children using persona dolls, MacNaughton (2005) shows how young children's present understandings of cultural diversity include past traces of colonialism. For example, most of the children in this study were able to sort the dolls according to color, a small group equated "white" with "Australian," and several Anglo and Asian-Australian children found white desirable and good.

Using these ideas in practice, Davis (2007) shows how the discourses of "whiteness" work to privilege white people and marginalize non-whites. By interrogating how she was using images and activities in the curriculum that were intended to highlight Indigenous peoples and their ways of knowing, she wonders if these strategies were beginning to "other" Indigenous culture or position these values and beliefs as insignificant. It is significant how Davis's critical reflections shift from questioning curriculum practices, to a more inward look at how she was ignoring certain issues, such as prejudice and discrimination, because they made her, a white Australian female teacher, too uncomfortable. Critical race theory, with its focus on the everyday realities of racism and how racism continues to privilege whites and disadvantage non-whites (Ladson-Billings, 1998), facilitated this shift and also forced Davis to question if her beliefs, assumptions, and intentions to include Indigenous knowledges in the curriculum were actually widening, rather than closing, the gap between white Australians and Indigenous peoples.

Examinations of the early childhood curriculum drawing on post-structural, feminist, queer, postcolonial, and critical race theories illustrate how child-centered curricula are often normative and limiting of children's and teachers' subjectivities (Ryan & Grieshaber, 2004). Some of these common practices include conducting child observations, reading stories to children, conducting group time, considering girls' interests in boyfriends as simply cute, and using culturally diverse materials and resources with children. Critical perspectives provide a set of conceptual tools that are useful for troubling these taken-for-granted curriculum practices by revealing the sociocultural and political dimensions of teaching and learning. They allow us to consider how common curriculum practices often reproduce inequities even when teachers claim to be engaging in social justice work. However, while there has been an expansion of research using postmodern theories (see reviews by Grieshaber & Ryan, 2006; Ryan & Grieshaber, 2004), little of this work goes beyond critique and not enough is about how practitioners are using these theoretical tools in their everyday work.

Moving from Critique Toward Reconstruction and Transformation

There is an emerging body of research and practice that is concerned with developing a different logic *with* teachers and therefore stimulating new capacities for transforming curriculum practices. Inspired by posthumanist philosophers such as Deleuze and Guattari (1983, 1987), Haraway (2008), and Barad (2008), new work is emerging (see Blaise, 2010b; Camden Pratt, 2009; Lenz Taguchi, 2010; Olsson, 2009; Palmer, 2010) for re-orienting how we think about learning, teaching, and curriculum. This work is important because, like postmodern theories, it tries to challenge Western logic but at the same time these newer forms of theorizing go beyond examinations of language and discourse to consider the relations between the material world and humans, and the human and non-human. Much of this work has been done with and by teachers and as a consequence illustrates how teachers might use critical theory in their everyday work.

Troubling Western Logic

Much of Western logic is based on binary thinking. Binaries or paired concepts are usually founded on opposites (adult/child, male/female, developmentally appropriate/developmentally inappropriate, etc.), with one side of the binary always positioned as more important than the other. In this logic ideas are unable to exist without each other and there is a fixed and final result. For instance, if you are not a developmentally appropriate educator, then you must be developmentally inappropriate.

Deleuze claimed that Western logic, with its aim on a fixed and final result, stops us from thinking and acting on the "in-betweens" of different ideas and their relations (Deleuze & Parnet, 1987), and he argues for a new logic that works against naturalized modes of difference and fixed notions of truth. As post-structuralists, Deleuze and Guattari's (1983, 1987) work is responding to the impossibility of founding knowledge either on experience or on systematic structures, such as language. Deleuze and Guattari did not see the impossibility of organizing life around closed structures as problematic. Instead, they saw this as an opportunity to experiment with, invent, and create different ways of knowing (Colebrook, 2002). Instead of focusing on representation and identification, which are related to knowing and determining what children can or cannot do, their work points towards how learning processes are produced and function, and what social effects they have. Deleuze and Guattari's intellectual project is an invitation to think differently about childhood and curriculum, and several early childhood scholars have taken up this challenge by using their philosophy to engage with difference.

A growing number of early childhood researchers and teachers are beginning to put some of Deleuze and Guattari's philosophical concepts to use at the micro level of preschools (Camden Pratt, 2009; Olsson, 2009) and early childhood teacher education (Lenz Taguchi, 2010; Palmer 2010). In doing so, these scholars are building on the important work regarding knowledge, power, and subjectivity enacted by postmodern theorists by now using slightly different tactics that are intended to unsettle old ways of thinking and encourage new pedagogical encounters with difference. That is, they are challenging binary thinking by attempting to make use of difference, rather than trying to reduce it to simplistic either/or thinking. One of the ways they are doing this is by using Deleuzian/Guattarian concepts, such as "lines of flight," "rhizomes," "becoming," etc.

Although Olsson (2009) uses several Deleuzian/Guattarian concepts with Swedish early childhood teachers to challenge binary thinking, "the rhythm of the heart" project shows how a group of teachers experiment with lines of flight. As a Deleuzian/Guattarian concept, lines of flight are moments when something new or different happens and as a result produces new meanings and knowledge. Since lines of flight are unpredictable and cannot be planned for, experimentation is required and this challenges teachers' desires to represent and recognize children's interests and learning. Olsson describes how teachers engaged with lines of flight, encouraging curriculum practices that work with the unknown and are concerned with the new.

In this project, four- and five-year-old children had been talking a lot about the heart and its rhythm. Because of these interests the teachers gave the children stethoscopes, paper, and pens, and asked them to illustrate how they understood the rhythm of the heart. The teachers observed and documented how the children engaged with this activity and their learning processes, and tried to understand how the children were using their illustrations to represent the rhythm of the heart beating. The teachers then discussed with each other different ways they might continue working with children's illustrations. While this type of planning using children's interests is how many teachers operate, the teachers working with Olsson went further with the children. Next, the teachers presented their pedagogical documentation to the children, but shared only part of their observations. The children reacted with disappointment because only part of their learning was recorded and represented, rather than everything they said or illustrated. The children were so upset that they did not want to investigate this idea any further.

A few days later, the teachers approached the group with all of their documentation, rather than just the parts they originally thought were relevant. This strategy works against a cause-and-effect logic because the teachers were no longer trying to extract a part of children's individual learning or interests to inform their curriculum practices. This strategy seemed to be successful as the children decided they did want to look for and illustrate more sounds outside. As the children began exploring sounds and illustrating them, the teachers' pedagogies shifted from trying to recognize and represent what individual children were learning, to instead focusing on how new understandings about sounds were being produced. The teachers noticed how one girl changed strategies for illustrating heartbeats by using her friend's technique and then inventing a new way to show a heart beating. This discovery then led the teachers to begin noticing what was happening "in-between" children, ideas, and materials. It was this moment when teachers were no longer trying to control what children would learn next, but instead allowing collective experimentation between children to occur, that let learning and ideas take off and in turn created lines of flight.

Lenz Taguchi (2010) finds inspiration from Deleuze and Guattari's (1987, 1994) rhizomatic logic and Barad's (2008) material feminism, which considers the intra-active relationship between all living organisms and the material environment. She works with preservice and inservice early childhood teachers as they move towards what she calls an "intra-active pedagogy" (Lenz Taguchi, 2010, p. 9), which understands learning and knowing as occurring in the interconnections that take place "in-between" different forms of matter. Lenz Taguchi is interested in what is happening relationally in the field and what might become, but she also includes the non-human. This kind of pedagogy requires teachers to shift their understanding of learning from a linear to a rhizomatic process that is multi-dimensional.

An example of how an intra-active pedagogy works is illustrated in a preservice teacher's project with two- and three-year-old children in Sweden (Lenz Taguchi, 2010). Using pedagogical documentation, the teacher shared how a group of boys were playing with wooden sticks, which quickly turned into gun play. After overhearing one of the boys shout that his gun was "alive," the teacher inquired further about the gun, including if it had a name, where it lived, etc. Soon, the boys became interested in the sticks beyond playing guns by turning the sticks into friends and decorating them in various ways. When shooting became impossible with the sticks, children began having different relationships with this material. The learning became more inclusive because the whole group was now interested in the sticks, and the discussions about the sticks evolved to include topics such as nature and science. An intra-activity pedagogy is employed by shifting the focus from the interpersonal interactions between the teacher and the boys and how this supports learning, to the multiple intra-active processes taking place in-between children and the materials and children's meaning making. A clear set of directions for meeting learning outcomes is not followed, but instead the teacher focuses on the in-betweens and the turning points where no one really knows what will happen. When the children start discussing nature and science, the teacher does not follow their interests and create a curriculum around the life cycle of nature. Instead, her focus is on what is emerging in the multiple inter-activities taking place. As a rhizomatic process, learning has no predetermined directions, but instead can begin anywhere and go any place. This requires teachers to be comfortable with not knowing where the learning will go or what will be produced. It is also important to recognize that the teacher did not have a preset agenda when she questioned the boys' play. Rather, she took a chance when she responded to the stick being "alive," and this turned the play and learning around because it activated the boys' interests in an unpredictable way. The teacher's actions set off multiple intra-activities, in which all are considered significant.

Lenz Taguchi argues that this intra-active pedagogy transgresses binary divides such as discourse/matter and theory/practice, and lines of flight have been made possible.

Together, these two studies inspire educators to reconsider the relations between teaching and materials in early childhood classrooms, to question our gaze on individual children and our efforts to use knowledge to impose curriculum events on them, and they suggest that we might think of curriculum making as momentary, less able to be planned, or viewed as theory into action.

The Importance of Critical Theories to the Early Childhood Curriculum

Critical theory is a range of theories that expose the biased and problematic aspects of everyday curriculum practices. The studies reviewed here show that practices as benign as periods for play, providing children with materials to act on the world, and observation and documentation are imbued with hidden meanings that have the potential to limit both teachers' and children's agency. Yet, as has also been illustrated in this review, critical theoretical constructs are complicated, somewhat elusive, and for some may seem irrelevant in an era of accountability and increasing standards-based reform. However, it is precisely because we live and work at this moment in the field's history that we believe we have no choice but to use critical theories.

The field has long had a commitment to improving the lives of young children and for at least 40 years now we have made various efforts to address inequity and injustice. The fact remains, however, that while the students we teach become increasingly diverse, we have yet to find ways to level the playing field so every child succeeds. Complicating this issue further is the reality that how children learn and the information and tools available to them with sophisticated technologies means that it is not possible for educators to apply generic theories of learning and development. Therefore even as policymakers attempt to standardize curriculum and impose research-proven practices, if educators are not aware of whose knowledge is being given authority in the curriculum, and how knowledge enacts a politics that marginalizes some students, then it will not be possible to be inclusive of every child's learning.

Early childhood teachers also need critical theory if they are to be able to understand how power is playing out in everyday classroom life. Studies of children's play using critical theory have shown children are active agents in the curriculum, regulating each other's subjectivities and yet also using spaces to subvert adult discourses. Teachers also are often unaware of their own positioning in various discourses and how their own subjectivity values particular ways of knowing and being, thereby constraining their pedagogical actions. In short, educators need critical theory to see how children are exercising power and what they might do pedagogically to engage with children in ways that build on the learning moment and also challenge children's presumptions about race, class, sexuality, gender, etc.

Teaching young children in the 21st century requires that we do things differently. In assuming that our developmentally based curricula are inclusive of all learners, we have been unjust to some students and families. Early childhood educators need critical theory because it enables them to examine the political nature of the curriculum, and in so doing challenges normative views of young children and outdated views of childhood. However, it is one thing to be able to use critical theory to uncover bias, and another to act on bias to change it. Like the teacher-researchers described in this chapter, we believe it is time for all of us to start engaging with some of the newer forms of critical theory, documenting and sharing our efforts, helping each other to engage with these concepts in ways that do not just trouble but reinvent what it means to teach young children in these new times.

References

Barad, K. (2008). Posthumanist performativity: Toward an understanding of how matter comes to matter. In S. Alaimo & S. Hekman (Eds.), *Material feminisms* (pp. 120–54). Bloomington: Indiana University Press.

Blaise, M. (2005). *Playing it straight!: Uncovering gender discourses in the early childhood classroom.* New York: Routledge.

——(2009). "What a girl wants, what a girl needs": Responding to sex, gender, and sexuality in the early childhood classroom. *Journal of Research in Childhood Education,* 23 (4), 450–60.

——(2010a). Kiss and tell: Gendered narratives and childhood sexuality. *Special Sexualities Issue: Australasian Journal of Early Childhood,* 35(1), 1–9.

——(2010b). New maps for old terrain: Creating a postdevelopmental logic of gender and sexuality in the early years. In L. Brooker & S. Edwards (Eds.), *Engaging play* (pp. 80–95). Maidenhead, UK: Open University Press.

Boldt, G. (1997). Sexist and heterosexist responses to gender bending in an elementary classroom. In J. Tobin (Ed.), *Making a place for pleasure in early childhood education* (pp. 188–213). New Haven, CT: Yale University Press.

Butler, J. (1993). *Bodies that matter: On the discursive limits of "sex."* New York: Routledge.

——(1999). *Gender trouble: Feminism and the subversion of identity* (2nd ed.). New York: Routledge.

Camden Pratt, C. (2009). Relationality and the art of becoming. In B. Davies and S. Gannon (Eds.), *Pedagogical encounters* (pp. 53–68). New York: Peter Lang.

Colebrook, C. (2002). *Gilles Deleuze.* New York: Routledge.

Davies, B. (1989). *Frogs and snails and feminist tales: Preschool children and gender.* NSW, Australia: Allen and Unwin.

Davis, K. (2007). Locating the "Other": Stories from practice and theory. *Childrenz Issues,* 11(1), 21–24.

Deleuze, G. and Guattari, F. (1983) *Anti-Oedipus: Capitalism and schizophrenia* (R. Hurley, M. Seem, & H.R. Lane, Trans.). London: Continuum.

——(1987). *A thousand plateaus: Capitalism and schizophrenia* (B. Massumi, Trans. and forward). London: Continuum.

——(1994). *What is philosophy?* (G. Burchell & H. Tomlinson, Trans.). London: Verso.

Deleuze, G. & Parnet, C. (1987). *Dialogues* (H. Tomlinson & B. Habberjam, Trans.). London: Athlone Press.

DePalma, R. & Atkinson, E. (Eds.). (2009). *Interrogating heteronormativity in primary schools: The No Outsiders Project*. Staffordshire, UK: Trentham Books Limited.

Foucault, M. (1978). *The history of sexuality: An introduction* (vol. 1) (R. Hurley, Trans.). New York: Pantheon Books.

——(1980). *Power/knowledge: Selected interviews & other writings, 1972–1977* (C. Gordon, Ed.; C. Gordon, L. Marshall, J. Mepham, & K. Soper, Trans.). New York: Pantheon Books.

Ghandi, L. (1998). *Postcolonial theory: A critical introduction*. New York: Columbia University Press.

Grieshaber, S. & Cannella, G.S. (Eds.). (2001). *Embracing identities in early childhood education: Diversity and possibilities*. New York: Teachers College Press.

Grieshaber, S. & Ryan, S.K. (2006). Beyond certainties: Postmodern approaches and research about the education of young children. In B. Spodek & O. Saracho (Eds.), *Handbook of research on the education of young children* (pp. 533–53). Mahwah, NJ: Lawrence Erlbaum Associates.

Gupta, A. (2006). *Early childhood education, postcolonial theory, and teaching practices in India: Balancing Vygotsky and the Veda*. New York: Palgrave Macmillan.

Haraway, D. (2008). *When species meet*. Minneapolis: University of Minnesota Press.

Hatch, A., Bowman, B., Jor'dan, J., Lopez Morgan, C., Hart, C., Diaz Soto, L., et al. (2002). Developmentally appropriate practice: Continuing the dialogue. *Contemporary Issues in Early Childhood*, 3(3), 439–57.

Kessler, S. & Swadener, B.B. (Eds.). (1992). *Reconceptualizing the early childhood curriculum: Beginning the dialogue*. New York: Teachers College Press.

Ladson-Billings, G. (1998). Just what is critical race theory and what's it doing in a nice field like education? *International Journal of Qualitative Studies in Education*, 11(1), 7–24.

Lenz Taguchi, H. (2010). *Going beyond the theory/practice divide in early childhood education: Introducing an intra-active pedagogy*. New York: Routledge.

Lubeck, S. (1998). Is developmentally appropriate practice for everyone? *Childhood Education*, 74(5), 283–92.

MacNaughton, G. (2005). *Doing Foucault in early childhood studies: Applying post-structural ideas*. New York: Routledge.

MacNaughton, G. & Davis, K. (Eds.). (2009). *"Race" and early childhood education: An international approach to identity, politics, and pedagogy*. New York: Palgrave and Macmillan.

Mansfield, N. (2000). *Subjectivity: Theories of the self from Freud to Haraway*. NSW, Australia: Allen & Unwin.

Olsson, L.M. (2009). *Movement and experimentation in young children's learning: Deleuze and Guattari*. New York: Routledge.

Palmer, A. (2010). Let's dance!: Theorising alternative mathematical practices in early childhood teacher education. *Contemporary Issues in Early Childhood Education*, 11(2), 130–43.

Pinar, W.F., Reynolds, W.M., Slattery, P., & Taubman, P.M. (1996). Understanding curriculum: An introduction. In W.F. Pinar, W.M. Reynolds, P. Slattery, & P.M. Taubman. (Eds.), *Understanding curriculum* (pp. 1–66). New York: Peter Lang.

Popkewitz, T.S. (1999). Critical traditions, modernisms, and the "posts." In T. Popkewitz & L. Fendler (Eds.), *Critical theories in education: Changing terrains of knowledge and politics* (pp. 1–16). New York: Routledge.

Renold, E. (2005). *Girls, boys and junior sexualities: Exploring children's gender and sexual relations in the primary school*. New York: RoutledgeFalmer.

Ryan, S. & Grieshaber, S. (2004). It's more than child development: Critical theories, research, and teaching young children. *Young Children*, 5(6), 44–52.

Semann, A. & DeJean, W. (Eds.). (2010). *The sexuality issue: Australasian Journal of Early Childhood*, 35(1). Canberra: Early Childhood Australia, Inc.

Taylor, A. & Blaise, M. (Eds.). (2007). *Special issue on queer theory: International Journal of Equity and Innovation in Early Childhood*, 5(2).

Taylor, A. & Richardson, C. (2005). Queering home corner. *Contemporary Issues in Early Childhood*, 6(2), 163–73.

Viruru, R. (2001). *Early childhood education: Postcolonial perspectives from India*. New Delhi, India: Sage.

Williams, L.R. (1992). Determining the curriculum. In C. Seefeldt (Ed.), *The early childhood curriculum: A review of current research* (2nd ed.) (pp. 1–15). New York: Teachers College Press.

Yelland, N. (Ed.). (2010). *Contemporary perspectives on early childhood education*. Maidenhead, UK: Open University Press.

8

USING CRITICAL THEORIES IN THE CURRICULUM

Betsy J. Cahill and Tammy L. Gibson

Introduction

The purpose of this chapter is to provide an examination of critical theory as enacted in early childhood classroom. We discuss how postmodern teachers might think about their work with young children and families. Using a critical lens, we deconstruct issues of developmentally appropriate practice (DAP) that influence curriculum and pedagogy. We believe that a postdevelopmental perspective opens possibilities for educators to envision a classroom that is inclusive of the multidimensionality of children.

Critical theory is an all-encompassing term for theoretical lenses such as postmodern, poststructural, feminist, and queer, that may be used by teachers to examine how knowledge is socially constructed. As suggested by Grieshaber (2008), to engage critically is to "challenge the assumed consensus that comes with the dominant group, to make way for the contradictions and inconsistencies that accompany all forms of diversity, and to undermine notions of homogeneity" (p. 515). As authors of this paper we position ourselves as feminist poststructuralists who examine ways in which social structures, gender, and sexuality are influenced by discourses of power and knowledge (Blaise, 2005; Robinson, 2002; Ryan & Grieshaber, 2005; Yelland, 2005). We have selected the following stories because of our own lived experiences and the shared goal of social justice and equity for all children.

In this paper, the tools of deconstruction are inspired primarily by Foucault's concepts of power and knowledge, which allow us to examine how children learn, who controls the knowledge children learn, and what knowledge counts as important (Foucault, 1982; MacNaughton, 2005). Using a critical perspective, all knowledge is tentative and contextualized; therefore there are multiple meanings for many words and concepts in the field of early childhood education. An example of using deconstruction is to wonder about one universally accepted definition of curriculum. Instead we ask, *how many meanings might there be for the word "curriculum"?* MacNaughton (2005), looking toward others, found quite a variety of contradicting metaphors and concepts, such as: (1) everything that happens in an educational setting; (2) a carnival; (3) an historical accident; and (4) a gift. These images offer differing ideas and possible enactments of a curriculum for teachers and young children.

To offer a critical look at curriculum and imagine possibilities, we use a definition from Bredekamp:

> Curriculum is a written plan that describes the goals for children's learning and development, and the learning experiences, materials and teaching strategies that are used to help children achieve those goals. The goals include the knowledge, skills, and dispositions that we want children to achieve.
>
> *(Bredekamp, 2011, p. 299)*

We chose this definition because it reflects popular discourse found in early childhood professional organizations and institutions within our context. To briefly describe our context, one of the authors, Tammy, is a graduate student and teacher of young children working at an accredited center and the other, Betsy, is a professor of early childhood teacher education. We are located near the border of Mexico and New Mexico, where we work with diverse families and children.

What follows are four sections within which phrases from the Bredekamp definition of curriculum are deconstructed to offer multiple responses, uncover underlying values, and question possible power relationships (Casper & Theilheimer, 2010) in the quest for a deeper dialogue about and for curriculum, children, teachers, and families. Questioning inherent power relationships is important in understanding how these relationships oppress or benefit children and families, but also make us think deeply about what we do or do not do as educators (MacNaughton, 2005). We share examples in order to examine how those working in a critical "tradition" have altered their thinking and classroom practices as they problematize what has been traditionally thought about curriculum.

Curriculum Is a Written Plan

The definition of curriculum by Bredekamp (2011) begins with the act of writing a plan. Writing down ideas and hopes for the day or week is helpful. Writing helps teachers organize their thinking, and clarify group and individual learnings in the classroom. A teacher knows how the room might be arranged and the resources prepared through planning ahead. A written plan may also legitimatize the work of teachers in a milieu of greater accountability.

It is our opinion, from years of observing and talking with teachers and student teachers, however, that the written plan appears to be both helpful and restrictive for children and teachers. Beyond this binary, the general messiness of learning is not easily captured or prepared for. Critical questions emerge, such as: Who benefits from having a written plan? How might a written plan limit the possibilities for teachers, children, and families? What are the many meanings to a written plan? What is the role of the teacher as connected to this written plan—author or instructor?

It has been noted elsewhere (McArdle & McWilliam, 2005) that early childhood teachers describe themselves as facilitators rather than instructors. Critical educators facilitate children's contributions to the curriculum, hence promoting children's power. For example, there is much attention in the field regarding the possibilities of negotiated learning as one possible approach to a more postmodern curriculum. If teachers are to negotiate learning with children, then how does a teacher script the day prior to the negotiated experiences?

An example of a critical shift in thinking about curriculum as a written plan occurred during professional development experiences with Betsy and teachers from a Head Start program. After much dialogue concerning emergent curriculum (a goal for these teachers) and the problems of a written plan, the teachers decided to complete their required written plans as documentation after the children left, through reflection on the day's interactions and encounters. The curriculum for tomorrow and beyond was thought about and prepared for based on what emerged during the day. It was the teachers' shift from planning and implementation to reflection and dialogue that opened possibilities for them to be present with children in deeper ways.

To question the need for written plans might be dangerous work in the current accountability arena, where a program serving families in poverty could lose funding and thus not exist. However, the teachers in this Head Start program engaged in theoretically grounded discussions and decisions about their daily experiences with children. Discussions of individual children moved toward an expanded understanding of the meanings of the multiple encounters for children in a larger socio-cultural context. Ryan and Goffin (2008) define curriculum as moment-by-moment encounters in the classroom, thereby asking teachers to find new ways to think about, represent, and express curriculum. These Head Start teachers are now planning differently, thus creating new dialogue and possibilities for the early childhood curriculum.

Goals for Children's Learning and Development

We return to Bredekamp's (2011) definition of curriculum as "a written plan that describes the goals for children's learning and development" (p. 299). Theories of development can help teachers understand, and hopefully accept, how children change over time. Yet knowledge of "ages and stages" does not necessarily translate into curriculum. Child development tells us a little about children, but not what to teach. The content of what we teach is often labeled "curriculum." When teachers select what to teach (content) based on their goals for children, and how to teach (instructional strategies) and pair these curricular ideas with their knowledge of child development, what might be missing is the rich context of the children's lives. As Cannella (2002) stated, "positioning children within predetermined discourses and expectations immediately devalues them by placing limits on how they see themselves, on how we see them, and on how we hear what they want to say" (p. 18).

Early childhood education stories from critical and queer theorists have shown this to be true for teachers and children. Robinson (2002) offers the following quotation from a research study in which early childhood professionals shared their child development knowledge of children's understandings of sexuality. An early childhood director stated:

> I think children are really too young to deal with sexuality issues ... they do get into playing house, mothers and father and getting married ... but that's normal everyday play. But beyond that, I don't think it's appropriate and it is not part of their experiences.
>
> *(quoted in Robinson, 2002, p. 421)*

What is perceived as normal sexuality is heteronormative play behavior and any other possible sexuality is not appropriate for young children. Yet we know that children explore multiple identities as they come to know themselves in the diverse world of race, gender, language, and sexuality (Theilheimer & Cahill, 2001).

In her work with children, Tammy offers an example of "doing" gender in her classroom toward the production of new knowledge. She shares:

> Two girls both approximately five years old were swinging. They were studying me, giggling and yelling something at me. As I walked over to the girls, one of them finally said, "I want to marry you." The other girl said, "Emily wants to marry you." I asked, "Do you think that would be o.k.?" They looked at each other, giggled, and said, "Yes."

Tammy chose not to respond with modernistic discourses such as "only girls marry boys" or "that's not appropriate" or to laugh and walk away. She believes that children need to be allowed to discuss gender possibilities as part of the curriculum. Although Tammy worried that the girls' parents might not like the conversation, she could, if need be, articulate a stance to families that the work of children involves gender exploration that includes understanding whom one can and cannot marry. By opening possibilities for children as they build understandings about relationships and marriage, Tammy was developing a social justice curriculum.

Fostering a critical disposition requires teachers to look beyond development as universal and unchanging. Blaise (2005) suggests that teachers invent new "post-developmental" pedagogies. Critical teachers are not dependent on any one theory to explain phenomena but accept that multiple and shifting perspectives are necessary when thinking about children's learning and development. Once a teacher is committed to expanding beyond a developmental lens, what is gained is a complex sense that is "spacious enough for children's diverse ways of being, within a time frame and on curriculum terrain that expands beyond adult prescriptions" (Genishi & Dyson, 2009, p. 10). Teaching from a critical stance is demanding of teachers and children as they form identities and shape and reshape their understanding of the classroom and the world.

Learning Experiences, Materials, and Strategies

The definition by Bredekamp (2011) states that curriculum is "the learning experiences, materials and strategies" (p. 299) that effective teachers implement to assist children toward the achievement of goals. Often, unfortunately, programs serving young children use a preplanned curriculum with a set of learner outcomes developed by the state or a corporation that most likely does not serve the diverse sociocultural communities in which children and teachers live. Instead, Hyun (2006) suggests that a critical teacher develop a conscious framework for an ever-changing interdependent learning community. This "lived curriculum" incorporates moment-to-moment phenomena that emerge from the children and families being served. Hyun also suggests that a critical teacher knows the children in her class, their "intellectual cultures" (p. 65) and self-expressions, and constantly checks for and enacts power-sharing in the curriculum. The curriculum, therefore, grows from, and with, the community.

A place to start is for the teacher to ask, "What learning experiences, materials, and teaching strategies do I consider are worthwhile for this learning community based on my limited understanding at this time?" A critical teacher begins with imagining what is possible rather than starting from the restraints of mandates and standards or a purchased curriculum. Without a pedagogy of wonderment and hope, educators can never be agents of change, advancing transformation among educators, families, and children (Freire, 2007).

This process may take the shape of a curricular approach discussed in other chapters, combined with the best theoretical ideas from different disciplines and perspectives. For example, Lenz Taguchi (2008) shared a research project where Swedish early childhood practitioners worked within a Reggio Emilia philosophical and curricular framework that was combined conceptually with poststructural dialogues about equality and power. This process of deconstruction, of looking at the taken-for-granted ideas about children and then working toward thinking differently, allowed for new meanings to be constructed. The curriculum then becomes the creation of a classroom context with content that allows the teacher and children to make contributions to their lives and the lives of others. The "learning experiences" would emerge uniquely with materials and effective teaching strategies that are defined by the specific context.

Knowledge, Skill, and Dispositions

In the Bredekamp (2011) definition of curriculum, we see that the learning experiences that teachers plan must be connected to goal achievements. Rather than thinking of goals as the "knowledge, skill and dispositions" (p. 299) that we have for children, critical teachers think about learning goals as educational priorities framed within critical actions. There is movement away from the concept of mastery of knowledge toward an examination of possibilities (Ryan & Grieshaber, 2005). What should the children know and act upon to make sense of and create their world? These priorities will change dependent on their relevancy for the children and community served. Yelland and Kilderry (2005) suggest that critical teachers be passionate and articulate, continuously interrogating theory, such as developmentally appropriate practice, that influences their work. In addition, critical teachers are investigators of important issues and actions that must take place in the classroom and beyond. And because knowledge informs practice, teachers must read, think, and question their beliefs in relationship to their work. It is this reciprocal process of theory informing practice and vice versa that prepares educators to engage critically with children.

As a teacher engages in educational priority-making within her diverse community, the goals will, most likely, promote inclusivity, with recognition of multiple and shifting positionings, identities, and belongings (Ang, 2010). This occurs because the teacher works as a careful observer of and dedicated listener to the children and families she serves. Furthermore, a critical lens involves self-reflection, questioning purpose, identity, position, and power as an early childhood educator. Part of this work is a constant rethinking of curriculum ownership. All the stakeholders (children, families, community) should be part of the curricular design dialogue. As Hyun (2006) suggests, early childhood educators need to approach curriculum decision-making as an ethical, critical, and reflective action.

One Teacher in Action

> One of my goals is for kids and parents to see school as a place of discovery and connection; to develop together a new concept of school as rich and desirable. And, I want this concept of school to serve as an entry point for the future.
>
> *(Jeanne)*

In this section we offer a brief glimpse at a teacher with a developing critical lens who: (1) develops curriculum from relationships and dialogue; (2) advocates for equity; (3) shares power with families; and (4) creates meaningful learning experiences that emerge from the local community context. Jeanne is a PreK tea-cher in New Mexico working for a program that serves four- and five-year-old children who will be attending kindergarten the following year at a school that did not meet "annual yearly progress" (AYP), as defined by the No Child Left Behind regulations. In her community, only three schools in the district made AYP. Jeanne stated that she likes the PreK program because it is free for families and the standards are not restrictive. She states that the curriculum standards were written as general learning outcomes for the children that appear applicable to the diverse communities in New Mexico. Each program can decide what, if any, specified curriculum will be used in the classroom. The teachers must, however, use the learning outcomes as goals that drive curriculum decision-making. Jeanne, her colleagues, and administrators chose not to use a specific curriculum but rather to build curriculum with each other, the children, and families. She said, "I feel pur-posefully planning is the core of our curriculum and this takes time—ongoing dia-logue. Indeed much more dialogue is needed when not using a prepackaged curriculum."

Although Jeanne spoke highly of the PreK program and its flexibility for creating community-based curriculum, she was concerned about the assessment measures and documentation of the children's learning. She stated:

> the rubrics are dependent on verbal ability rather than what kids know or can do. And it prejudices second language learners. I had a child that was doing double digit addition and subtraction and I wrote that on my assessment. My reviewer put a sad face [on the report] and said this does not prove the child can count. I just laughed … and then I contacted the author.
>
> *(Jeanne)*

Jeanne acted from a sense of agency that is used in advocacy for the children in her classroom. Her equity stance is an indication of her critical lens. She felt it was her job to talk to the people that developed and monitor the program's evaluation plan. Jeanne described her belief that change was always possible through conversation as "we are all fallible … everyone is in a growth process," so input is necessary for change.

Jeanne discussed how each school year she begins with questions and actions. These include: Who are my kids and families? Where do my families live? What languages are spoken (last year there were six)? And what cultures will be joining together to make a new classroom community? These questions demonstrate Jeanne's commitment to learning about the children and families without assump-tions and expectations. As do many early childhood teachers, Jeanne and her co-teacher visit each home before the school year starts. However, Jeanne does not stop at home visits. During class time and beyond the school day, Jeanne and the families from her classroom participate in regular outings and activities such as Saturday gatherings at the city pool. This commitment to knowing the children and families beyond the classroom walls represents an intentional coming together of curriculum and community. It is an example of power-sharing that has led to parental contributions to the curriculum in and outside of the classroom.

A goal Jeanne holds is to develop educational priorities and critical actions for her and the children at the beginning of each school year. This year an educational priority is to study citizenship and what it means to create a democratic community. Jeanne hopes to engage herself and the children in thinking deeply about this original intent of schooling, the creation of citizenship. Jeanne's definition of citizenship is inclusion of all members of society, regardless of legal status. She wants to build the disposition of "active participant" because that is how to make "things happen" in a democracy. It is interesting, perhaps taking a risk, to study citizenship in a community where the Border Patrol is an ever-present reminder of the contested tri-state intersection of Texas, New Mexico, and Chihuahua, Mexico. We serve a majority of Latino families, who may not have, or desire, citizenship status in America. We work with families who recently fled Mexico in fear for their lives, only to come to America, where immigration laws make it difficult to get a job, own a home, or go to school. Yet it is goal for Jeanne that the children and families know that they have a voice in our border community, regardless of citizenship status and immigration law. She hopes to make a change.

Conclusion

The application of critical theory, in service to social justice and equity, may take many forms (Yelland, 2005). Critical curriculum can be a small event in the classroom or, as suggested by Silin (2005), informed by an unbelievable catastrophe such as September 11, 2001. It may be the teacher that changes her theoretical gaze so that she expands her definition of families. It could be the educator that rearranges his environment to study and problematize exclusionary and gendered play. It might also be the trio of teachers that meet weekly to push each other toward revised ideas about children that open spaces for alternative concepts of lesson planning.

As seen with Jeanne and the examples above, educational intentions are developed from an anti-oppressive stance where possibilities for change are created, acted upon, and thereby transformed. The reality of the standardization movement in early childhood is neither ignored nor passively accepted. Instead, through reflection and praxis, critical educators reinvent the taken-for-granted and fixed notions of child development, curriculum, assessment, and what counts as knowledge. It is with these ideas that we offer an alternative definition of curriculum informed by our critical perspective: Curriculum is a community dialogue that creates and documents transformational possibilities for all children, families, and teachers.

References

Ang, L. (2010). Critical perspective on cultural diversity in early childhood: Building an inclusive curriculum and provision. *Early Years*, 30(1), 41–52.

Blaise, M. (2005). *Playing it straight: Uncovering gender discourses in the early childhood classroom.* New York: Routledge.

Bredekamp, S. (2011). *Effective practices in early childhood education.* Upper Saddle River, NJ: Prentice Hall.

Cannella, G. (2001). Natural born curriculum: Popular culture and the representation of childhood. In J.A. Jipson & R.T. Johnson (Eds.), *Resistance and representation: Rethinking childhood education* (pp. 15–22). New York: Peter Lang.

——(2002). *Deconstructing early childhood education: Social justice & revolution.* New York: Peter Lang.

Casper, V. & Theilheimer, R. (2010). *Early childhood education: Learning together.* New York: McGraw Hill.

Foucault, M. (1982). The subject and power. *Critical Inquiry,* 8(4), 777–95.

Freire, P. (2007). *Daring to dream.* Boulder, CO: Paradigm Publishers.

Genishi, C. & Dyson, A.H. (2009). *Children, language and literacy: Diverse learners in diverse times.* Washington, DC: National Association for the Education of Young Children.

Grieshaber, S. (2008). Interrupting stereotypes: Teaching and the education of young children. *Early Education and Development,* 19(3), 385–95.

Hyun, E. (2006). *Teachable moments: Re-conceptualizing curricula understandings.* (Counterpoints: Studies in the postmodern theory of education, vol. 297.) New York: Peter Lang.

Lenz Taguchi, H. (2008). An "ethics of resistance" challenges taken-for-granted ideas in Swedish early childhood education. *International Journal of Education Research,* 47, 270–82.

McArdle, F. & McWilliam, E. (2005). From balance to blasphemy: Shifting metaphors for researching early childhood education. *International Journal of Qualitative Studies in Education,* 18, 323–36.

MacNaughton, G. (2005). *Doing Foucault in early childhood studies.* New York: Routledge.

Robinson, K.H. (2002). Making the invisible visible: Gay and lesbian issues in early childhood education. *Contemporary Issues in Early Childhood,* 3(3), 415–34.

Ryan, S. & Goffin, S.G. (2008). Missing in action: Teaching in early care and education. *Early Education and Development,* 19(3), 385–95.

Ryan, S. & Greishaber, S. (2005). Shifting from development to postmodern practices in early childhood teacher education. *Journal of Teacher Education,* 56(1), 34–45.

Silin, J.G. (2005). Who can speak? Silence, voice and pedagogy. In N. Yelland (Ed.), *Critical issues in early childhood education* (pp. 81–95). Maidenhead, UK: Open University Press.

Theilheimer, R. & Cahill, B. (2001). A messy closet in the early childhood classroom. In S. Grieshaber & G.S. Cannella (Eds.), *Embracing identities in early childhood education: Diversity and possibilities* (pp. 103–13). New York: Teachers College Press.

Yelland, N. (Ed.). (2005). *Critical issues in early childhood education.* Maidenhead, UK: Open University Press.

Yelland, N. & Kilderry, A. (2005). Postmodernism, passion and potential for future childhoods. In N. Yelland (Ed.), *Critical issues in early childhood education* (pp. 243–48). New York: Open University Press.

Part III
Examining Curriculum Approaches and Their Applications

In this section, we provide examinations of various curricula in early childhood. We have made choices of what to cover here by considering questions such as: What approaches are dominant in the field? Where is there something interesting to further discussion about curriculum? Where do we believe curriculum is going?

We asked the contributors to cover similar key points. These included the origins and key components of the approach. We asked also that contributors consider contributions and critique of the curriculum or approach. Finally, each contributor was asked to consider how diversity is addressed in the approach.

Diane Horm, Carla Goble, and Kathryn Branscomb begin the section with an examination of curriculum for infants and toddlers (Chapter 9). It seems that, often, when the topic becomes teaching and learning we unconsciously redefine our field as constituting ages three to eight, rather than the commonly declared birth through age eight. In this sense, infants and toddlers seem to occupy another world. We contend, however, that the group deserves equal consideration regarding thoughtful analysis of the experiences provided to them in group settings. Horm, Goble, and Branscomb describe three curricular approaches, highlighting strengths and concerns for each.

We chose to include a chapter about Creative Curriculum and HighScope because they represent longstanding and widely used approaches in the preschool years. In Chapter 10 Sara Michael-Luna and Lucinda Heimer provide explanations of each curriculum, along with a summary of research they have conducted to more closely probe how dual-language learning is presented to curriculum users. While they discuss concerns about some aspects of these curricula, they also point out that they do continue a tradition within the field of teacher agency in planning and implementing curricula within a framework, rather than teaching within prescribed scripts.

The schools of Reggio Emilia have received wide recognition for excellence, both within dominant perspectives in early childhood and from reconceptualists (Dahlberg et al., 1999). Therefore, including a chapter from this perspective (Chapter 11) was an easy decision. The goal we held in common with the chapter's author, Andrew Stremmel, was to examine the Reggio approach as situated, and thus uniquely interpreted when applied to settings within the United States. Stremmel discusses his work in translating what he has experienced within the Reggio schools to classrooms in this country, taking inspiration from Reggio and framing locally contextualized programs.

Distinct from the other chapters, we decided to include coverage of *Te Whāriki*, a national curriculum from New Zealand. This decision was based upon our sense of unique aspects of this framework, well detailed within Chapter 12. We also believed that in an era of increasing top-down control of teaching and learning this national framework would be interesting to examine in more detail. As movement toward common core standards gains momentum in the United States, how does the New Zealand experience look in comparison? The authors of this chapter are Jenny Ritchie, a New Zealander who has written extensively about the national framework, and Cary Buzzelli, an American who spent several months living in New Zealand. Together, they provide a unique "insider/outsider" perspective that helps to bridge an understanding of the work in New Zealand for a U.S. readership.

The final chapter in this section, Chapter 13, is included in recognition of the growing influence that the publishing industry has on curriculum in this country. In our own undergraduate teacher preparation program we continue to teach a curriculum design course focused on helping students to think deeply about authentic and meaningful learning. But increasingly we wonder how much our graduates will be able to plan what they teach in the classroom, as instead teachers are handed prescribed and scripted curricula. Mariana Souto-Manning provides an insightful and revealing analysis of one published literacy curriculum, based in part on her experiences with it as a teacher. Her critical examination of teaching and learning in this curriculum reveals a curriculum fraught with difficulties for diverse learners.

In sum, this section provides readers with reviews of a range of curricular approaches. Some evidence promise for the future, based upon a vision of classrooms operating with empowered teachers making informed decisions about helping children understand their worlds. And yet, we are reminded as well of many ways in which diverse groups of children may not be well served by the curricula in place.

Reference

Dahlberg, G., Moss, P., & Pence, A. (1999). *Beyond quality in early childhood education: Postmodern perspectives*. London: Routledge.

9

INFANT TODDLER CURRICULUM

Review, Reflection, and Revolution

Diane M. Horm, Carla B. Goble, and Kathryn R. Branscomb

Introduction

The purpose of this chapter is to review three major infant toddler curricula, identifying key or unique features, discussing strengths and limitations, and reflecting on similarities and differences. The commonly used definition of curriculum in early childhood as "an organized framework" (Bredekamp & Rosegrant, 1992, p. 10) including the three components of content (what children are to learn), processes (classroom practices), and context (the physical and social-emotional environment) will be used. Resources for Infant Educarers (RIE), the Program for Infant/Toddler Care (PITC), and *Creative Curriculum for Infants & Toddlers* will be reviewed in the chronological order of their development. This review and reflection provides a platform for consideration of factors that will require a transformation or revolution in infant toddler care.

An examination of infant toddler curriculum is important for several reasons. One factor is the number of infants and toddlers in care. Recent reports document that approximately 50% of one-year-olds and 60% of two-year-olds experience regular nonparental care, averaging 30–32 hours per week (Kreader et al., 2005; Mulligan et al., 2005). Another factor is the low quality of available care coupled with the research base demonstrating that quality impacts young children's short- and long-term developmental outcomes. For example, the NICHD Study of Early Child Care (NICHD Early Child Care Research Network, 1996) found that three out of four infant caregivers provided only minimal stimulation of cognitive and language development and that higher quality early care was related to better cognitive and academic outcomes across preschool, primary, later elementary, and adolescence (Vandell et al., 2010). The child outcomes research combined with information emerging from neuroscience has led policy makers and others to increasingly focus on the content of infant toddler programs. For example, more and more states have established early learning guidelines for infant toddler programs (Scott-Little et al., 2008). These factors show the growing interest of families, practitioners, researchers, and policy makers in infant toddler curriculum.

Five topics are used to organize the reviews of the three infant toddler curricula. These topics are: origins and theoretical bases, key components, contributions to the field, consideration of diversity, and strengths and cautions. It is important to recognize the curricula reviewed here are only a sample of those available. These approaches were selected due to their extensive use. Other widely used approaches include published curricula such as HighScope and broader philosophical models such as Reggio Emilia.

Review of Contemporary Infant Toddler Curriculum

Resources for Infant Educarers

Origins and Theoretical Bases

Resources for Infant Educarers "is a non-profit world-wide membership organization, dedicated to improving the quality of infant care and education through teaching, supporting, and mentoring parents and caregivers" (RIE, 2007, p. 1). This approach emphasizes respectful care and the recognition of infants as competent self-motivated human beings. RIE views infants as the best guides of their own growth and discourages unnecessary adult interference in the natural unfolding of development. Magda Gerber, the co-founder and first director of RIE, believed that "all healthy, normal infants do what they can do and should be expected to do when they are ready. They should not be expected to do what they are not ready to do" (quoted in Jones, 2005, p. 76).

Gerber's philosophy of care emerged from her work with Dr. Emmi Pikler at the Pikler/Loczy Institute in Budapest. Pikler, a pediatrician, had developed a unique model of institutional care for orphaned infants that emphasized respect for the competence of the developing child. Infants at Loczy were given a safe environment in which to move freely, explore, and develop at their own pace. Attachment relationships between infants and their nurses (primary caregivers) were fostered through responsive, respectful interactions during caregiving routines (Owen & Petrie, 2006). Gerber was inspired by Pikler's approach and worked with her at the Loczy Institute until she moved to California in 1957. Gerber described herself as a bridge between Dr. Pikler and America and sought to bring Pikler's ideas to family and childcare center contexts (Gerber, 1998). In 1972, Dr. Tom Forrest, a Stanford University professor, invited her to co-direct the Demonstration Infant Project (DIP). In this program, Gerber worked with parents of high-risk infants with and without special needs to model respectful care, scaffold parents' abilities to observe and understand their individual infants' cues, and convey the importance of infants being allowed to engage in free, self-guided movement, independent play, and problem solving (Petrie & Owen, 2005). In 1978, Gerber and Forrest expanded the DIP model and established Resources for Infant Educarers (RIE) to offer courses for parents and childcare providers (Petrie & Owen, 2005). Certification and training courses are offered for center- and home-based providers, and pre- and postnatal courses are offered for parents (see http://www.rie.org).

No explicit developmental theories guide the Pikler/Gerber approach to care. However, scholars have drawn parallels between Pikler, Montessori, and Waldorf (Weber, 2003). All three approaches emphasize respect for the child, recognize the importance of the environment and play in children's learning, and embrace a maturationist view of development.

Key Components

Gerber (1998) stated that caregivers should "Observe more. Do less" (p. 63). Caregivers are urged to slow down, observe the infant, and not intervene in the infant's play unless this is necessary for safety. Gerber explained that "non-intervention, or non-interruption of play helps children develop competence in problem-solving skills" (Gerber & Johnson, 1998, p. 17). Infants are given freedom of movement and allowed to develop at their own pace, with unimpeded gross motor movement seen as a primary way for infants to learn and develop confidence (Abbott & Langston, 2006). Infants are grouped by developmental age, and classroom environments are designed to allow freedom of movement, age-appropriate challenges, and a moderate amount of stimulation (toys are simple and few). Caregiving routines (feeding, toileting) serve as the key times for relationship-building between children and caregivers.

Relative to infant curriculum, Gerber stated, "An infant always learns. The less we interfere with the natural process of learning, the more we can observe how much infants learn all the time" (RIE, 2007, p. 1). Gerber believed that infants' sense of self developed through their independent explorations and accomplishments as well as through their relationships with peers and adults in care (Triulzi, 2008). RIE caregivers observe infants closely, provide ample time for safe, free exploration on the floor, and serve as attachment figures. Environments are designed to be safe, quiet, and challenging, but skills are never explicitly taught (Petrie & Owen, 2005).

Contributions to the Field Beyond Direct Implementation

RIE's emphasis on motor development and freedom of movement is unique. This curriculum highlights the interconnections between children's motor development and social development, and the importance of being cognizant of how physical development is facilitated in care. RIE recognizes that all aspects of physical care impact infants' development of self (i.e. "educaring" as curriculum).

Consideration of Diversity

Gerber's parent–infant groups were conducted with high-risk children from diverse cultural backgrounds and abilities. RIE's emphasis on observing, recognizing, and responding to children's individual needs lends itself to individualized care. However, aspects of the approach may run counter to familial and cultural practices and children's temperamental differences. For example, many families and cultures swaddle infants, a practice that is strongly discouraged by RIE because the movement of the child is impeded.

Strengths

- RIE recognizes the importance of parents and provides tools to help parents implement RIE at home.
- RIE highlights the importance of designing environments to facilitate infants' motor development, independence, and exploration.

Cautions

- Pikler/Gerber's beliefs about child development emerged through their observations of infants. However, no underlying theoretical roots are explicitly articulated by RIE.
- RIE's implied maturationist approach does not adequately account for the importance of contextual factors.
- While over 60 years of observational research exists documenting infants' motor development, the effectiveness of RIE as a curriculum has not been evaluated.

Program for Infant/Toddler Care

Origins and Theoretical Bases

The Program for Infant/Toddler Care was developed in 1985 by Ron Lally and colleagues "in response to the low quality of infant/toddler child care found in the United States, the increased use of and demand for infant/toddler care, and the paucity of trainers and training materials available for the age period" (Lally & Mangione, 2009, p. 25). The philosophical basis for PITC (Lally & Mangione, 2009) is that infants and toddlers need close, emotionally responsive relationships; a safe, interesting, and developmentally appropriate environment; uninterrupted time to explore; and intellectually supportive interactions with adults. PITC advocates that relationships are facilitated through respectful, responsive daily caregiving routines. The approach recommends continuity of care, where infants and toddlers remain with the same caregiver(s) over long periods of time, with a primary caregiver assigned to each young child.

PITC is based in developmental theories, including the relationship approach emerging from the theories and research of Bowlby (1982), Ainsworth (Ainsworth et al., 1978), Maslow (1968), and Gerber and Pikler (Gerber & Johnson, 1998). Piaget's (1952) constructivist theory and Vygotsky's (1978) socio-cultural theory provide the basis for the PITC emphasis on providing an interesting environment, uninterrupted time to explore, and intellectually supportive interactions with peers and caregivers.

A developmentally appropriate environment with individual, group, and culturally appropriate approaches is a strong theme in PITC. Lally was a major consultant and contributor to the Zero-to-Three (2008; with earlier editions in 1995, 2004) publication *Caring for Infants and Toddlers in Groups: Developmentally Appropriate Practice.*

Key Components

PITC offers a set of program policies to create infant toddler programming "with a high probability of ensuring quality regardless of family and child circumstances" (Lally & Mangione, 2009, p. 26). The purpose of these policies is the establishment of a childcare experience focusing on the achievement of stable relationships and emotional connections for the child and family (Lally & Mangione, 2009). The six PITC program policies are:

- the establishment of a primary care system with each child and family assigned a primary care teacher;
- the creation of small groups of children and caregivers;
- the continuity of groups and teacher assignments over time;
- the establishment of personalized, responsive care focused on the individual needs, schedules, and abilities of each child;
- dialogue and collaboration with families to create cultural continuity between the program and each child's home;
- the inclusion and accommodation of children with special needs.

PITC proposes that infants and toddlers are both vulnerable and competent. To address the vulnerability and enhance competence, PITC identifies ten attributes of infancy as the center of the program philosophy (Lally & Mangione, 2009, p. 32–35):

- relationships are essential for infant toddler development;
- infants and toddlers learn holistically;
- infancy consists of three distinct developmental stages: young, mobile, and older infant;
- infants are active, self-motivated learners;
- infants are individuals with unique temperaments and relationship experiences;

- infants develop their sense of self through contact with others;
- home culture and family are fundamental to a child's developing identity;
- habits and language skills develop early;
- environments are powerful influences;
- caregiving routines are prime opportunities for learning.

PITC approaches curriculum for infants and toddlers as an ongoing process (Lally & Mangione, 2009) beginning with observation of each child's behavior, temperament, development, and interests. The observational information is documented and interpreted to provide a profile of that child. This individual developmental profile is the basis for planning and providing supportive tailored interactions. The teacher implements the plans and the cycle begins again. The curriculum process is ongoing, with the teacher continually observing, documenting, assessing, and planning enrichment opportunities for each child (for more information, see http://www.pitc.org).

Contribution to The Field Beyond Direct Implementation

PITC has developed a course of study and certification for professional trainers and infant toddler teachers. PITC training is divided into five modules, including readings, lecture, video, small and large group discussions, reflection, problem solving, and experiential learning with a focus on both infant toddler content and adult learning processes (Lally & Mangione, 2009).

Consideration of Diversity

PITC addresses diversity in both the curriculum and training modules. PITC consistently emphasizes and supports home cultural practices as well as the inclusion of young children with special needs. PITC recognizes the importance of children's home language and promotes family involvement. The PITC training videos and materials are available in English, Spanish, and Chinese (Cantonese).

Strengths

- PITC is based on developmental theories focusing on the whole child, with an emphasis on emotional and social development.
- The approach emphasizes respect for the unique individuality of each child and family, inclusion of young children with special needs, and cultural diversity.
- PITC has a comprehensive training system and credentialing process.

Cautions

- Teachers may not have the support or time to complete the ongoing assessments and to plan individual interactions.

- Continuity of care, while a sound principle, is often difficult to achieve even with a strong, highly competent staff. Given the high staff turnover and low staff qualifications common in infant toddler programs, continuity of care is challenging to implement in reality.
- Research on the approach is limited. However, Huston (2010) and colleagues are conducting a random assignment study of PITC training examining classroom variables and child outcomes.

Creative Curriculum

Origins and Philosophical Bases

Teaching Strategies first published *The Creative Curriculum for Infants & Toddlers* in 1997 (revisions 1999, 2006) in response to repeated requests from the field for guidance on working with infants and toddlers (Dombro et al., 1999). Diane Trister Dodge, the founder and president of Teaching Strategies, reports that the most recent 2010 revision includes a new expanded assessment system (personal communication, June 28, 2010).

Dodge, Rudick, and Berke (2006) note that *Creative Curriculum* focuses on the importance of meeting basic needs, fostering social-emotional development, developing secure attachments, and supporting cognition and brain development. Citations to support each of these major foci and information on how *Creative Curriculum* principles are based on specific theories are provided in their books and website (http://www.teachingstrategies.com). Teaching Strategies cites the work of Maslow, Brazelton, and Greenspan to support the creation of emotionally safe and secure environments, responsive caregiving, and individualized experiences. Erikson and Greenspan are credited as the basis for implementing trust-building and nurturing routines and helping children express their emotions. The attachment theories of Bowlby and Ainsworth, and Masten's work on resilience, are cited as the basis for assigning primary caregivers and facilitating children's development of self-control. Piaget and Vygotsky are referenced as the sources underlying *Creative Curriculum*'s uninterrupted time for children to explore and play, teacher scaffolding, and encouragement of peer learning through social interactions.

Key Components

In striving to be comprehensive and responsive to Head Start's standards, *Creative Curriculum* offers a review of infant toddler development, outlines experiences that support infants and toddlers in reaching broad developmental goals, provides information for staff and parents to facilitate development, and delineates the materials and settings needed to support implementation (Dombro et al., 1999). A central concept is the importance of building responsive relationships among teachers, children, families, and the community within the context of daily routines and activities (Dodge & Bickart, 2000). Teachers are considered "the foundation of the curriculum" (Dodge & Bickart, 2000, p. 34). The teacher's role is to create a warm inviting environment that ensures children are safe, and to implement practices that promote children's physical and mental health and learning (including individualizing, planning and evaluating, and guiding behavior). Routines are another core feature. The importance of using five routines (hello/good-bye, diapering/toileting, eating/mealtimes, sleeping/nap time, and dressing) as opportunities to build positive relationships and promote learning and trust is a key component. Individualized activities based on each child's stage, abilities, and interests are planned by the teacher and include experiences such as imitating and pretending, enjoying stories and books, or exploring sand and water (Dombro et al., 1999). *Creative Curriculum*'s 2010 Gold Assessment System, designed for children birth through kindergarten, lists 38 specific objectives organized into nine areas, including social-emotional, physical, cognitive, oral language, literacy, math, science and technology, social studies, and the arts. The 38 objectives are based on widely held expectations, drawn from the literature and state early learning standards, that are predictive of school success (Teaching Strategies, 2010).

Contributions Beyond Direct Implementation

Dodge believes *Creative Curriculum* validates the importance of the first three years of life by recognizing it as the foundation for all future learning (personal communication, June 28, 2010). *Creative Curriculum* also validates the early childhood personnel who work with infants and toddlers by emphasizing professional development.

Creative Curriculum has a variety of materials (books, videos, coach's guides) and delivery options (e.g. on-site at programs, e-learning) for professional development specifically designed for staff working with infants and toddlers. The scope of the materials ranges from products designed for those new to the field to those for seasoned professionals.

Consideration of Diversity

Dodge and Bickart (2000) note that *Creative Curriculum* is individualized and tailored to meet the unique needs of each child and family based on teachers' observations. Various races, ethnicities, socio-economic levels, and family structures are included in the vignettes describing children, caregivers, and families that are referenced throughout the training materials to illustrate concepts. The 2010 edition includes a specific section on dual language learners (Teaching Strategies, 2010).

Strengths

- The linkage of curriculum and assessment, aided by computerization, encourages teachers to use ongoing assessment to inform curriculum.
- Resources for training and professional development are available for a wide range of skill levels.
- Curriculum frameworks for preschool and primary levels have been developed, enabling continuity across several levels of early education.

Cautions

- The use of state early learning standards and inclusion of content disciplines (i.e. math, science, and technology) differ from traditional approaches relying on developmental domains as the organizing framework for infant toddler curriculum and assessment. This raises questions, not yet fully discussed or answered, about the proper balance of academic content with appropriate care and also the proper role of forces internal and external to the classroom in determining infant toddler curriculum.
- No systematic program of research to document child outcomes or teaching processes has been published to date.
- The approach can be viewed as a broad framework, rather than a curriculum, requiring a good deal of teacher expertise to implement as intended.

Reflection: Similarities and Differences

All three curricula address the components—content, processes, and context—used to define curriculum in early childhood. However, there are important similarities and differences in how each model addresses these components.

Content

All three curricula focus on facilitating development; with RIE focusing on motor and social-emotional development and the other two adding an enhanced focus on cognitive development. Relative to curricular goals, RIE emphasizes independence, free movement, and the development of self. PITC emphasizes development of strong attachments, an identity tied to culture, and the holistic nature of early learning. *Creative Curriculum* goes beyond broad goals in listing 38 specific objectives organized into nine areas and clearly situates infant toddler curriculum in the context of school success and state early learning standards.

Processes

All approaches address similar processes of teaching infants and toddlers, including the importance of observation, individualization, and routines. They differ in the role of the teacher, with RIE adopting a hands-off philosophy, emphasizing the natural unfolding of development and utilizing caregiving routines as the dedicated time for active interactions. PITC and *Creative Curriculum* embrace an interventionist role, with teachers actively designing tailored interactions and activities implemented throughout the day. Despite these differences, all three approaches advocate that specialized professional development is required to successfully implement each model.

Context

Relative to the physical environment, RIE stresses safe environments that allow for free motor explorations with few toys. PITC strives to provide an interesting environment that offers continuity between home and program, and extended periods of play and exploration with continual supportive interactions with primary caregivers. *Creative Curriculum* emphasizes a warm and inviting environment that ensures children are safe while promoting children's development in specific areas through planned activities related to school success.

Other Common Characteristics

Beyond these similarities and differences in elements that qualify each approach as a "curriculum," a number of other common characteristics emerge. For example, a noticeable limitation is the lack of research documenting implementation processes and child outcomes associated with each curriculum.

Another common characteristic is that each approach reflects the context and scientific theories prominent during the time of its development. This commonality underlies the major differences—in the scope of the curriculum's focus, the role of the caregiver/teacher, the nature of the environment, the view of families, the value of diversity—among the approaches. For example, RIE's origins were during a time period dominated by maturational theories and the primacy of observation as a child study technique. RIE's principle of "Observe more. Do less" captures this maturational focus, with caregivers giving children space and time to develop at their own pace with minimal adult interruptions. Additionally, RIE's emphasis on fostering a sense of trust and security in infants through respectful and consistent care routines may have roots in RIE's origins serving high-risk children who had experienced hardship and loss. PITC's focus on relationship-based care reflects the interest in and development of attachment theories in the 1970s and 1980s, and the concern with the potential of childcare to disrupt maternal–child bonds and be detrimental to development (e.g. White, 1988). The 1970s and 1980s also brought "The Amazing Newborn" (Klaus & Klaus, 1985) and "the competent infant" (Friedman & Vietze, 1972). PITC incorporated these concepts by addressing both the vulnerability and competence of infants and toddlers. *Creative Curriculum*, the most recently developed of the three approaches, shares these features with PITC but provides more structure in its approach to ongoing assessment by offering a computerized system of organizing teacher observations and linking these to suggested classroom activities across multiple domains. *Creative Curriculum*'s 2010 revision addresses contemporary interest in state standards and school readiness by placing infant toddler curriculum on the continuum of experiences leading to school success.

Given this interplay between the zeitgeist and curricular approaches, open questions are: What theoretical advances will drive new innovations in infant toddler curriculum? What future social, cultural, and historical factors will influence the content of infant toddler curriculum?

Future Directions: A Revolution?

Continued Attention

It is anticipated that the current interest in the care and education of infants and toddlers will continue, with enhanced focus on the content of programs. What led to this prediction?

- *The needs of families*: In 2008, 48% of the requests for childcare received by resource and referral agencies were for infant care (NACCRRA, 2008).
- *The growing body of research findings highlighting the value of starting early*: The persistence of achievement gaps, coupled with promising research findings documenting the lasting positive outcomes of young children's participation in high quality early intervention programs (Camilli et al., 2010), has encouraged educators and researchers to investigate interventions with younger and younger children. It will be important to monitor the appropriateness of new interventions, including the curriculum, and assess any potential risks for young children in addition to the intended benefits.
- *Practitioners' continuing discussions of how to appropriately integrate rich content in a relationship-based approach to care*: While this discussion has largely occurred among teachers staffing programs designed for older children, it is increasingly a focus of infant toddler teachers as expectations for content/learning are pushed further down (Kucharski, 2008).
- *State and federal policy makers increasingly view infant toddler programs as the "frontier" of school readiness*: One example is Oklahoma's State Pilot Program to Expand and Enhance Infant/Toddler Services (see Goble & Horm, 2009). The doubling of Early Head Start in 2009 is an example of the growing federal interest in infants and toddlers. As infant toddler services expand, the meaning and role of "school readiness" will need to be critically examined to reconcile external expectations that focus on children's future success with traditional practice that prioritizes infants' current developmental needs.

This increased attention, and associated issues, will demand further evolution of infant toddler programs, with specific attention to proven curricula and the necessary teacher skills and supports to implement curricula with fidelity. As public expenditures increase so will the calls for accountability and the formalization or "professionalization" of infant toddler care and education.

Professional Development Challenges

These demands place a spotlight on the infant toddler workforce and specialized professional development. The infant toddler workforce has been found to have lower rates of formal education than the workforce serving older children (e.g. Norris et al., 2003). Hiring practices often do not prioritize college coursework or degrees when selecting infant toddler staff (Howes et al., 1992). Specialized professional development opportunities are limited, with only 29% of U.S. colleges or universities offering an early childhood teacher preparation program including content on children age four and younger (Early & Winton, 2001), and only 46% of programs offering at least one dedicated infant toddler course (Maxwell et al., 2006).

The need for future research on curriculum also calls for increased attention to professional development. There is a shortage of infant toddler specialists at every level of the career ladder. More infant toddler specialists with graduate degrees are needed to administer programs; to fill higher education faculty positions; and to design and conduct needed research, including the development of new measures and approaches to document curriculum delivery, classroom quality, teacher effectiveness, and child outcomes.

The Revolution

Infant toddler programming and curriculum require a revolutionary change to adequately meet current and future challenges. This need presents both opportunities and risks related to curriculum, including:

- *Offering research-based infant toddler curriculum versus implementing approaches based on external pressures*: Curriculum and theory emerge, in part, as a response to social, cultural, and historical contexts. Today, the field faces political, social, and economic pressures—how the field responds will have important implications. If external pressures assume greater precedence than research-based knowledge, will infant toddler care be able to establish itself as a true profession? Can quality curriculum be offered if practices are reactionary rather than intentional?
- *Conducting systematic research on the processes and outcomes of infant toddler curricula versus no robust research*: The most widely used curriculum models currently lack systematic research on the effectiveness of their processes and outcomes. How can practitioners choose a curriculum model wisely if evidence does not exist? How can we assure families and policy makers that infants are receiving care that is growth promoting and not harmful if no systematic research has been conducted?

- *Inappropriately pushing down academic content versus valuing infants' present, holistic development*: Recent pressures for school readiness have introduced a false dichotomy: Should we focus on infants' present or spend our time preparing them for the future? However, "school readiness" and developmentally appropriate care are not mutually exclusive. Quality infant care supporting infants' current developmental strengths and needs will foster the development of the whole child in the present, ensuring that the child is better prepared for the future. In addition, as advocated in the *Creative Curriculum* approach, rich content knowledge can be appropriately integrated into play-based infant toddler care without introducing formal academic instruction or inappropriate expectations. Will the field be able to reconcile and communicate this? Will lack of an adequately prepared workforce preclude implementation of curricular approaches that embrace both high quality "present" care and appropriately rich and diverse content?

Conclusion

The three curricula reviewed in this chapter provide similar, yet unique, approaches. Formalized curriculum frameworks such as these are part of a larger movement towards the professionalization of the field of early care and education. This professionalization, and resolution of the issues described above, will best be supported by robust research examining the effectiveness of different infant toddler curriculum models and systematic efforts to embrace evidence-based knowledge and practices to guide the future of the field.

References

Abbott, L. & Langston, A. (2006). *Parents matter: Supporting the Birth to Three Matters Network*. New York: McGraw-Hill.

Ainsworth, M.D.S., Blehar, M.C., Waters, E., & Wall, S. (1978). *Patterns of attachment: A psychological study of the strange situation*. Hillsdale, NJ: Erlbaum.

Bowlby, J. (1982). *Attachment*. New York: Basic Books.

Bredekamp, S. & Rosegrant, T. (Eds.). (1992). *Reaching potentials: Appropriate curriculum and assessment for young children* (vol. 1). Washington, DC: National Association for the Education of Young Children.

Camilli, G., Vargas, S., Ryan, S., & Barnett, W.S. (2010). Meta-analysis of the effects of early education interventions on cognitive and social development. *Teachers College Record*, 112(3), 579–620.

Dodge, D. & Bickart, T. (2000). *How curriculum frameworks respond to developmental stages: Birth through age 8*. Paper presented at the Lilian Katz Symposium, University of Illinois, Urbana-Champaign, IL, November 5–7. Retrieved from http://ceep.crc.uiuc.edu/pubs/katzsym/dodge.html.

Dodge, D., Rudick, S., & Berke, K.L. (2006). *The Creative Curriculum for infants, toddlers, and twos*. Washington, DC: Teaching Strategies.

Dombro, A.L., Colker, L.J., & Dodge, D. (1999). *Creative Curriculum for infants & toddlers* (rev. ed.). Washington, DC: Teaching Strategies.

Early, D.M. & Winton, P.J. (2001). Preparing the workforce: Early childhood teacher preparation at 2- and 4-year institutions of higher education. *Early Childhood Research Quarterly*, 16, 285–306.

Friedman, S. & Vietze, P.M. (1972). The competent infant. *Peabody Journal of Education*, 49 (4), 314–22.

Gerber, M. (1998). *Dear parent: Caring for infants with respect.* Los Angeles, CA: RIE.

Gerber, M. & Johnson, A. (1998). *Your self-confident baby: How to encourage your child's natural abilities from the very start.* New York: Wiley.

Goble, C.B. & Horm, D.M. (2009). Infant–toddler services through community collaboration. *Zero to Three*, 29(6), 18–22.

Howes, C., Whitebook, M., & Phillips, D. (1992). Teacher characteristics and effective teaching in child care: Findings from the National Child Care Staffing Study. *Child & Youth Care Forum*, 21, 399–414.

Huston, A.C. (2010). *Evaluation of the Program for Infant and Toddler Care (PITC)*, August 1. Retrieved from http://www.he.utexas.edu/web/EECCR/.

Jones, S. (2005). *Comforting your crying baby: Why your baby is crying and what you can do about it.* New York: Innova.

Klaus, M.H. & Klaus, P.H. (1985). *The amazing newborn.* Reading, MA: Addison-Wesley.

Kreader, J.L., Ferguson, D., & Lawrence, S. (2005). *Infant and toddler child care arrangements.* (Research-to-Policy Connections no. 1.) New York: Child Care & Early Education Research Connections. Retrieved from http://www.nccp.org/publications/pdf/text_628.pdf.

Kucharski, L. (2008). What role does content learning have in a toddler classroom? Unpublished manuscript, Department of Curriculum and Instruction, University of Wisconsin, Milwaukee, WI.

Lally, J.R. & Mangione, P.L. (2009). The program for infant/toddler care. In J.L. Roop-narine & J.E. Johnson (Eds.), *Approaches to early childhood education* (pp. 25–47). Upper Saddle River, NJ: Pearson.

Maslow, A.H. (1968). *Toward a psychology of being.* New York: Van Nostrand Reinhold.

Maxwell, K., Lim, C.-I., & Early, D.M. (2006). *Early childhood teacher preparation programs in the United States: National Report.* Chapel Hill, NC: University of North Carolina, Frank Porter Graham Child Development Institute.

Mulligan, G.M., Brimhall, D., West, J., & Chapman, C. (2005). *Child care and early education arrangements of infants, toddlers, and preschoolers: 2001, statistical analysis report* (NCES 2006–39). Washington, DC: U.S. Department of Education, Institute of Education Sciences.

National Association of Child Care Resource and Referral Agencies (NACCRRA). (2008). *Covering the map: Child care resource & referral agencies providing vital services to parents throughout the United States.* Arlington, VA: NACCRRA.

NICHD Early Child Care Research Network. (1996). Characteristics of infant child care: Factors contributing to positive caregiving. *Early Childhood Research Quarterly*, 11(3), 269–306.

Norris, D.J., Dunn, L., & Eckert, L. (2003). *"Reaching for the stars" center validation study final report.* Oklahoma City, OK: Department of Human Services, Division of Child Care.

Owen, S. & Petrie, S. (2006). "Observe more … do less": The approaches of Magda Gerber to parent education. In L. Abbott & A. Langson (Eds.), *Parents matter: Supporting the Birth to Three Matters Network* (pp. 127–37). New York: McGraw-Hill.

Petrie, S. & Owen, S. (2005). *Authentic relationships in group care for infants and toddlers: Resource for Infant Educarers (RIE) principles into practice.* Philadelphia, PA: Kingsley.

Piaget, J. (1952). *The origins of intelligence in children.* New York: Norton.

RIE. (2007). *Resources for Infant Educarers: The RIE approach by Magda Gerber.* Retrieved from http://www.rie.org.

Scott-Little, C., Kagan, S.L., Frelow, V.S., & Reid, J. (2008). *Inside the content of infant–toddler early learning guidelines: Results from analyses, issues to consider, and recommendations.*

Greensboro: University of North Carolina. Retrieved from http://ccf.tc.columbia.edu/pdf/Inside%20the%20Content%20of%20Infant-Toddler%20ELGs-Full%20Report.pdf.

Teaching Strategies. (2010). Research foundation: Teaching Strategies GOLD Assessment System. Retrieved from http://www.teachingstrategies.com/content/pageDocs/GOLD-Research-Paper-Web.pdf.

Triulzi, M. (2008). Do the Pikler and RIE methods promote infant–parent attachment? (unpublished master's thesis). Smith College School for Social Work, Northampton, MA.

Vandell, D.L., Belsky, J., Burchinal, M., Steinberg, L., Vandergrift, N., & NICHD Early Child Care Research Network. (2010). Do effects of early child care extend to age 15 years? Results from the NICHD study of early care and youth development. *Child Development*, 81(3), 737–56.

Vygotsky, L.S. (1978). *Mind in society*. Cambridge, MA: Harvard University Press.

Weber, S. (2003). The lives and work of Emmi Pikler and Magda Gerber. Retrieved from http://www.waldorflibrary.org/Journal_Articles/picklergerber.pdf.

White, B.L. (1988). *Educating the infant and toddler*. Lexington, MA: Lexington Books.

Zero-to-Three. (2008). *Caring for infants and toddlers in groups: Developmentally appropriate practice* (2nd ed.). Washington, DC: Zero-to-Three.

10

CREATIVE CURRICULUM AND HIGHSCOPE CURRICULUM

Constructing Possibilities in Early Education

Sara Michael-Luna and Lucinda G. Heimer

Introduction

The primary public funding sources for early education in the US are the federal government (in the form of Head Start, with 6.8 billion in 2005) and, increasingly, states. States are entering the funding picture (2.84 billion in 2004–5) through the support of public preschool programs (ACF, 2006). As of 2005, 57% of the teachers in a multi-state study of public pre-K reported using either Creative Curriculum or HighScope (NCEDL, 2005). The classrooms in the NCEDL study consisted of public pre-K classrooms defined as those either partially or fully funded by the state; interestingly, the majority (59.1%) of Head Start programs have also adopted HighScope or Creative Curriculum (ACF, 2003). Between Head Start and public pre-Ks, Creative Curriculum and HighScope Curriculum are currently the most extensively used early childhood curricula. Both curricula were established in the 1970s, a decade which historians consider a "high water-mark" for public responsibility for the education and care of young children (Beatty, 1995), as more women entered the workforce and the need for more extensive early care and education rose. Both HighScope and Creative Curriculum developed models of child-centered, experiential learning for children three to five years of age. While these two popular curricula have weathered the test of time, some recent research that reflects a reconstruction of early childhood learning and growth has highlighted drawbacks to using these two curricula.

In this chapter, we focus on: (1) the origins of each approach as well as how theory and their foundational values are utilized; (2) the key components of these approaches; (3) an example of the way that each curriculum addresses diversity, specifically English language learners; and (4) the implications, contributions, and opportunities of each approach. Throughout the chapter, we carefully consider the roles that developmental universalism and socio-cultural context play in both curricula, as well as review the research that critiques Creative Curriculum and HighScope for their short-term and long-term outcomes. Although no curriculum is neutral (Apple, 2000, 2004), we suggest that the open, unscripted curriculum presented in Creative Curriculum and HighScope leaves room for teacher agency in creating child-centered, culturally appropriate classrooms.

Origins: Developmental Foundations

The development of HighScope and Creative Curriculum resulted from two preschool intervention studies. Both were framed in a developmental perspective on child learning and growth. The two studies, the Perry Preschool and the Abecedarian Study, were the result of increased attention during the 1960s to psychologists, such as Piaget, Bloom, and E. Erikson, and to development in the first years of life. The four domains of development reflected in both the curricula and currently defined developmentally appropriate practice are: (1) social-emotional; (2) physical; (3) cognitive; and (4) language (Copple & Bredekamp, 2009).

HighScope

As a part of President Johnson's War on Poverty, researchers during the 1960s turned an eye to how to "break the cycle of poverty" through education. One of the best-known efforts from this era, the Perry Preschool, 1962–7, resulted in the development of HighScope curriculum. The Perry Preschool, as developed by David Weikart and his colleagues, selected 123 African American children living in poverty and at high risk of not completing school, and provided a preschool experience for them. The core group of children who received the "treatment" of preschool were then followed for decades of their lives, and a cost–benefit analysis was conducted for the preschool experience. The outcomes were based on interviews and demographic surveys completed at the ages of 15 (Erikson, 1977), 27 (Barnett, 1985), and 40 (Belfield et al., 2006). Comparing the preschool group to the non-preschool group, researchers found significant differences for the children through age 27. For example, there were decreases in the likelihood of involvement in crime (from 35% to 7%), and the high school graduation rate jumped from 54% to 71%. Based on this work, Barnett calculated that for every dollar spent on preschool, there was a $7.16 return (Barnett, 1996). The participants' success, compared to the control group who did not receive a preschool experience, helped to lay the groundwork for the federal government's funding of Head Start.

Creative Curriculum

Creative Curriculum emerged in the late 1970s (the first edition of the Creative Curriculum was 1978) as a way to help preschool teachers organize their classrooms into well-defined areas of interest. The Creative Curriculum approach was based on the child–adult interactive learning experiences that were developed as the curriculum for the Abecedarian Studies (1972–2009), a decade after the Perry Preschool. Based in Chapel Hill, North Carolina, the Abecedarian Early Childhood Intervention Project was a full-day, year-round program serving low-income children through age eight years. Initially, 101 "at risk" African Americans, with low birth weight babies targeted, were selected to engage in experiential learning activities (Sparling et al., 2007). The effect of their early learning experience was followed for decades and the following outcomes were reported: higher IQ; improved reading and math; and fewer special education placements (Campbell et al., 2002). These findings spurred the refinement of the Creative Curriculum, which continues to be a popular curricular approach in a variety of early education classrooms today.

Theoretical Underpinnings and Values: Balancing Developmentalism and Socio-Cultural Theories of Learning

Although HighScope and Creative Curriculum share a strong foundation, both based on developmentalism, both curricula also claim to draw upon socio-cultural understandings of learning. In addition to Piaget and E. Erikson, HighScope Curriculum developers report that they draw upon learning theories from Dewey, Smilansky, and Vygotsky in order to create learning experiences where children co-construct knowledge, or actively build ideas about the world, through direct experiences with their social, cultural, and material environments. Similarly, in addition to Maslow, E. Erikson, and Piaget, Creative Curriculum claims to draw from Vygotsky, Gardner, and Smilansky specifically, as the curriculum focuses on creating environments where experiential learning through designed play is encouraged. In both curricula, child-based assessment and observation draw from developmentalist stages (as currently reflected in developmentally appropriate practice, or DAP—Copple & Bredekamp, 2009), and interactions and the classroom environment appear to draw from constructivist theories of learning.

It is clear in both packages that the foundation for learning begins with the child and that the child is constructing new experiences and subsequent knowledge through experimenting with the environment, peers, and teachers. This foundation builds upon mainstream stage theories (Erikson, 1959; Maslow, 1943; Piaget, 1952) and the notion that all children develop along similar trajectories. While E. Erikson's developmental stages and Maslow's hierarchy of needs focus attention on comple-tion of tasks at each "stage" or "need" (e.g. developing trust or having basic needs met), both curricular packages place cognitive constructivism at the center of the curriculum.

The influence of a universal notion of development through various stage theories was and continues to be prevalent in some areas of psychology. While there are many academics who have questioned and critiqued this universal perspective in education (see, for example, Cannella, 1997; MacNaughton, 2003; Fendler, 2001), the popularity of the developmental theoretical foundation is embodied in these packages. The knowledge, assumptions, and culture in curriculum are not neutral (Apple, 2000). One might suggest that the popularity of these packages simply reflects the academic knowledge of our time; however, a critical reflection on the 1970s movement to create early childhood curriculum could also be viewed as a form of social control over low-income families. This formal indoctrination into school "ways of knowing" is communicated through universal assumptions regarding child development and acquisition of knowledge. In a sense, the developmentally appropriate practices cited by both Creative Curriculum and HighScope act in much the same way as academic standards in K-12 education. Apple's (2000, 2004) work suggests a closer look at the power in curriculum. In this case, power is employed through a positivist developmental perspective that creates a hegemony in which developmental milestones are held as equalizers—suggesting all "normal" children, regardless of home background (or cultural and linguistic origins), should perform particular tasks by a certain age. Through the mainstream popularity of constructivism and the creation and endorsement of developmentally appropriate practices (DAP) by the National Association for the Education of Young Children (NAEYC), curricular choices presented to the field become "packaged" and more powerful.

Both HighScope and Creative Curriculum also acknowledge socio-cultural and contextual influences through theorists such as John Dewey and Lev Vygotsky. Dewey's focus on education as an equalizer in our society is clearly reflected in the historically significant underpinnings of both curricula (Dewey, 1902/1990). Similarly, Vygotsky's later work not only considered the role of inner speech and peer scaffolding but also offered a complex cultural component that pushed the consideration of new ways to scaffold learning. His *zone of proximal development* is reflected in the role teachers are encouraged to play in children's learning. By focusing on environment and individual child-driven experiential learning, both Creative Curriculum and HighScope set up possibilities for teachers to support child problem-solving through scaffolding. Through experimentation and sharing, this interaction may produce co-constructed early understandings regarding concepts such as gravity or geometry. These concepts can be supported through teacher or peer questioning that pushes the learner's competence (Bodrova & Leong, 2007).

Socio-cultural perspectives on learning can provide the opportunity for teachers to explore their role and agency with both Creative Curriculum and HighScope curriculum (Apple, 1986). Unlike prescriptive or scripted curriculum packages, both Creative Curriculum and HighScope provide space for teachers to make moment-to-moment decisions regarding content, distribution of time and space, as well as interactions with individual children and groups. Neither of the curriculum packages offers overt scripts for teachers to follow, but, rather, each one presents teachers with vignettes and sample observation notes to model appropriate interactive strategies. While this ability to influence the curriculum creates a model of respect for individual child development and needs, it unfortunately also leaves Creative Curriculum and HighScope easy targets for critics who feel curriculum must be "teacher proof" (Apple, 2004; see, for example, Mokros & Russell, 1995).

The extent and depth to which both curricula appear to engage and embody the socio-cultural aspects of these theories in recent editions have waned. As the field of early childhood has adapted to the trend of outcome-based assessments and standards, both curricula have echoed the outcome-based movement in their 54 "key developmental indicators" (HighScope) or 38 "objectives for development and learning" (Creative Curriculum). There is no provision of in-depth application and overt explanation of socio-cultural and contextual influences. In a later section of this paper (pp. 126–27), describing a case study on English language learners, we further examine the dangers of superficial application of socio-cultural and contextual influences in both Creative Curriculum and HighScope (Michael-Luna & Heimer, 2009).

Key Components

Both Creative Curriculum and HighScope highlight the importance of the environment and support for following the interest and abilities of the children in the class. While these packages build on a constructivist foundation, there are both explicit and subtle differences in the packages.

HighScope

The multi-volume HighScope Preschool Curriculum uses direct, hands-on experiences with people, objects, events, and ideas. The curriculum (HighScope, 2007) addresses four areas:

- a set of teaching practices for adult–child interaction, arranging the classroom and materials, and planning the daily routine;
- curriculum content areas for three- to five-year-olds;
- assessment tools to measure teaching behaviors and child progress;
- a training model to help caregivers implement the curriculum effectively.

By creating an environment where children and teachers can actively co-construct knowledge during purposeful play, HighScope suggests that learning is a four part process: (1) adult–child interaction which should encourage child problem-solving; (2) prepared environment that presents areas and resources for child exploration and discovery of knowledge; (3) planned daily routine that includes the Plan–Do–Review cycle of learning and also takes into consideration small and large group interactions; and (4) assessment of individual children's learning needs through teacher observation. The interaction and communication between teachers and children and teachers and parents are emphasized in HighScope. The teacher's role is that of facilitator.

A HighScope teacher works to "promote initiative and independence" (Epstein, 2007, p. 13) in child decision-making and participation in classroom activities. Even in activities that are initiated by teachers, HighScope advises teachers to encourage children to supply their own ideas and choose how to use the materials available to them. HighScope also provides teacher training on how to "share control" between adults and children, and supports child-based problem-solving around academic content as well as social conflict.

Creative Curriculum

Creative Curriculum fosters an educational environment that supports age-appropriate learning through purposeful play by using the developmental domains consistent with DAP (Copple & Bredekamp, 2009): social/emotional, physical, cognitive, and language. A Creative Curriculum classroom is set up to maintain ten interest areas: blocks, dramatic play, toys and games, art, sand and water, library, discovery, music and movement, cooking, computers, and also the outdoors.

Each classroom establishes a daily routine that becomes predictable and familiar to young children. It is suggested in the curriculum that this routine establishes a positive classroom climate in which the socio-emotional needs of the children are met. The daily routine includes: (1) taking attendance; (2) large group meeting, in which teachers are encouraged to present "calendar time" and touch on the events of the day and community happenings; (3) small group time, where a small group of children and the teacher work on introducing a new skill, concept, activity, or materials; and (4) choice time, where children select and work in one of the pre-prepared interest areas such as the sand table or the dramatic play area. Creative Curriculum gives special emphasis to transition times, the time where children move from one activity to another, meal times, and rest time. The recent move to content knowledge in early childhood is also reflected in Creative Curriculum's emphasis on seven content areas: literacy (including phonological awareness and print concepts); mathematics (number sense and patterns); science; social studies; the arts; technology; and process skills (observing, problem-solving, and communicating information). The teacher's role in Creative Curriculum is that of observer, teacher, and assessor. Teachers are encouraged to use the Developmental Continuum (Dodge et al., 2002) when objectively observing children in the context of the classroom. Creative Curriculum also supports a range of teaching approaches, including child-initiated learning and teacher-directed learning, and offers advice for how to adapt instruction to different types of learners, including those with special needs, gifted children, and second language learners. Creative Curriculum guides teachers to use naturalistic forms of assessment which directly contribute to supporting individual learning as well as to program evaluation. In the next section, we discuss how both Creative Curriculum and HighScope address the individual learning of English language learners through the brief description of a case study.

Curriculum Quandaries: An Investigation into the Construction of English Language Learning in HighScope and Creative Curriculum

Given the historical, theoretical, and pragmatic overview of both packages, we now shift our focus and consider one specific critique of the packages as they relate to working with diverse populations. More than one-quarter of young children under the age of six live in households in which no one over age 13 speaks English fluently (US Census, 2000). Many of these children participate in preschool. However, early childhood curriculum has been slow to support teacher knowledge on the linguistic development of multilingual children, or English language learners. Approximately 27% of the children enrolled in Head Start programs speak a language other than English at home (Head Start Bureau, 2001). In a previously reported text analysis study, we uncovered several areas where Creative Curriculum and HighScope missed opportunities for teacher knowledge of multilingual language development (Michael-Luna & Heimer, 2009). These holes in knowledge are not unique to HighScope or Creative Curriculum, but rather are symptomatic of a larger monolingual-focused education framework in the United States (Crawford, 1999; Cummins, 2001).

Differentiating English Language Learners and Monolinguals

Both HighScope and Creative Curriculum indirectly, and perhaps inadvertently, draw from a deficit perspective on language learning and development that is prevalent in the United States. The deficit perspective, which positions monolingual language development as the norm and bilingual language development as secondary, suggests that bilingual development in young children is cognitively harmful, or that young bilinguals do not develop as quickly as monolinguals. Language acquisition research has long disproved this (Bialystok, 2001, 1991). While Creative Curriculum and HighScope do not use such strong assertions in their curriculum, both curricula use metaphoric language which equates second language acquisition with cognitive delay. Creative Curriculum uses a comparison between the variation in children with disabilities and bilingual development: "Just as children with the same disability may have very different strengths and needs, children learning English as a second language vary greatly" (Dodge et al., 2002, p. 38). HighScope uses the federal government's term "Limited English Proficiency" (LEP) throughout its text. This terminology is problematic as it portrays a deficit perspective. The more commonly accepted term "English language learner" (ELL) focuses on the potential of learning rather than on the "limit" of the language. While neither curriculum package asserts that multilingual language development is cognitively harmful to young children, the use of this terminology suggests that both curricula frame English language learners as problematic to some degree. Both curricula support dual language learning, however, most notably English–Spanish, and produce versions of their curriculum in a variety of languages.

Language Development of English Language Learners

Language acquisition and development research suggests that within monolingual (Hart & Risley, 1995) and bilingual populations (Pearson et al., 1993; Marchman et al., 2004) there is individual variation in children's vocabulary acquisition rates and levels. These differences are linked to the children's home environment, for both monolinguals and bilinguals, and the balance between the two developing languages for bilinguals (De Houwer, 2009). By the age of two and a half years, a child raised in a bilingual environment will be able to function effectively in both (or all) the languages of his/her family environment (Bialystok, 2001); however, "the two languages are distinct and the representation for them is unique" (p. 120) and directly effects children's learning.

Application of ELL Knowledge

Both Creative Curriculum and HighScope made an effort to include knowledge on English language learning and young children in their descriptive text; however, both miss the opportunity to apply the knowledge through examples—an important learning tool for teacher education. In HighScope, we found that there were possible second language explanations in five out of six vignettes presented in their multicultural curriculum text. Creative Curriculum also misses this same opportunity when reporting sample observation notes. In the nine sample observation notes, only one observation presents an opportunity to examine the child's language learning; but even in that case, the observation focused on the cultural differences between the children and their school environment or peers. The role of language acquisition, and how a teacher can and should support it, was not discussed (Michael-Luna & Heimer, 2009).

The use of this study as a critique of the two curricular approaches illuminates the need to continually evaluate the shifting context in which the curriculum is implemented. In the following section we build on the exploration of the influence of context on curriculum as we consider the connections between early education curriculum and current education policy for K-12 that emphasizes standards and particular forms of assessment.

Implications, Opportunities, and Contributions

In our final section, we discuss the implications, contributions, and opportunities present in each curriculum package approach. Here, we review recent, somewhat controversial, research on short-term and long-term outcomes for Creative Curriculum and HighScope. We consider how Creative Curriculum and HighScope have struggled to address the tension between K-12 and early childhood through balancing play and skills-based instruction. Additionally, we discuss the opportunities and contributions both curricula make to early childhood education as well as to the broader field of education in terms of teacher knowledge and agency.

While both curricula draw on a foundation of developmental universalism that limits how the curricula address socio-cultural contexts, this imbalance also creates an opportunity for teacher agency. Teacher interpretation and agency are possible through local, culturally relevant application of moment-to-moment strategies. The curricular emphasis on learning environment, resources and materials, and the importance of child and teacher interactions creates an opportunity for engaging young children in contextual discovery learning through an unscripted curriculum.

In the current larger educational context, however, open, flexible, learner-centered and play-based curricula are being questioned in relation to outcome-based assessments in specific content areas such as math and language (NCER, 2008; Zigler et al., 2004). In three separate site-based evaluations described in the National Center of Education Research report (NCER, 2008), Creative Curriculum did not prove to be a statistically significant curriculum for improving children's reading, phonological awareness, or oral language. In the results of this standardized assessment, such instruments as the Peabody Picture Vocabulary Test (PPVT) or Test of Oral Language Development (TOLD), the short-term outcomes in reading readiness, are in sharp contrast to the positive long-term demographic data, such as the link to higher graduation rates, reported in both the Abecedarian Projects (Campbell et al., 2002). With the release of the National Early Literacy Panel report (NELP, 2009), early childhood researchers have been reinforced in moving toward outcome-based interventions focusing on specific literacy skills. The NELP (2009) report reviews intervention programs, many highly scripted and controlled, which show statistically significant results in literacy learning. To further complicate matters, the Head Start Impact Study (OPRE, 2010) suggests that while short-term gains were positive when compared to a control group, long-term gains were mixed. However, these studies also must be weighed against other, non-content-driven values. In current early childhood curricula, we are concerned that the socio-emotional and physical development have taken a back seat to some forms of cognitive and language development (Miller & Almon, 2009). A four-year-old classroom looks like first grade, with children reciting the alphabet and working on phonemic (letter–sound) coordination worksheets (Miller & Almon, 2009). In HighScope and Creative Curriculum, this classroom culture shift is further exacerbated by the recent attempt to create literal links between their curriculum and either national or state standards (see, for example, http://www.teachingstrategies.com/page/alignments-creative-curriculum-preschool.cfm). One defense for connecting curriculum to standards is the need to *translate* young children's growth and development in a way that is accepted and understood based on early elementary school criteria. Our concern is that the movement toward creating/adapting early childhood curriculum with the main purpose of meeting universal standards as defined in elementary settings will limit the potential of the early childhood classroom. Early childhood education practitioners, policy makers, and researchers have begun to debate what curriculum in early childhood should look like, and how to weigh life-long effects versus short-term content-specific goals, such as vocabulary growth.

As HighScope and Creative Curriculum are currently written, teacher agency, control, and flexibility are core principles. Teachers are encouraged to create a daily routine with their students, but neither of the curriculum packages mandates specific content, lesson plans, or "scripts" for teacher–student interactions. As discussed earlier, the findings of NCER (2008), NELP (2009), and Office of Planning, Research and Evaluation (OPRE, 2010) reports, compared to the long-term outcomes found in previous research (Kirp, 2007; Barnett, 1996; Campbell et al., 2002), paint a complex picture of competing educational values and norms. The juxtaposition of these reports may foreshadow a bleak future for early childhood teacher agency. A balance between acceptance of flexible child-centered curriculum and the need to legitimize the curriculum through evidence of student attainment of knowledge, skills, and abilities based on standards or developmental milestones is problematic to achieve.

Conclusion

As more attention is placed on the early education community in terms of kindergarten proficiency and readiness, both HighScope and Creative Curriculum offer a helpful reminder that flexibility in curriculum provides greater opportunity for student success. Clearly tension exists between the need for verification of student attainment of short-term outcomes and the larger picture in which the milestones and benchmarks are reached at variable intervals. While we have questioned the popularity of a universal approach to teaching, our concern is the lack of urgency from policy makers, administrators, researchers, and teachers to shift curricular approaches to meet the needs of *all* children and families. Creative Curriculum and HighScope are not centered on discrete lesson plans; rather they encourage facilitation that offers room for interpretation. Curriculum and assessment are beginning to "cross over" between the early childhood and public school systems; one positive of these "packages" is the ability for teachers to interpret the curriculum and "use" environment as a facilitator for early learning. We are hopeful that teachers, researchers, and policy makers will appropriate the latitude similar to that offered in the Creative Curriculum and HighScope and use it to inform the K-12 world regarding the importance (and effectiveness) of individualized curriculum for respecting and supporting cultural, social, and intellectual knowledge, skills, and abilities. Our call is to build on the idea of child-centered curriculum with an emphasis on the importance of genuine integration of the child's context/culture. Teachers need support in order to accomplish these goals. Resources and knowledge to teach diverse populations, as well as respect for multiple forms of assessment (such as authentic portfolio, documentation, etc.), must be provided and accepted as legitimate forms of teaching and learning. We hope teachers, teacher educators, and policy makers will not accept the "push down" of standardized curriculum and assessment without also proposing a "push up" of child-centered open-ended curriculum into the primary grades.

References

Administration for Children and Families (ACF). (2003). *Federal and state funding for early care and education*. Retrieved January 15, 2011 from http://nccic.acf.hhs.gov/poptopics/ecarefunding.html.

——(2006). *Head Start FACES 2000: A whole-child perspective on program performance*. Retrieved January 15, 2011 from http://www.acf.hhs.gov/programs/opre/hs/faces/reports/executive_summary/exec_summary.pdf.

Apple, M. (1986). *Teachers and texts: A political economy of class and gender relations in schools*. New York and London: Routledge and Kegan Paul.

——(2000). *Official knowledge: Democratic education in a conservative age*. New York: Routledge.

——(2004). *Ideology and curriculum* (3rd ed.). New York: Routledge.

Apple, M. & Teitelbaum, K. (1986). Are teachers losing control of their skills and curriculum? *Journal of Curriculum Studies*, 18, 177–84.

Barnett, W.S. (1985). Benefit–cost analysis of the Perry Preschool Program and its policy implications. *Educational Evaluation and Policy Analysis*, 7, 333–42.

——(1996). *Lives in the balance: Age-27 benefit–cost analysis of High/Scope Perry Preschool Program*. Ypsilanti, MI: HighScope Educational Research Foundation.

Beatty, B. (1995). *Preschool education in America: The culture of young children from the colonial era to the present*. New Haven, CT: Yale University Press.

Belfield, C.R., Nores, M., Barnett, W.S., & Schweinhart, L.J. (2006). The High/Scope Perry Preschool Program: Cost–benefit analysis using data from the age-40 follow-up. *The Journal of Human Resources*, 41, 162–90.

Bialystok, E. (Ed.). (1991). *Language processing in bilingual children*. London: Cambridge University Press.

——(2001). *Bilingualism in development: Language, literacy and cognition*. New York: Cambridge University Press.

Bodrova, E. & Leong, D. (2007). *Tools of the Mind: The Vygotskian approach to early childhood education*. Upper Saddle River, NJ: Prentice Hall.

Campbell, F.A., Ramey, C.T., Pungello, E., Sparling, J., & Miller-Johnson, S. (2002). Early childhood education: Young adult outcomes from the Abecedarian Project. *Applied Developmental Science*, 6, 42–57.

Cannella, G. (1997). *Deconstructing early childhood education: Social justice and revolution*. New York: Peter Lang.

Copple, C. & Bredekamp, S. (2009). *Developmentally appropriate practice in early childhood programs*. Washington, DC: National Association for the Education of Young Children.

Crawford, J. (1999). *Bilingual education: History, politics, theory and practice* (4th ed.). Los Angeles: Bilingual Educational Services, Inc.

Cummins, J. (2001). *Language, power, and pedagogy: Bilingual children in the crossfire*. Clevedon, UK: Multilingual Matters.

De Houwer, A. (2009). *Bilingual first language acquisition*. Buffalo, NY: Multilingual Matters.

Dewey, J. (1902/1990). *The child and the curriculum*. Chicago, IL: University of Chicago Press.

Dodge, D., Colker, L., & Heroman, C. (2002). *Creative curriculum for preschool* (5th ed.). Florence, KY: Thomson Delmar Learning.

——(2004). *The Creative curriculum for preschool* (Spanish Ed.). El Currículo Creativo para educación preescolar. Florence, KY: Thomson Delmar Learning.

Early, D., Barbarin, O., Bryant, D., Burchinal, M., Chang, F., Clifford, R., et al. (2005). *Pre-kindergarten in eleven states: NCEDL's multi-state study of pre-kindergarten & study of state-wide early education programs (SWEEP)*. Preliminary descriptive report. Retrieved June 2, 2005 from http://www.fpg.unc.edu/~ncedl/pages/products.cfm#sweep_ms.

Epstein, A.S. (2007). *Essentials of active learning in preschool: Getting to know the High/Scope Curriculum*. Ypsilanti, MI: HighScope Educational Research Foundation.

Erikson, E.H. (1959). *Identity and the life cycle*. New York: International Universities Press.

Erikson, K. (1977). *Everything in its path*. New York: Simon and Schuster.

Fairclough, N. (1995). *Critical discourse analysis*. London: Longman.

Fendler, L. (2001). Educating flexible souls: The construction of subjectivity through developmentality and interaction. In K. Hultvquist & G. Dahlberg (Eds.), *Governing the child in the new millennium* (pp. 119–42). New York: RoutledgeFalmer.

Hart, B. & Risley, T.R. (1995). *Meaningful differences in the everyday experience of young American children*. Baltimore, MD: Paul H. Brookes.

Head Start Bureau. (2001). *Head Start program performance standards and other regulations (Standards)*. Alexandria, VA: Administration on Children, Youth and Families.

HighScope. (2007). *Preschool curriculum*. Retrieved June 2, 2007 from http://www.highscope.org/Content.asp?ContentId=63.

Kirp, D. (2007). *The sandbox investment: The preschool movement and kids-first politics*. Cambridge, MA: Harvard University Press.

Kruse, T. (2006). *Building a High/Scope program: Multicultural programs*. Ypsilanti, MI: HighScope Press.

MacNaughton, G. (2003). *Shaping early childhood: Learners, curriculum and contexts*. Maidenhead, UK: Open University Press.

Marchman, V.A., Martines-Sussmann, C., & Dale, P.S. (2004). The language-specific nature of grammatical development: Evidence from bilingual language learners. *Developmental Science*, 7, 212–24.

Maslow, A.H. (1943). A theory of human motivation. *Psychological Review*, 50, 370–96.

Michael-Luna, S. & Heimer, L. (2009). *Early childhood English language learners: Unpacking the dominant discourse of commonly used UPK Curriculum*. Paper presented at annual meeting of the American Educational Research Association, San Diego, CA, April.

Miller, E. & Almon, J. (2009). *Crisis in the kindergarten: Why children need to play in school*. College Park, MD: Alliance for Childhood.

Mokros, J. & Russell, S.J. (1995). *Investigations in number, data, and space*. Palo Alto, CA: Dale Seymour Publications.

NCEDL. (2005). NCEDL pre-kindergarten study. *Early Developments*, 9(1). The University of North Carolina at Chapel Hill: FPG Child Development Institute.

National Center of Education Research (NCER): Preschool Curriculum Evaluation Research Consortium. (2008). *Effects of preschool curriculum programs on school readiness (NCER 2008–9)*. Washington, DC: National Center for Education Research, Institute of Education Sciences, U.S. Department of Education. Washington, DC: U.S. Government Printing Office.

National Early Literacy Panel (NELP). (2009). *Developing early literacy: A scientific synthesis of early literacy development and implications for intervention*. Washington, DC: National Institute of Literacy.

National Institute of Child Health and Human Development. (2000). *Teaching children to read: An evidence-based assessment of the scientific research literature on reading and its implications for reading instruction* (NIH Publication No. 00–4769). Report of the National Reading Panel. Washington, DC: U.S. Government Printing Office.

Pearson, B.Z., Fernandez, S., & Oller, D.K. (1993). Lexical development in bilingual infants and toddlers: Comparison to monolingual norms. *Language Learning*, 43, 93–120.

Piaget, J.P. (1952). *The origins of intelligence in children*. New York: International Universities Press.

Office of Planning, Research and Evaluation of the U.S. Department of Health and Human Services (OPRE). (2010). *Head Start impact study and follow up: 2000–2011*. Retrieved January 1, 2011 from http://www.acf.hhs.gov/programs/opre/hs/impact_study/.

Schickedanz, J. & Dickinson, D.K. (2005). *Opening the World of Learning: A comprehensive literacy program*. Parsippany, NJ: Pearson Early Learning.

Sparling, J., Ramey, C.T., & Ramey, S.L. (2007). The Abecedarian experience. In M. E. Young (Ed.), *Early child development—From measurement to action. A priority for growth and equity* (pp. 81–99). Washington, DC: The World Bank. http://www.worldbank.org/children.

US Census. (2000). Language use and English-speaking ability: 2000. United States Census Bureau. Retrieved on January 23, 2007 from http://www.census.gov/prod/2003pubs/c2kbr-29.pdf.

Zigler, E.F., Singer, D.G., & Bishop-Josef, S.J. (2004). *Children's play: The roots of reading*. Washington, DC: Zero to Three Press.

11

A SITUATED FRAMEWORK

The Reggio Experience

Andrew J. Stremmel

Introduction

Reggio Emilia is a city in northern Italy that has become noted for its development of an early educational system known as the Reggio experience. The principles and methods of the Reggio experience have been embraced by early childhood educators the world over. Teachers, university professors, and eminent scholars from many countries have visited Reggio Emilia, only to be impressed with the possibilities and potentials that the Reggio Emilia philosophy offers. This experience is epitomized by key components that are now viewed by most early childhood educators as critical to highly effective, high quality early childhood education. These include the image of the child as a competent learner; the environment as a challenging and joyous place for learning; the view of the teacher as a co-learner and researcher; the role of parents as partners; the importance of project work (*progettazione*) as a catalyst for exploration and investigation; and documentation of learning as an effort to make learning visible among children, teachers, parents, and all who contribute to the educational system. Each of these components will be discussed briefly, followed by a critique of the approach. First, I discuss the origins of the Reggio Emilia experience and its epistemological and philosophical underpinnings.

Origins of the Reggio Emilia Experience

The northern Italian region of Emilia Romagna has had a long history and tradition of political activism and cooperative work in all areas of economy and organization. The roots of what has become known as the Reggio Emilia experience or approach are deeply embedded in the city's historical and political struggles against social injustice and its alliance with socialist and communist ideals (Edwards et al., 1998).

The end of Fascism and the Second World War brought about a new society guided by a desire to rebuild, materially, socially, and morally, a new way of life (Barazzoni, 2000). The inspiration for the development of the Reggio schools came from parents, particularly women, who wanted to build an exemplary system of early education. This educational system featured schools that reflected the beliefs and values of the community and promoted in children skills of critical thinking and collaboration essential to reconstructing a democratic society. Loris Malaguzzi, an educator at the time, was so impressed by a group of parents wanting to build new and better schools for their children that he became their philosophical leader and spokesman and helped open the city's first municipal preschool in 1963. Today there are more than three dozen preschools and infant–toddler centers serving roughly half the city's young children (New, 2007). The Diana school of Reggio Emilia has been recognized by *Newsweek* magazine as the best early childhood program in the world (*Newsweek*, 1991), and four versions of The Hundred Languages of Children exhibition, incorporating examples of children's learning, have traveled the world.

As will be discussed in the pages that follow, the pedagogical and cultural phenomenon known as the Reggio Emilia experience is not a method or prescribed curriculum to be copied. It is a socially and culturally embedded philosophical approach, a response to a strong desire for a new vision of democratic education driven by a fundamental core of Italian values which include the idea that education is a shared process of knowledge construction and a right of each child as a citizen.

Ideological and Theoretical Underpinnings

An examination of many of the principles underlying the Reggio experience will reveal the influence and inspiration of progressive educators and developmental theorists who have informed much of what American educators and practitioners know and believe about children and how they learn and develop. In fact, many of the ideas that have informed and continue to shape the thinking of educators in Reggio Emilia originated in the United States, and are now returning to their point of origin (Gandini, 2002). The work of John Dewey, David Hawkins, Jerome Bruner, Howard Gardner, and Urie Bronfenbrenner, as well as European theorists Jean Piaget and Lev Vygotsky, has influenced the practice and thinking of Reggio educators. Anyone who has read Vivian Paley, Bill Ayers, Maxine Greene, Nel Noddings, or Eliot Eisner will see remarkable similarities in thinking about children as active and competent learners, teaching as an intellectual and ethical endeavor, and schools as places for democratic conversation, critical thinking, and caring relationships.

The practices and principles of the Reggio Emilia approach resonate with the premises and promises of progressive education, including the ideas that children are protagonists in the their own development and that schools prepare children for life in a democratic society. They also provide clear challenges to the Piagetian interpretation of the child as a lone scientist who constructs knowledge of the world individually while progressing through a series of developmental stages. Notwithstanding, Piaget's theory of constructivism is important to the Reggio philosophy. Piaget was one of the first theorists to take seriously children's thinking and experience. But it was Vygotsky's assumptions about socially and culturally constructed knowledge that have found favor in an approach that views education as a system of relationships, in which children and adults collaborate and negotiate meaning through their experiences (Edwards, 1998). While Piaget has inspired Reggio educators to pay close and respectful attention to what children do, say, and think, Vygotsky has inspired educators to create environments that promote interactions, dialogue, reflection, collaborative inquiry, and negotiated learning.

Social constructivism underpins all practice in Reggio classrooms. Social constructivism is the epistemological and philosophical notion that mental activity is constructed from negotiated relationships between individuals and the social-cultural context (Rogoff, 1990). Loris Malaguzzi was inspired by Vygotsky's (1978) notion that learning leads development and that learning occurs in social contexts, in particular interactions through which children engage in problem solving and conduct open-ended investigations under the sensitive guidance of adults and in collaboration with more capable peers. In these contexts, children and adults co-construct knowledge and understanding. The principle that education happens in relationships and that educational settings should be places for dialogue, relation, and partnerships is the fundamental premise for Malaguzzi's philosophy and pedagogy (Edwards, 1998; Rinaldi, 2006).

Although the ideological roots of the Reggio Emilia approach are fundamentally child centered, progressive, and social constructivist, the approach to curriculum and pedagogical orientation also is "emancipatory." That is, children are seen from a "social constructionist" perspective as powerful agents who can challenge and transform ideas (and indeed society) through discourse with adults and other children (Dahlberg & Moss, 2006). Moreover, Reggio teachers constantly reflect on and question the content and methodology of their practice as they strive to create just and democratic learning environments for children and families.

Key Components of the Reggio Emilia Experience

The Image of the Child

In Reggio Emilia, the starting point for all practice is the child, who is seen as a strong and competent individual having rights and capable from the moment of birth of forming relationships and making meaning (Malaguzzi, 1998; Rinaldi, 1998). The idea of the child as a competent social being is based on the social constructivist perspective that learning occurs in a social context. Children are viewed as competent in the sense that they are open to the world, able to understand, know and learn, and ready to learn from the first moment of life. They are competent in constructing an identity and their own theories. Children are strongly motivated because they must "know" in order to live and to make sense of their world. Children from all socioeconomic and educational backgrounds attend the programs, and children with disabilities are given first priority for enrollment and fully mainstreamed in the schools, following Italian law (Gandini, 2002). This optimistic way of looking at children underscores the entire Reggio Emilia philosophy and approach to educating young children. For a more comprehensive examination of the image of the child as a historical and cultural construction, I refer the reader to Stremmel (2002) and Hill, Stremmel, and Fu (2005).

The Environment as Third Teacher

In Reggio, educators believe that children have the right to be educated in thoughtfully designed spaces that support the development of their many languages. Careful consideration is given to the design and organization of children's space because the environment is viewed as another teacher having the power to enhance children's sense of wonder and capacity for learning (Ceppi & Zini, 1998; Gandini, 2002). The environment, both indoors and out, offers children opportunities to express what they know, wonder, feel, and imagine as they encounter and make sense of a wide variety of materials, activities, and experiences.

Schools are designed to reflect the structure of the community. In Italy piazzas are gathering places in the community. In the schools they serve as comfortable meeting places for children, parents, and teachers. The walls hold the history of the life within the school in the form of documentation that chronicles children's daily experiences and their meanings.

The classroom environment supports the educational and cultural values of the school and community in other ways. Each classroom is thoughtfully laid out to provide a rich multi-sensory experience, and materials are arranged to invite interest, curiosity, and exploration. Dialogue is rich and vibrant, as children are free to make choices, collaborate with others, and listen to and construct new ideas. Children's own time and rhythms in the daily life of the school are respected, and they are given extended and unhurried time to explore and do their best work. They are not artificially rotated or asked to move to a different learning center or activity when they are still productively engaged and motivated by a piece of creative work. The classroom climate reflects the encouragement and acceptance of mistakes, risk-taking, innovation, and uniqueness; and, most importantly, the environment encourages social relationships, which are basic to the learning process and to the construction of meaning.

The Image of the Teacher

The Reggio Emilia approach challenges the traditional view of the teacher as a transmitter of knowledge and the view of the teaching–learning relationship as unidirectional. Reggio educators refer to the need for a constant dialogue between theory and practice, and their practice may be described as a holistic anthropological approach derived from careful and respectful observation of the child (Rinaldi, 2006). Teachers stay close to the experiences and encounters of children by constantly observing, reflecting, discussing, and debating what is occurring in the classroom.

The schools in Reggio Emilia may be viewed as laboratories for teachers (New, 2007). Teachers do not follow any particular theorist or curriculum; they are not dependent on prescribed teaching methods; and they do not claim to be experts. Instead, they see themselves as co-learners in the journey to construct meaning and understanding with the child. Teachers who embrace a Reggio approach need to possess an attitude of inquiry, a disposition of curiosity, and the desire to know and understand. Adopting this stance, theory and practice are placed in a relationship of reciprocity, and the roles of practitioner, theorist, and researcher are all inseparable and unifying elements of what it means to be "teacher." One does not teach without theorizing, and when one theorizes, it often is the implicit part of one's teaching. Because teachers continuously investigate, analyze, and interpret their practices, leading them to formulate new theories, new hypotheses, and new strategies about teaching and learning, they are researching (Gandini, 2002). Thus, what teachers do every day in the classroom is inquiry into the wonders and mysteries of the experiences of children, and through practical inquiry teachers seek to construct new understanding of their practice with children.

Documentation: Visible Listening

Paying close attention to children's work and making visible their learning are accomplished through careful and detailed documentation, which is founded on the pedagogy of listening (Rinaldi, 2006). Listening is a hallmark of the classroom environment in Reggio (see Edwards, 1998; Forman & Fyfe, 1998) because it legitimizes a view of children who can act and think for themselves and whose ideas are worth listening to, or documenting (Dahlberg et al., 1999; Rinaldi, 2006). Therefore, documentation, often referred to as "visible listening," is part of the larger process of giving the child a sense of place in the community, a legitimate voice to be made visible and respected (Rinaldi, 2006).

The documentation of children's learning makes visible traces of experience from which we infer learning. These traces include children's learning strategies and processes; their encounters with materials, peers, and adults; and their questions, thoughts, and ideas that emerge in the course of their work. Documentation typically includes samples of a child's work at several different stages of completion, and may be in the form of photographs showing children's dialogue and work in progress; video-taped observations and reflective comments; or transcriptions of children's discussions, comments, and explanations of their intentions in a given activity. What is important is that documentation doesn't occur after the fact or process, but during and throughout; it is an integral part of the procedures aimed at fostering learning. Furthermore, what teachers choose to observe and the means for observing it always represent a partial perspective that can only be beneficial to the extent to which multiple documents of the same event are produced and multiple observers are involved using different media, and multiple perspectives on the event are shared and considered.

This last point is critical to understanding the process of pedagogical documentation. Documentation includes making teachers' perspectives and interpretations explicit and contestable through debate, dialogue, and negotiation. This need for rigorous subjectivity (see Rinaldi, 2006) allows for the sharing of multiple perspectives and for individual interpretations to be subject to dispute and disagreement. Documentation is a social process in which individual meanings give way to socially constructed ones. Because the aim of documentation is to get close to the child's way of thinking and seeing reality, it is important to have the ideas and perspectives of others to see what might not have been seen otherwise (Gandini & Goldhaber, 2001). As a tool for democratic meaning making, it is an ethical and subjective means of assessing what children know and understand, in contrast to a process for judging, measuring, or critically examining children's work in relation to some standard of acceptability. Documentation enables teachers to assume the roles of co-learner and co-researcher with children in the classroom and, as such, to negotiate the curriculum.

The Negotiated Curriculum

What we typically refer to as curriculum in the United States is viewed differently in the Reggio experience. In Reggio schools, like those in the United States, children have opportunities to engage in free play and informal learning activities. However, because teaching is deeply influenced by the ideas and assumptions of Vygotsky, much of the curriculum centers on projects or investigations in which both children and adults question, hypothesize, explore, observe, discuss, and represent their ideas and understandings, and then revisit these ideas to clarify and refine their thinking (Forman & Fyfe, 1998). The idea is that the teacher's challenge is to pay careful attention to children, make decisions based on their ideas and choices, and reflect on the process of teaching and learning. As teachers examine and discuss their recorded observations together, they make predictions and hypotheses about children's interests, questions, and understandings. They think carefully about and discuss children's ideas to determine which ones should be pursued and how they might be supported in the context of flexible planning and curriculum.

This negotiated curriculum is neither child centered nor teacher directed; rather, it is child originated and inspired and teacher framed and supported (Forman & Fyfe, 1998, p. 240). This notion is consistent with Dewey's (1902) "both/and" view of the child and curriculum. According to Dewey, the child, and not the subject matter, determines both the quality and quantity of learning (p. 187). But we can neither leave the child to his/her own unguided spontaneity nor inspire direction upon him/her from without. The curriculum is seen as a continuous reconstruction moving reciprocally from child to subject matter. Vygotsky's influence is evident here, also. The key role of the teacher is to know the children well, to be present without being intrusive, to anticipate their thinking and the possible directions in which an idea or activity might lead before intervening, and to negotiate understanding through dialogue. The teacher recognizes and suggests aims for children's activities, but the aims emanate from the activity itself and not from the teacher's belief about where the activity should take the child. This is in contrast to the kind of teaching, often seen in the United States, in which the teacher seldom intervenes in children's activities, but leaves it to them to discover and explore unassisted.

In Reggio, educators prefer the word *progettazione*, as opposed to "project," to describe the in-depth and long-term investigations that occur in the schools. *Progettazione* is a term that does not translate well into English, though it literally means "to project ahead." Therefore it appears similar to van Manen's (1991) notion of anticipatory reflection, in which a plan of action is flexibly based on teachers' anticipation of the experiences they and children will have as a result of their decisions. Investigations or projects are flexible, dynamic, and fluid, involving a continual negotiation between children and adults regarding decisions and choices of what to do and where to go next. Projects have a beginning, but seldom is there a definite path to where they are going. They may begin from a chance event, a nagging question, a problem posed by a single child, or even a provocation by the teacher, who has closely observed children's questions and interests. Projects are pursued over an extensive period of time to allow children to test their hypotheses, reflect on and revisit them, and generate new ideas and assumptions, as learning proceeds.

Parents as Partners

In the Reggio experience, parents have the right to be involved in all aspects of the school experience, and they are supported as powerful agents in their children's development (Gandini, 2002). The role of parents is not limited to one of sharing knowledge about their children, or of participating minimally in the classroom when asked. Reggio educators highly value parents' abilities to help them understand children's experiences, and parents are seen as welcome partners in the formation, implementation, and documentation of projects. Parents contribute actively to the pedagogical experience of their children, researching with teachers ways to enhance learning. *Partecipazione* (participation by parents and families) is one of the defining characteristics of the Reggio schools and denotes the sharing and co-responsibility of families in the organization and design of the schools and the activities that occur within them (Rinaldi, 2006). This sense of shared responsibility begins when children first enroll in the infant–toddler centers as teachers invite parents to remain in the center for as long as they think is necessary, which may be for a period of weeks or months (New, 1999). The goal is to ensure the formation of positive relationships for the child and reciprocal and collaborative relationships between parents and teachers. In this way, the child serves as a catalyst for parents and teachers to interact, which will lead to continued collaboration of adults and children toward the goal of designing positive learning experiences and nurturing environments (New, 1999).

Critical Analysis of the Reggio Experience

The Reggio experience is somewhat of a paradox. It is seen as a refreshing and distinct approach, yet it can be difficult to understand and implement. Much of what is written about it is positive, yet it has been met with both favor and resistance. What are the challenges of implementing the Reggio experience? And to what extent is it transferable?

Reggio Emilia is part of a region where civil society has existed for centuries, a unique place where local people have come together to pursue the common goal of creating a culture and community made by their own vision and focused on creating connections and building relationships (Gardner, 2008; New, 2007). The development of the Reggio Emilia approach is rooted in a particular time and place, and is influenced by principles that place high value on the rights and abilities of children. Without the hard work of committed members of the community, Reggio Emilia could never have achieved distinction in early childhood education. "They asked, in effect, what kinds of citizens do we want to produce?" (Gardner, 2008, p. 131). If we are to hope for anything comparable, we must ask the same question.

It has been argued that, in our society, we have surrendered to others the power to determine the kind of communities and schools we should want to create for ourselves (McKnight & Block, 2010). We have abdicated responsibility for community life and have entrusted the education of our children to corporations, agencies, and institutions that have diminished our role as citizens. We wait for others to regulate and define us in a society impatient for results. We confuse education with schooling and its obsession with increasing test scores and higher levels of achievement. Alternatively, in Reggio Emilia education is a shared experience in a democratic society of which schools are a part and whose citizens take responsibility for all children. School is a public space for ethical and political practice, a place for interaction and dialogue among its citizens living together in community. Together, citizens see themselves as creators and producers of their future. Those who wish to embrace the Reggio experience must choose to reclaim their citizenship and become reengaged with the larger purposes of education in a democracy.

This tension between consumerism and citizenship has contributed, I believe, to the question of whether the principles and ideals of Reggio Emilia can be transferred to other educational settings. The dominating discourse in American education is rooted in the belief that education's role is to transmit and perpetuate cultural knowledge and values, and then assess how well this has been achieved. It is a discourse embedded in ideologies that view teachers as technicians whose primary role is to deliver a product, a specified curriculum, to a passive, homogenized student. Nowhere is this tension about the purposes of education greater than as it pertains to the concept of assessment.

In the United States, standardized tests are viewed as the primary means of assessing important intellectual proficiencies. In Reggio Emilia, documentation is considered to be an instrument for reflective practice and democratic learning, not assessment in the way American educators view it (Dahlberg et al., 1999; Gandini & Goldhaber, 2001). However, documentation often is criticized as an "add-on" activity, as opposed to an integral part of what teachers do in the classroom. Students have been heard to ask, "How can I interact effectively with children if I am always documenting what they do?" In Reggio Emilia, teaching means getting close to the processes of learning through careful, systematic, and ongoing observation and reflection. This is not a view of teaching with which many are comfortable in our culture. The idea and practice of documentation feel strange to teachers, especially new and prospective teachers, who lack confidence in their abilities or who do not trust the capacity of children to learn without the use of methods that demand conformity and obedience, or the use of well-specified, linear lesson plans.

Another tension or paradox is associated with the idea of order or structure. American teacher educators who have tried to recast the Reggio Emilia approach in their settings often have discovered that their students view it as an unstructured "anything goes" approach. Typically, those who hold this view equate structure with discipline, order, and a narrow conception of teaching and learning. The need to feel in control of the classroom and the learning process is ingrained in student teachers, who understand from their own experiences that the fundamental law of school is to follow orders. Malaguzzi (1998) believed that structure is built into the choice of what to investigate, the preparation of the learning environment to support investigation, and the nature of the relationships children have among themselves and with adults. Teacher educators will be challenged to help their students understand that meaningful structure involves everything from the construction of the environment to the experiences of both children and adults in the classroom.

Resistance to the Reggio experience often stems from the feeling one gets when visiting Reggio, or reading about it as described and endorsed by American and Italian scholars and practitioners, that the approach is all positive, without flaws, or superior to others. "Can it be true?" they ask. I, myself, have wondered, "What are those teachers really saying to the children?," vowing not to return to Reggio Emilia until I can speak and better understand Italian.

Educators who return home from a trip to Reggio Emilia are highly enthused and inspired to make changes to their programs, and they attempt to do so for one or more of the following reasons: They want to look differently at curriculum, drawing more deeply on children's perspectives and curiosities about the world; they are amazed at the aesthetic quality of the schools and the beautiful art of children; or, they are astounded by the rich documentation of children's work. But often they become discouraged when their plans to implement the principles and practices they observed in Reggio Emilia are not immediately realized.

In my own experience, I have found that the extraordinary quality and beauty of the physical environment is what appears to first attract educators to the Reggio approach. I have observed more than a few programs return from Reggio only to duplicate the look and feel of a Reggio school, without the necessary and ongoing thought and dialogue required to make their school their own. The idea of the environment as third teacher is much more than how the school looks. It focuses our attention on the very kind of schools we should want for our own children.

Reggio teachers spend many hours in the schools reflecting on and debating their experiences with children. These teachers have adopted a particular way of thinking about education that is unfamiliar to most teachers outside of Reggio Emilia. The level of commitment demonstrated in Reggio teachers is not easy to imitate. It requires openness, dialogue, and a willingness to rethink our practices on a regular basis. It requires being able to trust and have confidence in one's choices and abilities, and to have faith in children's ability to learn.

Discussions about the traditions and history that have informed practice in one's current setting can be a starting place for change that focuses on what it means to teach, to learn, and to educate young children within a particular cultural and community context. Teachers who are serious about education must be willing to examine their beliefs and practices. Programs, also, must be willing to commit to the ongoing study, discussion, reflection, and reinterpretation of what it means to educate young children. Moreover, educators who are serious about implementing a Reggio-inspired approach must be willing to question and examine the principles and ideals of the Reggio approach within the context of their own experience, culture, and community values. It has taken over 15 years of continual study, dialogue, reflection, and rethinking for me to have reached the views I hold today. But these views have been and continue to be challenged by others as I strive more deeply to make sense of what it means to be Reggio inspired.

Although much of what we have come to know and believe about the Reggio experience is positive, it should be pointed out that there is little systematic research on Reggio practices and child-related outcomes. Child outcomes research, in particular, is not intrinsic to the Reggio experience (Edwards, 2002). Reggio and Reggio-inspired educators question the validity and usefulness of outcome research (Dahlberg et al., 1999; Rinaldi, 2006), preferring instead to view schools and classrooms as places for documenting learning and development. Nevertheless, there is a need for empirical research, particularly research utilizing innovative and mixed-methods designs, to examine ways of effectively measuring lasting child-related outcomes and program quality in Reggio schools (e.g. see Giudici et al., 2001).

Final Thoughts: What Does the Reggio Experience Offer to American Educators?

The discourse of the competent, intellectual child is associated historically with the early childhood pioneers of progressive education, and there are many progressive American educators, starting with John Dewey, who believe that education in its truest form is an invitation to explore, to honestly question, and to charge directly at topics of real meaning (e.g. Ayers, 2001; Dewey, 1938). What has drawn so many educators, including myself, to the Reggio experience is this idea of teaching as an inquiry process. If we believe, as Dewey did, that the goal of education is to prepare children for life in a democratic society, then we need to create situations and encounters that arouse curiosity and invite children to ask their own probing questions, and create classrooms where the focus is on what children are doing rather than how well they are doing it.

Although the Reggio Emilia approach should not be viewed as a blueprint for best practice, it is rightly viewed as a philosophical way of thinking about children and early childhood education that may lead to "promising practices." The Reggio experience is a powerful alternative voice emphasizing critical and reflective thought and attitude toward what educators do and why they do it. Therefore, it is best to talk about what it means to be Reggio inspired, as opposed to being a Reggio school or implementing the Reggio approach (Cadwell, 1997; Sisson, 2009; Rinaldi, 2006).

On a practical level, to be Reggio inspired means creating schools where children and adults can develop meaningful relationships as they work together to construct new knowledge and understandings; where children are seen as cognitively and socially capable, not labeled by their deficits; where teachers can develop a professional life with one another, dialoguing and debating in order to maximize learning in the classroom; where teachers and children have some control over the content and conduct of their work; and where parents can be real partners, exercise meaningful choice in their child's education, and be meaningfully involved.

Further, to be inspired by Reggio is about educating young children in *our* communities. In South Dakota, where I live, I encourage early educational programs that want to be informed by the Reggio experience to be "South Dakota inspired." This means to see South Dakota as a place of encounter and dialogue about the educational realities of our early childhood educational system, and to be transformed in the way we think and talk about children in our communities. To be inspired by Reggio as a philosophical approach, then, is to create opportunities to question the role of the school in the particular communities they reside in, and to carefully and regularly consider what it means to teach, to learn, and to be educated. It is an opportunity for understanding others, self, and the why of what we do, not an attempt to offer recipes (Rinaldi, personal communication, May 30, 2000).

Finally, the Reggio experience is a constant reminder that we must be committed to teaching as a serious and moral endeavor which requires us to challenge our realities and transform ourselves daily. It is a constant reminder that there are many possibilities in how we educate children, many choices to make based on our answers to critical questions such as "What is our image of the child?" and "What does it mean to be a teacher?" Our challenge is not how to copy Reggio; nor is it to find one best practice to adopt. Our challenge is to explore how best to meet the educational needs of children and families in our communities based on meaningful, ongoing, and committed dialogue on what it means to teach and to learn from young children in those communities.

References

Ayers, W. (2001). *To teach: The journey of a teacher* (2nd ed.). New York: Teachers College Press.

Barazzoni, R. (2000). *Brick by brick: The history of the "XXV April" people's nursery school of Villa Cella*. Reggio Emilia, Italy: Reggio Children.

Cadwell, L.B. (1997). *Bringing Reggio Emilia home: An innovative approach to early childhood education*. New York: Teachers College Press.

Ceppi, G. & Zini, M. (Eds.). (1998). *Children, spaces, relations: Metaproject for an environment for young children*. Reggio Emilia, Italy: Reggio Children.

Dahlberg, G. & Moss, P. (2006). Introduction: Our Reggio Emilia. In C. Rinaldi (Ed.), *In dialogue with Reggio Emilia: Listening, researching, and learning* (pp. 1–22). New York: Routledge.

Dahlberg, G., Moss, P., & Pence, A. (1999). *Beyond quality in early childhood education: Postmodern perspectives*. London: Routledge.

Dewey, J. (1902). *The child and the curriculum*. Chicago, IL: University of Chicago Press.

——(1938). *Experience and education*. New York: Scribner.

Edwards, C. (1998). Partner, nurturer, and guide: The role of the teacher. In C. Edwards, L. Gandini, & G. Forman (Eds.), *The hundred languages of children: The Reggio Emilia approach—advanced reflections* (2nd ed.) (pp. 179–98). Greenwich, CT: Ablex.

——(2002). Three approaches from Europe: Waldorf, Montessori, and Reggio Emilia. *Early Childhood Research & Practice*, 4, 1–13.

Edwards, C., Gandini, L., & Forman, G. (Eds.) (1998). *The hundred languages of children: The Reggio Emilia approach—advanced reflections* (2nd ed.). Greenwich, CT: Ablex.

Forman, G. & Fyfe, B. (1998). Negotiated learning through design, documentation, and discourse. In C. Edwards, L. Gandini, & G. Forman (Eds.) *The hundred languages of children: The Reggio Emilia approach—advanced reflections* (pp. 239–60). Greenwich, CT: Ablex.

Fu, V., Stremmel, A., & Hill, L. (Eds.). (2002). *Teaching and learning: Collaborative exploration of the Reggio Emilia approach*. Upper Saddle River, NJ: Merrill/Prentice Hall.

Gandini, L. (2002). The story and foundations of the Reggio Emilia approach. In V. Fu, A. Stremmel, & L. Hill (Eds.), *Teaching and learning: Collaborative exploration of the Reggio Emilia Approach* (pp. 13–21). Upper Saddle River, NJ: Merrill/Prentice Hall.

Gandini, L. & Goldhaber, J. (2001). Two reflections about documentation. In L. Gandini & C. Edwards (Eds.), *Bambini: The Italian approach to infant/toddler care* (pp. 124–45). New York: Teachers College Press.

Gardner, H. (2008). *5 minds of the future*. Boston: Harvard Business Press.

Giudici, C., Rinaldi, C., & Krechevsky, M. (2001). *Making learning visible: Children as individual and group learners*. Cambridge, MA: Project Zero, Harvard Graduate School of Education and Reggio Children, Italy.

Hill, L., Stremmel, A., & Fu, V. (2005). *Teaching as inquiry: Rethinking curriculum in early childhood education*. New York: Allyn & Bacon.

McKnight, J. & Block, P. (2010). *The abundant community: Awakening the power of families and neighborhoods.* San Francisco: Berrett-Koehler Publishers.

Malaguzzi, L. (1998). History, ideas, and basic philosophy. In C. Edwards, L. Gandini, & G. Forman (Eds.), *The hundred languages of children: The Reggio Emilia approach—advanced reflections* (pp. 49–97). Greenwich, CT: Ablex.

New, R. (1999). What should children learn? Making choices and taking chances. *Early Childhood Research & Practice,* 1(2). Retrieved August 2008 from http://ecrp.uiuc.edu/v1n2/new.html.

——(2007). Reggio Emilia as a cultural activity theory in practice. *Theory into Practice,* 46(1), 5–13.

Newsweek (1991). The 10 best schools in the world, and what we can learn from them. *Newsweek,* December 2, 50–59.

Rinaldi, C. (1998). Projected curriculum constructed through documentation—progettazione: An interview with Lella Gandini. In C. Edwards, L. Gandini, & G. Forman (Eds.), *The hundred languages of children: The Reggio Emilia approach—advanced reflections* (pp. 113–26). Greenwhich, CT: Ablex.

——(2006). *In dialogue with Reggio Emilia: Listening, researching, and learning.* New York: Routledge.

Rogoff, B. (1990). *Apprenticeship in thinking.* New York: Oxford University Press.

Sisson, J.H. (2009). Making sense of competing constructs of teacher as professional. *Journal of Research in Childhood Education,* 23(3), 351–66.

Stremmel, A. (2002). The cultural construction of childhood: United States and Reggio perspectives. In V. Fu, A. Stremmel, & L. Hill (Eds.), *Teaching and learning: Collaborative exploration of the Reggio Emilia Approach* (pp. 37–49). Upper Saddle River, NJ: Merrill/Prentice Hall.

van Manen, M. (1991). *The tact of teaching: The meaning of pedagogical thoughtfulness.* Albany, NY: SUNY Press.

Vygotsky, L. (1978). *Mind in society.* Cambridge, MA: Harvard University Press.

12

TE WHĀRIKI

The Early Childhood Curriculum of Aotearoa New Zealand

Jenny R. Ritchie and Cary A. Buzzelli

Introduction

Since its publication in 1996, *Te Whāriki. He whāriki mātauranga mō ngā mokopuna o Aotearoa: Early childhood curriculum*, known simply as "*Te Whāriki*," has made a tremendous contribution to the field of early childhood education both in its home country and abroad. In this chapter we present a brief history of the development of *Te Whāriki*, a discussion of its distinctive features, its contributions to the peoples of Aotearoa New Zealand and to the field of early childhood education. We end the chapter with a critique of the curriculum, but we frame it so as to offer points for consideration to those involved in curriculum development. The authors of this paper present a collaboration of "insider" and "outsider" perspectives. Jenny Ritchie is an early childhood teacher education academic from Aotearoa New Zealand, whose work has focused on supporting early childhood teachers in understanding the expectations contained within *Te Whāriki*, in relation to the indigenous language and culture. She writes from the "insider's" perspective. Cary Buzzelli is a teacher educator whose research has examined the moral dimensions of teaching. He is writing from the "outsider's" perspective.

Background to *Te Whāriki*

The writing collaboration that led to the distinctiveness of *Te Whāriki* (Ministry of Education, 1996) is hugely significant in that it reflects the relationship between the indigenous people of New Zealand, the Māori, and those who came to share their country as a result of the 1840 Tiriti o Waitangi (Treaty of Waitangi). In signing this treaty, Māori allowed for governance by Great Britain, although they could not at that time have imagined the collateral damage that would ensue from this colonization process.

The uniqueness of *Te Whāriki* comes both from the unique national context and, in particular, from the respect for indigeneity evident in its conceptualization and eventual format. When in 1991 Helen May and Margaret Carr of the University of Waikato began work on a project to develop this first national early childhood curriculum guideline, they realized that their process must adhere to the obligations contained within Te Tiriti o Waitangi, and in particular the Article Two commitment to Māori that their tino rangatiranga, or self-determination, would be protected (May, 2001). Consequently, a partnership model was employed in the curriculum development process, through Carr and May working closely with Tilly and Tamati Reedy, who had been delegated by the National Te Kōhanga Reo Trust[1] to work on their behalf, thus bringing a Māori conceptual framework to the design and content of the document from the outset. The document's name, *"Te Whāriki,"* refers to the woven flax mats traditionally used as floor coverings, and uses the metaphor of the curriculum offering philosophical principles and guiding strands, which are intended to be woven together in distinctively particular ways by each particular early childhood setting.

Aotearoa New Zealand is geographically remote, and this sense of isolation contributes to a national characteristic of independence and autonomy as an island nation of just over four million people. The early childhood curriculum development project was part of the New Zealand Ministry of Education's curriculum reforms, which had been initiated by the Labour government of the late 1980s and were continued after the National Party became the government in 1990. The fact that the national early childhood curriculum was conceived by a Labour government but subsequently delivered as *Te Whāriki* by a National government demonstrates a cross-party consistency of response to the Māori-instigated renaissance of their language and culture in the face of the "relentless psychic, economic and social displacement of Māori under European colonisation" (Cederman, 2008, p. 125). The Māori philosophical foundation of *Te Whāriki* was not foisted on an unsuspecting early childhood education community, but instead reflected widespread commitments that various early childhood organizations had already made during the late 1980s, in the lead-up to and following on from the bicentenary of the signing of Te Tiriti o Waitangi in 1990 (Cubey, 1992; Ritchie, 2002).

The vision for the development process of this first curriculum document for Aotearoa New Zealand was responsive to the diversity and complexities of the early childhood sector (May, 2001). May and Carr established a range of working parties of early childhood educators to represent and contribute the perspectives of each of these groups: Māori; Pacific Islands early childhood services; infants and toddlers; young children; children with special needs; and home-based care and education services. Consultation within the sector was a necessarily strong feature of the process if there was to be both widespread acceptance within the early childhood education community as well as government endorsement.

In addition to the distinctive features of the indigenous philosophical grounding and content, Carr and May determined that a broadly sociocultural theoretical stance should be adopted, moving beyond a solely developmentalist approach (Ministry of Education, 1993b; Nuttall, 2003a). Educational thinking in the late 1980s had been provoked by theorists challenging educators to consider the complexities of children's social and cultural identity, to reflect upon the nature of the life experiences that shaped it, and on the power relations backgrounding children's sociocultural positioning (see, for example, Rosaldo, 1989). *Te Whāriki* has been described as a process-orientated curriculum document, which "defines learning outcomes in terms of processes, summarized as dispositions and working theories" (Cullen, 2008, p. 8). This focus on process rather than predetermined measurable outcomes is consistent with its learner-centered, holistic, integrated, and sociocultural philosophy.

Components of *Te Whāriki*

Te Whāriki, then, is a curriculum document that situates children within their sociocultural contexts, their families, and their communities. Children are respected as active agents in their own learning process, viewed as competent and confident learners and communicators. *Te Whāriki* reflects a holistic understanding of children's growth, development, and learning through the integral engagement of body, mind, and spirit. There are four foundational "principles," and five key "strands," outlined in Part A of the curriculum document. A distinct section (Part B), written in the Māori language, explains these from a Māori conceptual framework. Part C illuminates the strands. Threaded throughout the strands are specific goals and learning outcomes, accompanied by "questions for reflection" which encourage educators to adopt a disposition of critique and analysis (Ritchie, 2005). A final section (Part D), outlines links with the then-national curriculum framework for the primary and secondary school sector (Ministry of Education, 1993a), which has recently been revised (Ministry of Education, 2007).

The four key principles of *Te Whāriki* are to be reflected in all early childhood care and education pedagogical practice in Aotearoa New Zealand. They are as follows: Empowerment—Whakamana; Holistic Development—Kotahitanga; Family and Community—Whānau Tangata; and Relationships—Ngā Hononga. In addition to these principles, the five strands provide another key curriculum layer and more specifics of early childhood practice: Well-being—Mana Atua; Belonging—Mana Whenua; Contribution—Mana Tangata; Communication—Mana Reo; and Exploration—Mana Aotūroa. Each of these strands has a set of goals and examples of learning outcomes for infants, toddlers, and young children. Each goal is followed by a list of learning outcomes, which are the anticipated knowledge, skills, and attitudes that will be achieved through the responsive pedagogy of the educators. Successful implementation of a goal can be seen in the desired outcomes listed for that goal.

The philosophical rather than technicist nature of the document can be seen in the explanation of the principle of Holistic Development—Kotahitanga, which acknowledges that "Cognitive, social, cultural, physical, emotional, and spiritual dimensions of human development are integrally interwoven" (Ministry of Education, 1996, p. 41). Learning and development are to be facilitated through the provision of

> opportunities for open-ended exploration and play; consistent, warm relationships that connect everything together; recognition of the spiritual dimension of children's lives in culturally, socially, and individually appropriate ways; [and] of the significance and contribution of previous generations to the child's concept of self.
>
> *(Ministry of Education, 1996, p. 41)*

This holistic perspective is well illustrated again within the strand of "Well-being," which requires that "The health and well-being of the child are protected and nurtured." Three goals are listed. "Children [are to] experience an environment where: their health is promoted; their emotional well-being is nurtured; [and] they are kept safe from harm" (Ministry of Education, 1996, p. 45). Particular Tiriti o Waitangi obligations are stipulated here also, as they are throughout the document:

> Adults working with children should have a knowledge of Māori definitions of health and wellbeing and an understanding of what these concepts mean in practice. Adults should acknowledge spiritual dimensions and have a concern for how the past, present, and future influence children's self esteem and are of prime importance to Māori and Tagata Pasefika families.
>
> *(Ministry of Education, 1996, p. 45)*

Te Whāriki's Contributions to Early Childhood Education

As can be seen in the preceding section, the development and implementation of *Te Whāriki* led to a number of significant and innovative contributions to early childhood education. In this section we discuss three aspects of *Te Whāriki* that have made and will continue to make a significant contribution to curriculum development and teaching practices. Our discussion of each will include comparisons to other teaching contexts. The three contributions are: (1) an affirmation of indigeneity; (2) a recognition of spirituality as an important aspect of well-being to be nurtured in children; and (3) a non-descriptive orientation to curriculum and teaching which values teacher reflexivity, and teacher knowledge and practical wisdom.

Affirmation of Indigeneity

From the beginning, the developers of *Te Whāriki* had a strong commitment to Māori as the indigenous people of Aotearoa New Zealand. This commitment is reflected in the recognition of Māori tino rangatiranga (self-determination) and the inclusion of Reo Māori (the Māori language) and taonga (valued aspects such as the Māori worldview and culture) in *Te Whāriki*. This commitment also is due to the nature of Aotearoa New Zealand as a bicultural rather than multicultural nation, albeit with an increasingly diverse population. An example of this commitment is the recognition of spirituality for inclusion in the curriculum as discussed here on pp. 150–52.

In the United States, through revisions of the position statement on Developmentally Appropriate Practice (DAP) (Copple & Bredekamp, 2009), its authors have striven to be more committed and sensitive to issues of diversity and culture. This is indeed laudable; however, some may continue to call for DAP to be yet more specific in addressing these issues even after the most recent revision. Yet it is important to note the significant differences between these two contexts. The Māori are the indigenous people of Aotearoa New Zealand and *Te Whāriki* was produced as a document for a country which has come some way to redressing its colonialist legacy by honoring the language and culture of its indigenous people. The United States presents a very different context. Many metaphors (the melting pot and the salad bowl are two of the most common) have been used to represent the diversity of peoples living the United States, and despite a similar history of colonization, the many and diverse indigenous peoples are not often accorded specific recognition within state or federal educational documents. Each metaphor that has appeared is an attempt to present an understanding of how people from many cultures and languages live alongside each other. The notion of what it means to be an American is continually evolving, but what remains is the fundamental idea of somehow many becoming one. Put differently, each metaphor tries to make sense of "E Pluribus Unum." The idea, then, of one coming from many precludes a bicultural country with a bicultural curriculum document reifying indigenous cultures alongside many others. While done in very broad strokes, this brief explanation seeks to outline some of the challenges in translating or transporting inspiration from *Te Whāriki* into the American context.

Inclusion of Spirituality

The inclusion of spirituality in *Te Whāriki* as a component of well-being sets forth for the first time in any such a document, be it a national curriculum or position statement, a vision of children which explicitly claims spirituality as a dimension that is to be recognized and nurtured. *Te Whāriki* states that "Learning and development will be integrated through … recognition of the spiritual dimension of children's lives in culturally, socially, and individually appropriate ways" (Ministry of Education, 1996, p. 41). It also suggests that "Adults should acknowledge spiritual dimensions and have a concern for how the past, present, and future influence children's self-esteem and are of prime importance to Māori" (p. 46).

In addition, the inclusion of spirituality acknowledges the influence of the Māori worldview on *Te Whāriki* and, with it, the recognition of the centrality of the spiritual in the Māori culture (Bone, 2007; Reddy, 2003). Reddy makes the point that the spiritual dimension of life is a central element of the Māori worldview, and thus to exclude it would be as radical as the exclusion of other dimensions of what the Māori consider as taonga, or treasures, such as their language, te reo.

Many early childhood educators, especially some in the United States, may find it difficult to grasp the important role spirituality has in *Te Whāriki*. However, whether influenced by *Te Whāriki* or not, recognition of spirituality and spiritual development in children now appears in national curricula for primary education in both England and Australia. In England the new primary curriculum states the following under the guideline "Learning Across the Curriculum":

> All National Curriculum subjects provide opportunities to promote pupils' spiritual, moral, social and cultural development. ... Pupils' spiritual development involves the growth of their sense of self, their unique potential, their understanding of their strengths and weaknesses, and their will to achieve. As their curiosity about themselves and their place in the world increases, they try to answer for themselves some of life's fundamental questions. They develop the knowledge, skills, understanding, qualities and attitudes they need to foster their own inner lives and non-material wellbeing.
>
> *(Qualifications and Curriculum Authority, 2010, n.p.)*

Similarly, in Australia the following appears in the Melbourne Declaration of Educational Goals for Young Australians:

> The curriculum will enable students to develop knowledge in the disciplines of English, mathematics, science, languages, humanities and the arts; to understand the spiritual, moral and aesthetic dimensions of life; and open up new ways of thinking.
>
> *(Ministerial Council on Education, Employment, Training and Youth Affairs, 2008, p. 13)*

That a spiritual dimension to children's development is included in curriculum documents from Aotearoa New Zealand, England, and Australia makes the absence of any such recognition in the most recent revision of Developmentally Appropriate Practice (Copple & Bredekamp, 2009) all the more conspicuous given its focus on a holistic orientation to children's development. Yet, some early childhood programs in the United States do include recognition of children's spiritual development. Numerous programs acknowledge children's spirituality through direct teaching of the faith communities' beliefs and practices. There also are programs, some based on the writing of well-known early childhood theorists and educators, that do not espouse a specific faith orientation, but do address spiritual issues. Both Maria Montessori and Rudolf Steiner wrote about the importance of the spiritual dimension in their work and both have inspired early childhood programs. It is important to note, though, that the extent to which spirituality is included in any particular program varies tremendously.

Non-prescriptive Curriculum and Teacher Reflexivity

Te Whāriki was designed as a non-prescriptive curriculum (Blaiklock, forthcoming; Nuttall, 2003b; Ritchie, 2003a), and as such there is a high expectation of teacher reflexivity. *Te Whāriki* co-writer Helen May explained that the philosophy of the curriculum "resisted telling staff what to do, by 'forcing' each programme to 'weave' its own curriculum pattern" (May, 2001, p. 246). "It was intended that each organization, service, centre and teacher 'weave' its own curriculum as appropriate to its particular needs, philosophy, community or cultural interests and most importantly, its children. There would be many possible woven 'patterns'" (May, 2006, p. 260).

May has acknowledged, however, that this "holistic and bicultural approach to curriculum of *Te Whāriki*, inclusive of children from birth, was a challenge to staff who were more familiar with the traditional focus on play areas and activities for children" (May, 2001, p. 248). The integrity of the consultation processes that were integral to the writing and promulgation of *Te Whāriki* had enabled early childhood educators within Aotearoa to embrace the new curriculum, albeit with caution on the part of some, particularly those who found its complexities daunting. The curriculum contains a series of "questions for reflection," woven throughout each goal, which demand a certain degree of reflective engagement. Educator confidence in the document was subsequently strengthened through a Ministry of Education-funded program of professional development contracts, which were carefully managed to optimize the support provided to the sector in the implementation of the new curriculum.

These two features make it possible for programs based on a variety of educational philosophies to each "weave its own curriculum pattern." The Educational Review Office (ERO) has issued reports examining both the quality of programs implementing various early childhood curricula and the extent to which the programs are consistent with the values of *Te Whāriki*. Recent investigations have been conducted for Montessori, Steiner, and Te Reo programs, as well as programs serving parents and whānau of Māori children, and the communities of Pacific peoples (ERO, 2007a, 2007b, 2007c). These reports provide evidence that a program's adherence to *Te Whāriki* does not present barriers to a program implementing a particular education philosophy. The reports also indicated areas for improvement in certain programs. Attention to those aspects of programs cited for improvement by the ERO reports would raise both the quality of the program and its adherence to its specific program philosophy. In this sense, *Te Whāriki* provides a flexible framework for curriculum development, implementation, and assessment.

In this section we have considered how *Te Whāriki's* non-prescriptiveness encourages teacher reflexivity. Yet, it also is important to examine the other side of non-prescriptiveness and teacher reflexivity, namely, does *Te Whāriki* guide and nurture the development of teacher reflexivity by influencing teacher education programs in Aotearoa New Zealand?

Based on the first author's extensive experience with early childhood teacher education degree accreditation panels in Aotearoa New Zealand, *Te Whāriki* does play a significant role in teacher preparation because such programs are focused on preparing teachers to deliver the curriculum. Granted, the implementation of *Te Whāriki* can be within the context of a program based on Montessori, or Steiner, or in a program for Pacific Islanders. Here we see the interplay of *Te Whāriki's* emphasis on non-descriptiveness and teacher reflexivity as well as its influence in teacher education.

In the United States, the National Council for Accreditation of Teacher Education (NCATE) accredits teacher education programs at both the baccalaureate and advanced degree levels for many colleges and universities. For a teacher education program to receive NCATE accreditation, it must provide evidence that its candidates demonstrate competence and meet specific content area standards. NCATE has adopted the standards for professional education for a number of specialty professional associations (SPAs). The National Association for the Education of Young Children (NAEYC) is one of the SPAs. The NAEYC position statement on professional preparation (NAEYC, 2009) lists DAP as one of the resources upon which its professional preparation standards are based. DAP clearly has a significant influence on the preparation of early childhood professionals, both through its influence on accreditation standards and as a document guiding pedagogical practices. Additionally, each state also has criteria for the accreditation of teacher education programs. The specific requirements and standards programs must meet to receive accreditation vary from state to state, as does the process used by each state to determine and assess candidates' proficiency in meeting its standards. The NCATE standards and those of the SPAs, including NAEYC, do allow for both the non-descriptiveness and teacher reflexivity described above. Pressure for more prescribed teaching approaches and content may come from state and local sources such as school boards.

Implementation Issues and Quality

A recent report to the New Zealand Ministry of Education found that parents rated supporting children's social development and emotional development as the two most important reasons for using early childhood services (Robertson et al., 2007). Support of children's language and cultural identity were the next two highest rated reasons. However, for non-European parents, meeting the cultural needs of the child and family were very important reasons. When asked to rate the importance of factors influencing their decision on whether or not to use early childhood services, parents rated program quality as the most important factor (p. 52). Given that these results point to the importance of program quality in parents' decision making concerning the use of early childhood services, we can now ask: What influence does the implementation of *Te Whāriki* have on program quality?

In 2007, the New Zealand Council for Educational Research published its first national survey of early childhood services (Mitchell & Brooking, 2007). The survey gathered data from teachers, directors, and parents on a number of indices related to service, program quality, and level of satisfaction. The results provide some answers to this question. Overall results show that parents had a high degree of satisfaction with the quality of early childhood services. The concerns parents did express included an increase in services for children under two years of age and a broader range in times, days, and number of hours when programs are open. On items related to *Te Whāriki*, teachers reported a greater confidence in using *Te Whāriki*, in creating environments that support children's learning, in meeting the individual needs of children, and in collecting assessment data for use in curriculum planning and for sharing with parents. However, results show that some aspects of *Te Whāriki* were more challenging for teachers to implement, and as a result did have some bearing on program quality. Teachers reported speaking te reo Māori every day, but this was primarily limited to greetings and commands. Additionally, 38% of the teachers reported placing a lot of emphasis on biculturalism, while 52% placed little emphasis on it. Similar data are reported for multiculturalism: It was highly emphasized by 29% of teachers, whereas 59% placed little emphasis on it. Multi-culturalism was most emphasized in programs enrolling more than five non-English speaking children (Mitchell & Brooking, 2007).

In the United States, several lines of research have examined the relationship between the implementation of DAP and issues of quality. One line of research has examined the influence of DAP on children's experiences in classrooms and a variety of outcomes. Most representative of this line of research are the "LSU [Louisiana State University] studies" (Charlesworth et al., 1993). Overall, the studies, begun in the 1990s, found that children in classrooms with developmentally appropriate curriculum exhibited lower levels of stress and had higher scores on the California Achievement Test than those experiencing less appropriate curriculum (Charlesworth, 1998). However, a recent review of other studies questions the influence of DAP on children's academic achievement (Van Horn et al., 2005).

A second line of research examining the influence of state-mandated standards and educational reforms contained in No Child Left Behind on teaching practices and curriculum in early childhood classrooms found a movement away from practices aligned with DAP as teachers struggle to comply with such com-peting demands (Goldstein, 2007, 2008). These two lines of research indicate that teaching practices and curriculum as outlined in DAP do have an influence on the ways teachers teach and on children's classroom experiences. However, quality is a contested term, and whether or not DAP delivers the type of quality parents, policy makers, and others want remains an open question.

Critique

It is paradoxical that a number of the critiques of *Te Whāriki* are leveled at its distinctive and groundbreaking features. It is the case that some of *Te Whāriki*'s most distinctive features pose a significant challenge to willing but unprepared practitioners. Alternatively, some critiques may result from the inability of some practitioners and programs to rise to the expectations set by *Te Whāriki* or from those who have not bought into the philosophical and theoretical tenets of *Te Whāriki*. A final set of critiques include calls for legitimate improvements and changes.

A first critique challenges the non-prescriptive nature of *Te Whāriki* and the quality of implementation. Negotiating and applying such a complex and challenging curriculum places a huge responsibility on the shoulders of early childhood educators. The impact of *Te Whāriki* in raising the "quality"[2] of early childhood education in Aotearoa New Zealand can only be understood in the context that its introduction was followed by a state commitment to increasing the level of teacher qualifications. The introduction of *Te Whāriki* posed challenges for early childhood programs, which, unlike state-funded kindergartens, were at that time largely staffed by untrained teachers. A new approach to early childhood education was required in which each early childhood center's educators were to work with parents and children to "weave" their own curriculum "whāriki." Joy Cullen has expressed a concern that teachers "have considerable autonomy in their use of the curriculum and also considerable potential for undervaluing the theoretical underpinnings of *Te Whāriki*. Because *Te Whāriki* is principled rather than prescriptive it relies heavily on teacher qualities to guide teaching practices" (Cullen, 2008, p. 10). This non-prescriptiveness, whilst empowering for well-qualified early childhood teachers, is clearly more problematic where staff are not well prepared to deliver on its expectations.

In 1997, one year after *Te Whāriki* was published, Helen May and Margaret Carr, co-writers of *Te Whāriki*, expressed their desire to ensure that the curriculum be implemented to its fullest potential. They urged that the government assume responsibility to ensure that the structural fabric of funding levels, quality staffing, and training requirements be put in place, without which the new curriculum "will not make much of a difference for children" (May & Carr, 1997, p. 235). Fortunately, the Labour-led government elected in 1999 demonstrated a commitment to the early childhood sector, recognizing the need to support early childhood educators to gain sufficient understanding of "the theoretical complexities of *Te Whāriki*" and "the necessary professional skills to enable them 'to weave' their centre's curriculum whāriki" (May, 2007, p. 138). This government instigated a sector-wide consultation process, resulting in a 10-year strategic plan for the early childhood sector (Ministry of Education, 2002) which aimed to ensure that by 2012 all early childhood educators would require a three-year tertiary-level minimum qualification. This expectation has recently been eroded by the current National Party-led government to an 80% expectation, with only 50% of staff working with under two-year-olds required to be qualified.

Te Whāriki has been critiqued for its non-prescriptiveness in relation to the domains of literacy and numeracy (Blaiklock, forthcoming; Education Review Office, 1998). Subsequent to the promulgation of *Te Whāriki*, the Ministry of Education produced national exemplars of assessment, *Kei Tua o te Pae* (Ministry of Education, 2004), which use narrative documentation or "learning stories" to record children's experiences. This method has been critiqued for the possibility that its open, responsive, subjective format may not consistently demonstrate whether children are reaching particular outcomes around literacy and numeracy (Blaiklock, 2010).

Another critique addresses the difficulties experienced by the mostly mono-cultural educator workforce in implementing *Te Whāriki*'s commitments pertaining to honoring the Māori language and cultural values and practices (Ritchie, 2003b). With regard to these expectations contained within *Te Whāriki*, the ERO, the national education auditing agency, has produced reports which indicate that the application of the cultural expectations as articulated in *Te Whāriki* is patchy (ERO, 2004), and that many centers are failing to develop strong relationships with their Māori families (ERO, 2010). Many teachers have reported struggling to include more than brief greetings and commands in the Māori language, such as "Haere mai ki te whāriki"—"Come to the mat." These usages can be viewed as tokenistic, when further, deeper ways of including Māori values are not being implemented. Further, researchers have pointed to the lack of research into the long-term effectiveness of *Te Whāriki*-based curriculum with regard to educational outcomes for children (Blaiklock, forthcoming; Cullen, 2008; Nuttall, 2005).

Conclusion

Te Whāriki continues to evolve as a curriculum, as does its implementation, which was not without difficulties for some teachers and directors, and its professional development. Yet, the development and implementation of *Te Whāriki* offer a template for how a national early childhood curriculum might be conceptualized and then put into practice. Through its distinctive features, some of which were new to the field of early childhood education, *Te Whāriki* has set a standard for curriculum development and implementation that marks a significant contribution to our field.

Notes

1 Kōhanga Reo is a national Māori-instigated and run movement focusing on the revitalization of te reo Māori through the provision of early childhood education

programs grounded in Māori values and culture, and utilizing the Māori language as the medium of instruction.
2 Recognizing that notions of "quality" are culturally and contextually bound, as per Tobin (2005).

References

Blaiklock, K. (2010). The assessment of children's language in New Zealand Early Childhood Centres. *New Zealand Journal of Education Studies*, 45(1), 105–10.
——(forthcoming). The effectiveness of Te Whāriki, the New Zealand Early Childhood Curriculum.
Bone, J. (2007). Breaking bread: Spirituality, food and early childhood education. *International Journal of Children's Spirituality*, 10, 307–17.
Cederman, K. (2008). Not weaving but drowning? The child.com in early childhood pedagogies. *International Journal of Early Childhood*, 40, 119–30.
Charlesworth, R. (1998). Developmentally appropriate practice is for everyone. *Childhood Education*, 74, 274–82.
Charlesworth, R., Hart, C.H., Burts, D.C., & DeWolf, M. (1993). The LSU studies: Building a research base for developmentally appropriate practice. *Advances in Early Education and Day Care*, 5, 3–28.
Copple, C. & Bredekamp, S. (Eds.). (2009). *Developmentally appropriate practice in early childhood programs serving children from birth through age 8*. Washington, DC: National Association for the Education of Young Children.
Cubey, P. (1992). Responses to the Treaty of Waitangi in early childhood care and education (unpublished M.Ed. thesis). Victoria University of Wellington, Wellington, New Zealand.
Cullen, J. (2008). Outcomes of early childhood education: Do we know, can we tell, and does it matter? Paper presented at the Jean Herbison lecture, New Zealand Association for Research in Education (NZARE) Annual Conference, Palmerston North, New Zealand, December.
Education Review Office (ERO). (1998). *Use of Te Whāriki*. Wellington, NZ: Education Review Office.
——(2004). *Catering for diversity in early childhood services*. Wellington, NZ: Education Review Office.
——(2007a). *The quality of education and care in Montessori early childhood services*. Wellington, NZ: Education Review Office.
——(2007b). *The quality of education and care in Steiner early childhood services*. Wellington, NZ: Education Review Office.
——(2007c). *The quality of education and care in Pacific early childhood services*. Wellington, NZ: Education Review Office.
——(2010). *Success for Māori children in early childhood services*. Wellington, NZ: Education Review Office.
Goldstein, L.S. (2007). Beyond the DAP versus standards dilemma: Examining the unforgiving complexity of kindergarten teaching in the United States. *Early Childhood Research Quarterly*, 22, 39–54.
——(2008). Kindergarten teachers making "street-level" education policy in the wake of No Child Left Behind. *Early Education and Development*, 19, 448–78.
May, H. (2001). *Politics in the playground: The world of early childhood in postwar New Zealand*. Wellington, NZ: Bridget Williams Books and New Zealand Council for Educational Research.
——(2006). "Being Froebelian": An Antipodean analysis of the history of advocacy and early childhood. *History of Education*, 35, 245–62.
——(2007). "Minding", "Working", "Teaching": Childcare in Aotearoa/New Zealand, 1940s–2000s. *Contemporary Issues in Early Childhood*, 8, 133–43.

May, H. & Carr, M. (1997). Making a difference for the under fives? The early implementation of Te Whāriki, the New Zealand National Early Childhood Curriculum. *International Journal of Early Years Education*, 5(3), 225–232.

Meade, A. (1988). *Education to be more: Report of the Early Childhood Care and Education Group*. Wellington, NZ: Government Printer.

Ministerial Council on Education, Employment, Training and Youth Affairs. (2008). *Melbourne Declaration of Educational Goals for Young Australians*. Carlton South, Victoria, Australia: Curriculum Corporation.

Ministry of Education. (1988). *Before five: Early childhood care in New Zealand*. Wellington, NZ: Government Printer.

——(1993a). *The New Zealand curriculum framework*. Wellington, NZ: Learning Media.

——(1993b). *Te Whāriki, draft guidelines for developmentally appropriate programmes in early childhood*. Wellington, NZ: Learning Media.

——(1996). *Te Whāriki. He whāriki mātauranga mō ngā mokopuna o Aotearoa: Early childhood curriculum*. Wellington, NZ: Learning Media.

——(2002). *Pathways to the Future: Ngā Huarahi Arataki. A 10-year strategic plan for early childhood education*. Wellington, NZ: Ministry of Education.

——(2004). *Kei Tua o te Pae. Assessment for learning: Early childhood exemplars*. Wellington, NZ: Learning Media.

——(2007). *The New Zealand curriculum for English-medium teaching and learning in years 1–13*. Wellington, NZ: Learning Media.

Mitchell, L. & Brooking, K. (2007) *First NZCER national survey of early childhood education services*. Wellington, NZ: New Zealand Council for Educational Research, Te Runanga O Aotearoa Mo Te Rangahau I Te Mataurnaga.

NAEYC. (2009). *NAEYC standards for early childhood professional preparation programs*. Washington, DC: National Association for the Education of Young Children.

Nuttall, J. (2003a). Exploring the role of the teacher within Te Whāriki: Some possibilities and constraints. In J. Nuttall (Ed.), *Weaving Te Whāriki: Aotearoa New Zealand's early childhood curriculum document in theory and practice* (pp. 161–87). Wellington, NZ: New Zealand Council for Educational Research.

——(2003b). Introduction. In J. Nuttall (Ed.), *Weaving Te Whāriki: Aotearoa New Zealand's early childhood curriculum document in theory and practice* (pp. 5–15). Wellington, NZ: New Zealand Council for Educational Research.

——(2005). Looking back, looking forward: Three decades of early childhood curriculum development in Aotearoa New Zealand. *Curriculum Matters*, 1, 12–28.

Qualifications and Curriculum Authority. (2010). National primary curriculum. Retrieved from http://curriculum.qcda.gov.uk/key-stages-1-and-2/learning-across-the-curriculum/spiritual-moral-social-and-cultural-development/index.aspx. Accessed April 30, 2010.

Reddy, T. (2003) Toku rangatiratanga na te mana-matauranga "Knowledge and power set me free … " In J. Nuttall (Ed.), *Weaving Te Whāriki: Aotearoa New Zealand's early childhood curriculum document in theory and practice* (pp. 51–79). Wellington, NZ: New Zealand Council for Educational Research.

Ritchie, J. (2002). "It's becoming part of their knowing": A study of bicultural development in an early childhood teacher education setting in Aotearoa/New Zealand (unpublished Ph.D. thesis). University of Waikato, Hamilton, NZ.

——(2003a). Te Whāriki as a potential lever for bicultural development. In J. Nuttall (Ed.), *Weaving Te Whāriki: Aotearoa New Zealand's early childhood curriculum document in theory and practice* (pp. 79–109). Wellington, NZ: New Zealand Council for Educational Research.

——(2003b). Whakawhanaungatanga: Dilemmas for mainstream New Zealand early childhood education of a commitment to bicultural pedagogy. Paper presented at the 11th Reconceptualizing Early Childhood Conference, Tempe, Arizona, January.

——(2005). Implementing Te Whāriki as postmodern practice: A perspective from Aotearoa/New Zealand. In S. Ryan & S. Grieshaber (Eds.), *Practical transformations and transformational practices: Globalization, postmodernism, and early childhood education* (vol. 14, pp. 109–36). Amsterdam: Elsevier.

Robertson, J., Gunn, T.R., Lanumata, T., & Pryor, J. (2007). *Parental decision making in relation to the use of early childhood services.* Wellington, NZ: Ministry of Education.

Rosaldo, R. (1989). *Culture and truth: The remaking of social analysis.* Boston: Beacon Press.

Tobin, J. (2005). Quality in early childhood education: An anthropologist's perspective. *Early Education & Development,* 16, 421–34.

Van Horn, M.L., Karlin, E.O., Ramey, S.L., Aldridge, J., & Snyder, S.W. (2005). Effects of developmentally appropriate practices on children's development: A review of research and discussion of methodological and analytic issues. *Elementary School Journal,* 105, 325–51.

13

PUBLISHERS IN THE MIX

Examining Literacy Curricula

Mariana Souto-Manning

Origins of the Approach: Commodifying Reading in the Early Years

The current context for early reading development is heavily laden with the necessity to conform to timely performance of certain behaviors and an accelerated trajectory toward conventional reading. Such a context is greatly influenced by the No Child Left Behind (NCLB) legislation (U.S. Department of Education, 2002). With the mandate that students must be reading by the end of third grade or risk never catching up academically, the intent of NCLB was "to ensure that every student can read at grade level or above ... [by] the end of grade 3" (Heath, 2005). Thus, much academic pressure has been placed on the early childhood years, including the push down of elementary curriculum (Genishi & Dyson, 2009) and the implementation of more standardized schooling experiences.

The concept of commodifying reading skills and behaviors gained a new meaning when funding for schools became tied to how students performed on test scores and on the trajectory and speed of their mastery of conventional reading. Schools and districts, especially those with lower tax bases (Kozol, 2005), sought a way of securing such funding, which could quickly go down the drain if a scientifically based (read governmentally defined) reading program was not implemented.

Scientifically based reading research, as defined by the federal government, favors certain companies and practices, thereby fostering the marketization and commodification of reading. According to Reading First, U.S. Department of Education:

> Scientifically based reading research (SBRR) uses rigorous, systematic, and objective procedures to obtain knowledge about reading development,

reading instruction, and reading difficulties. This type of reading research involves controlled experiments with data analysis and a thorough peer-review process.

(Reading First, U.S. Department of Education, 2007, para. 1)

Although federal sources claim that there is no prescribed list of SBRR programs, according to the Renaissance Learning website Accelerated Reader is one such official program. Principals and school districts may anticipate that purchasing the program will fantastically accelerate the reading development of young children prior to fourth grade—the federally mandated point of mastery.

In order to document students' reading development and to ensure that they will read at or above grade level by the end of third grade, students must develop reading skills more quickly and schools must find a way to quantify these skills. Young children are perceived in terms of needing to be fixed, as not possessing literacy in their homes (Genishi & Goodwin, 2008). In order to remedy this problem, to eliminate this deficit, accelerated reading programs were needed— programs that would quickly provide children with literacy skills and compensate for the apparent paucity of literacy practices, particularly in the homes of children from lower socioeconomic status backgrounds.

As a response to this mandate, Reading First federal grants were created to support high-quality reading instruction that is grounded in scientifically based reading research to ensure that every student can read at or above grade level by the end of third grade (U.S. Department of Education, 2002). The Reading First grants (including Early Reading First) program gave states both the funds and the tools they needed to help eliminate the reading deficit. The Reading First program was authorized under the federal Reading Excellence Act. It mandated the time by which children had to master a set of skills as opposed to considering the "real time" a child would take (which of course varies from child to child) to develop as a reader (Genishi & Dyson, 2009). It mandated a specific learning time and ignored individual differences.

High stakes and high accountability movements have been seized and commercialized by publishing companies, who package and sell programs labeled "Scientifically Based Reading Research." With the push down of elementary curriculum and teaching into early childhood classrooms (Genishi & Dyson, 2009), publishers entered the early childhood classroom with influence and power, providing programs that claim to accelerate reading comprehension. Their impact has been widespread and in many cases resulted in less child-centered and more curriculum-focused practices.

The purpose of this chapter is to critically examine the sources, aims, and features of early literacy programs which are (over)determined by scores, questions, and book levels. To do so, I take a close look at the Accelerated Reader program as such a representation.

A Situated Representation: Key Components and Features of Accelerated Reader

Accelerated Reader (commonly referred to by its initials, AR) is a computerized reading management program and a situated representation of standardized early literacy programs. It aims to accelerate reading comprehension and instill a love of reading in students. Over 65,000 schools have bought the rights to accelerate reading development by embracing the concept of the Accelerated Reader program, marketed by Renaissance Learning, Inc. By purchasing this program, schools engaged in a movement regarded as the commodification or marketization of reading (Biggers, 2001; Hibbert & Iannacci, 2005) along two dimensions: (1) purchasing a program to guarantee reading acceleration; and (2) measuring students' progress by points obtained through multiple choice tests, which could in turn be traded in a capitalist manner for external motivators such as tangibles (toys, erasers, candy) and social opportunities (e.g. ice cream parties).

According to creator Renaissance Learning, Inc. (2007), AR consists of the following steps:

1   Child reads a story within his/her zone of proximal development (ZPD).
2   Child takes a computerized multiple choice test of 5–20 questions that claims to assess comprehension.
3   Child receives a score and a number of points calculated according to the rate of accuracy (score of test taken) in combination with the level of the book. For example, chapter books such as *Charlotte's Web* (White, 1952) are worth many more points than picture books such as *Brown Bear, Brown Bear, What Do You Hear?* (Martin, 1967).

With the AR program, ZPD is commonly associated with specific colors and/or shapes that mark the books and not with the Vygotskian concept (1978) which extends the learner's knowledge and is defined as "particularly promising area[s] just beyond the child's reach" (Lindfors, 1999, p. 20). While the Accelerated Reader program promises to hasten reading development in primary grades, it provides little more than a management program for keeping track of the books students have read. It consists of a software program to generate multiple choice tests that claim to determine students' reading levels (such as the STAR report, which is generated from the STAR Early Literacy test) and understanding/comprehension of reading materials (such as the TOPS report, The Opportunity to Praise Students—based on the percentage of correct responses generated via a multiple choice test).

The role of the teacher is to support the publisher's program—giving praise whenever the computer indicates praise is due, mandating that students only read books within the level(s) identified by computer programs (Brown et al., 2010). The early childhood teacher is thus constructed as a proctor for publishers, such as Reading Renaissance, who seek to establish and implement teacher-proof curricula. The roles of children in such publishers' early literacy curricula fit the banking system of education (Freire, 1970), with little regard to issues of authenticity, interest, and motivation (Lindfors, 2008).

While AR establishes a daily period of uninterrupted independent reading, which alone would improve reading skills, there are many immediate issues surrounding such a system, including the lack of choice in book selection. Research studies regarding teachers' beliefs about motivation (Nolen & Nicholls, 1994) and reading (Sweet et al., 1998) have pinpointed that children need choice regarding what they read in order to progress toward independence in reading (Turner, 1995).

The practice of accelerating reading development has a dire impact on early literacy practices when children are in lock step with the No Child Left Behind clock as opposed to employing the concept of real time. As Genishi and Dyson (2009) eloquently described, real time is the period it takes each child to develop authentic language and literacy skills in purposeful and authentic ways. Distorting the time it takes a child to develop language and literacy can have very grave effects on a child's future as a reader specifically, and as a learner in a broader sense. Some of the ways that the Accelerated Reader program can hinder children's reading development are described below.

Uncovering Myths of AR Curriculum: Real Detriments to Early Childhood

In this section, I seek to uncover some of the myths propagated by the Accelerated Reader program and examine the real detriments of such a program in the field of early childhood education. I discuss these in the contexts of explaining the reasons why AR is not a magic formula and why AR is mostly prejudicial to children from low socioeconomic backgrounds. I draw on data collected in my second grade classroom in a public school within an urban area of the Southern United States serving a high-poverty population—around 80% qualified for free and/or reduced lunch.

Here I offer examples representing recurring patterns and themes from cases (Brown et al., 2010; Souto-Manning, 2010). These are cases, situated representations of prevalent patterns and trends (Dyson & Genishi, 2005), documented by other studies throughout the country. I relate my experiences of how the commodification of reading and the Accelerated Reader program impacted children as learners and readers. While my experiences may shed light on other contexts, the phenomenon of the marketization of reading and the use of publishers' literacy programs to make children's literacy development conform to the expectations of NCLB legislation will present itself differently across contexts.

Below I outline the relationship between such a pressing phenomenon and the particular issues that emerged in my second grade classroom. To document such instances, I collected audio recordings, anecdotal records, artifacts, and journal writings. I coded the data in terms of what I had been told by the publisher (institutional discourses, which I refer to as myths) and observations (presented here as narratives).

Myth #1: AR + External Rewards = Increased Motivation

It has been widely documented that reading development is closely linked to interest and motivation (Dweck & Leggett, 1988; Eccles et al., 1998; Gee, 2007; Guthrie & Wigfield, 2000; Nolen & Nicholls, 1994; Sweet et al., 1998; Turner, 1995). Children as young as three, four, and five read extremely complex texts in order to play video games and engage in Web 2.0 technology activities (Gee, 2007; Vasquez, 2010). Practices that focus on competition and comparing children in terms of extrinsic motivators (e.g. points in the AR program) can lead to less motivation and hinder intrinsic motivation and behaviors toward reading (Eccles et al., 1998). Guthrie and Wigfield (2000) found that "becoming an excellent, active reader involves attunement of motivational processes with cognitive and language processes in reading" (p. 408).

When students' selections of books are restricted to a certain level, as with the Accelerated Reader program, students' interests are placed in check. According to the Accelerated Reader program, students are to read within a certain level until they can score a certain percentage across a number of books within that fixed level. This is how they gain access to the following level. Nevertheless, in my second grade classroom students grew discouraged by such a process, which deeply and negatively affected reading behavior and motivation. This is illustrated by the representative passage below:[1]

DANIEL: I used to like reading.

TEACHER: Really? And you don't like it anymore?

DANIEL: No. I don't like to read at school. Only at home. At school I have to read these dumb books. They are stupid. At home I get to read Harry Potter and other stuff. Just 'cuz I don't understand every word, it doesn't mean I don't understand the story, you know?

Such feelings were expressed by many students, who indicated that pink books (referring to zero level books) didn't make sense and were consequently harder due to the fact that they had to be memorized rather than being memorable. Other students had expressed their disappointment toward reading by saying that because they were blue, or green, or red level readers, they could not read the same book as their peers and join in book discussions.

According to Rosenheck, Caldwell, Calkins, and Perez (1996), there seems to be no correlation between the use of Accelerated Reader and students' positive attitudes toward reading. In fact, studies (e.g. Carter, 1996; Stevenson & Camarata, 2000) have shown that the Accelerated Reader program devalues the act and concept of reading as it diminishes reading to being validated by a percentage score on a multiple choice test as indicated by the TOPS reports. Reading is only valued (or was in my school) if it yielded a score of 80% or above on the AR test. Otherwise, regardless of what it encompassed, it was deemed unsuccessful.

From such a stance, one that commodifies reading as extrinsic points worth goods (e.g. erasers, candy, and other tangibles) and/or social opportunities (e.g. ice cream socials), errors result in non-payment (no points). This practice completely ignores the fact that all learners make mistakes and that such mistakes are wonderful learning opportunities. In terms of detriments to early childhood classrooms, "such programs are not meeting the needs of readers but are destroying the desire to read" (Stevenson & Camarata, 2000, p. 10).

Myth #2: Purchasing AR = Getting a Reading Management Program + Books

Regardless of the implementation of the new reading program in my school, there was little money to purchase new books. Much of our budget was going toward purchasing the Accelerated Reader tests and computer programs which did not include books. This became a problem on two grounds. First, students could not find books that matched their interests, as many of the books available had been purchased years prior to their birth. Second, students could not find themselves in the books—characters were not always representative of students' backgrounds.

The money left after purchasing the Accelerated Reader program was limited. To make optimal use of the funds invested in AR tests, the media specialist (read librarian) invested in purchasing multiple copies of books already available in the library, so that each test could be used by many students. While this approach served the AR program well, it did not serve students well, as they could not find books that represented their interests or experiences. One case in point was a book on computer games, pop culture, and Japanese manga. These and other books that interested students, and books in languages such as Spanish, were unavailable because those particular AR tests had not been purchased or because they were not part of the AR program. Students were heavily discouraged from checking out books that would not yield points via the AR program.

One of my students, Gabriel, decided he would like to read several Harry Potter books. They were not part of his AR level and each time he went to the library, he received a lecture from the media specialist. As reported by Gabriel, she'd say, "You are such a smart reader, but no one will know if you keep checking out these books that are not in your level and don't give you points." According to the program, Gabriel would not receive points for tests taken out of his ZPD (read color and/or level). Without a doubt, AR affected students' self-perception and self-efficacy as readers, as reflected by the representative conversation between Levi and Gabriel below:

LEVI: You should definitely read Harry Potter … I mean, the new one.
GABRIEL: But, I can't. I tried to.
LEVI: Wha' [do] you mean?
GABRIEL: I went to the media center.

LEVI: Yeah. They have a copy there. You should definitely check it out!

GABRIEL: But, I'm only a red dot, so I can't get it.

(Souto-Manning, 2010, p. 109)

The very definition and concept of a good reader within the context of the school became defined in terms of how many points were generated and at what level one was reading. According to the AR system in place, Gabriel was not a "good enough" reader to read Harry Potter. The AR program overprivileged products (i.e. test scores) rather than in-depth, meaningful learning processes. Students are greatly influenced by schools' curricular expectations and practices. Thus, when teachers believe that overall understanding is more important than obtaining high test scores, they instill a sense that a focus on the learning process is more valuable (Roeser et al., 1996). However, when performance on a test and competing against peers are the focus (as with the AR program), there is less engagement and less learning as a result (Dweck & Leggett, 1988). The AR program sought to instill in teachers the belief that the focus of reading in the early grades should be on competition and performance, greatly disadvantaging students such as Gabriel.

In addition to focusing on product rather than on process, the AR program indirectly limited our library's holdings. This happened because there was no money to buy new books at my school due to the high cost of the AR program, which did not come with books. Thus, the shift in student population within the school was not represented by dated library holdings. Within the previous 10 years, the school had undergone great demographic changes, going from a 30% to about 80% free and reduced lunch rate. In addition, it had shifted from majority White to less than 15% White. African American and Latino student populations had ballooned. Nevertheless, the majority of students could not find books in the library in which they saw themselves (Sims Bishop, 2007).

Books in the media center portrayed African American characters who acted, talked, and dressed in White ways, and didn't portray their rich cultural background and history. They were just "colored White folk," as William (one of my students) voiced. According to Rudine Sims Bishop (2007), "the dearth of suitable material connected to the lives of Black children ... the persistent presence of stereotyped images of Blacks and assumptions of the natural superiority of whites ... lingered in one form or another in children's literature" (p. 24). In addition to these more systemic and inherent issues, the expense of the newly adopted reading management program meant there was no funding to diversify the library holdings as the student population diversified. This was detrimental to embracing diversities in the early childhood classroom.

These two realities linked to the lack of funds for purchasing books can be associated with the marketization of reading and represent real detriments of the AR curriculum. The program claimed to identify whether a student understood a book, sanctioned a reader's zone of proximal development, and censored what could be read. Thus, censoring and limiting choice of books were direct results of this program.

Myth #3: Accelerated Reader = More Reading + Increased Comprehension

The Accelerated Reader program requires that children must have daily uninterrupted independent reading time. Research on literacy development has highlighted the importance of reading practice as a means for improving reading rate and comprehension (Topping & Paul, 1999). With the growing discussion on the benefits of reading practice, more attention has been given to AR as a tool for increasing the amount of reading practice in schools. Nevertheless, while increased reading can certainly serve to improve reading practices, there is a lack of evidence indicating that employing AR specifically contributes to such advancements.

The research on the relationship between AR and early literacy development found that children who engaged in AR were encouraged to read more books compared to those who did not participate in AR (Krashen, 2002; Topping & Paul, 1999). While AR sets up daily independent reading time (which *per se* can be a positive thing), there is no evidence that taking the tests and being restricted to a certain number of leveled books have any positive effect.

While the time allocated to reading is positive, the lack of choice and the extrinsic motivation system established by the AR program can be damaging to young students. Instead of conceptualizing miscues as happy mistakes guiding instruction and growth (Goodman, 1969), AR penalizes students' mistakes in multiple choice questions. Instead of using such miscues to teach responsively, the AR test punishes students by not understanding or contextualizing miscues.

Often in my second grade classroom, regardless of whether they understood the story, students had difficulty answering the multiple choice AR questions due to decoding issues. For example, more than once Ky'isha called me to the computer to justify her answer choice, which was often logically valid, yet not recognized by the computer system. In addition, her use of African American Language (a language not acknowledged by AR) created a break in communication and great frustration. Ky'isha came to refuse to take such tests.

Overall, detriments of this curriculum included: (1) ignoring home literacy practices and cultural legacies as valuable resources; and (2) promoting assimilationist processes of erasure which sought to replace African American Language, Spanglish, and many other complex linguistic systems with the officially sanctioned AR language—Mainstream American English.

Publishers' Commodification of Reading as a Segregationist Practice

As I problematize the commodification of reading, I find the most difficult issue is how programs such as AR sponsor a segregationist atmosphere in which the children from upper SES backgrounds are provided assets (in terms of points and/or entry to social events), while those from lower SES backgrounds are simultaneously punished (Kozol, 2005). This happens because the AR program is built on the premise that students already understand the use of cue systems and can engage in reading as a process that encompasses the orchestration of semantic, syntactic, and graphophonemic cues within the context of Mainstream American English. It does not teach strategies used by proficient readers.

For example, when proficient readers come to words they don't know, they might think about what would make sense, return to the beginning of the sentence, skip the word and read on while looking for a forthcoming clue, go back and confirm, or check the illustration. The use of such strategies is essential for children to progress from emergent to more conventional readers—especially in a Discourse (Gee, 1996) which is secondary to many students. Trial and error and hypotheses testing are part of the process. AR's right or wrong approach to comprehension and disregard for nuances and approximations of emergent reading became problematic in my classroom. Seven- and eight-year-old students articulated how AR privileged students familiar with the school Discourse (Gee, 1996), typically those of White middle-class backgrounds. An example follows:

> As I listened to students in my classroom, it became obvious that they understood various problems associated with AR ... there was a clear understanding that children from ... higher socio-economic status performed better on AR tests ... Through the voices of my students, I perceived how AR was serving to darken the segregationist lines in my school ...

WILLIAM: Why [is it that] bus rider don't go to those AR parties?
TEACHER: What? That's not right. Sofia is a bus rider and she is at the party.
WILLIAM: Yeah, but I mean, most.
TEACHER: Why are you saying this?
WILLIAM: 'Cuz the [Central Project Housing] folk like me, Ci'Erikka, Tyrone, never go there. And like Levi, Anna, Jill, I mean car riders are always getting ice cream. And Sofia, when she miss the bus, her father bring her to school. She a car rider of sorts.

> Beyond socioeconomic status, it was clear that quite often White children were rewarded and African American and Latino/a children were excluded from AR parties ... AR was therefore further dividing the school in terms of demographics and opportunities, placing students in segregated groups and denying some the opportunity to build upon their background knowledge and home literacies. AR honored middle class literacies (c.f. Gee, 1996) and did not recognize the multilingual backgrounds of students in my classroom.

(Souto-Manning, 2010, p. 111)

AR continued to define good readers in a very biased way: White middle-class children were labeled good readers. The lack of such a label attributed to African American and Latinos was at best problematic, and at worst devastating to children's self-perception as readers.

In The Mix: Publishers and Early Literacy Programs

While publishers' early literacy programs such as AR (overdetermined by multiple choice tests and leveled books) claim to have the potential to provide some helpful resources for teachers and students regarding literacy development (such as allocating time for independent reading), they have degraded teachers and students to consumers of pre-packaged educational products available only for purchase (Carter, 1996; Hibbert & Iannacci, 2005). Accelerated Reader becomes the decision-making mechanism in the classroom, assessing and sanctioning student progress in terms of reading skills, comprehension, and choice. Regardless of me telling students that they were wonderful readers, my words were challenged and negated by a computer management program that crushed students' self-perception as readers as it rejected scores of 60% and below. As a teacher who attended the Reading Renaissance training, I was told to wait for a TOPS report before praising a student. Had I complied, the same students would be praised over and over while others would never hear a positive word from me.

From the perspective of AR, the publisher's program is a receptacle of expert knowledge, and teachers are limited in providing their own voice and knowledge in the classroom (Hibbert & Iannacci, 2005). The program institutes the banking system of education so criticized by Freire (1970) because it rejects students' historicity and sociocultural backgrounds. Such a perspective conceptualizes students as empty banks to be filled; if there is already another currency in the vault, it must be emptied out and replaced with the preferred currency. Such a practice promotes a process of erasure of home literacies.

According to this reading program, teachers aren't allowed to identify educational materials for their students and negotiate the design and delivery of their chosen curriculum (Hibbert & Iannacci, 2005; Shannon, 2001). In this sense, it is highly necessary that teachers engage in ongoing, authentic assessment of their students' needs, their program performances, and their own professional development when selecting and delivering products for stimulating critical thinking, thereby problematizing the purchase and use of such products (Stevens, 2003). While some claim that the AR program can supplement reading programs, in many schools it is the sole program available (Stevenson & Camarata, 2000).

The problem with the lack of teaching for strategies (and not engaging in ongoing assessment of students' needs) in a meaningful and authentic manner meant that those who had already acquired strategies employed by successful readers (such as drawing on semantics, syntax, and graphophonics, as well as identifying clusters within words) would continue making progress. Such students' home Discourses (Gee, 1996) were extremely similar to their school's Discourse.

Nevertheless, students who had not been previously immersed in schooling Discourses at home and had not acquired successful strategies for reading would fail without much assistance from their teacher. Often in these cases students came to believe that they were not successful readers. They had experienced plenty of negative reinforcement through repeated low scores in the AR TOPS report.

In terms of the impact of the AR program on children's literacy development, while external rewards for reading may boost students' reading practice, they frequently become obstacles to realizing pleasure and motivation from reading itself (Biggers, 2001; Carter, 1996; Krashen, 2002). The AR program promotes the commodification of the very act of reading, proposing that students are to be paid points (read external rewards) for the act of reading and selecting appropriate responses from a list. As such, this program corrupts students. AR promotes the stance that reading for the joy of reading is not a valid task—reading is only valid following a successful TOPS report.

For improving students' reading ability, their own choice of books is the primary and beneficial feature according to AR literature. However, because students' choices are limited by their level (ZPD as defined by the Reading Renaissance company), this feature of AR has been recognized as a major restriction to the development of lifetime readers (Carter, 1996). Choice has boundaries and is associated with a color (signifying a level). Hence, while the AR program proposes that students have choices, it assigns them identities, such as a red dot reader, who can only read books identified by red dots. Such markers are even placed on library cards, so as to censor what students can and cannot read.

Though short quizzes have been promoted as an immediate feedback for enhancing reading rates and skills, this trait of AR demonstrates the limitation that children's reading practice is central to the test rather than to the act of reading and thereby discourages diverse opinions and personal responses (Carter, 1996; Krashen, 2002). The Accelerated Reader program does not value children's approximations, means by which they learn to read, through hypotheses testing and miscues. It fails to recognize that children employ background knowledge and deep structure when reading. Additionally, because a computer-generated test is likely to provide students with few opportunities for extended activities beyond reading and interacting with text, reading practice is internalized as an isolated activity (Biggers, 2001; Stevenson & Camarata, 2000), and is therefore very problematic. In sum, reading practice as conceptualized by publishers and exemplified by the AR program bears the potential that children perceive reading as a competitive activity through answering questions generated by a computer and earning points toward prizes.

Note

1 Due to confidentiality issues, the names of all students portrayed in this chapter have been substituted by pseudonyms.

References

Biggers, D. (2001). The argument against Accelerated Reader. *Journal of Adolescent & Adult Literacy*, 45(1), 72–75.

Brown, S., Souto-Manning, M., & Laman, T.T. (2010). Seeing the strange in the familiar: Unpacking racialized practices in early childhood settings. *Race Ethnicity and Education*, 13(4), 513–32.

Carter, B. (1996). Hold the applause! Do Accelerated Reader & Electronic Bookshelf send the right message? *School Library Journal*, October, pp. 22–25.

Dweck, C.S. & Leggett, E.L. (1988). A social-cognitive approach to motivation and personality. *Psychological Review*, 95, 256–73.

Dyson, A. & Genishi, C. (2005). *On the case: Approaches to language and literacy research.* New York: Teachers College Press.

Eccles, J.S., Wigfield, A., & Schiefele, U. (1998). Motivation to succeed. In N. Eisenberg (Ed.), *Handbook of child psychology* (5th ed., vol. 3, pp. 1017–95). New York: Wiley.

Freire, P. (1970). *Pedagogy of the oppressed.* New York: Continuum.

Gee, J. (1996). *Social linguistics & literacies: Ideology in discourse.* London: Taylor & Francis.

——(2007). *What video games have to teach us about learning and literacy* (2nd ed.). New York: Palgrave.

Genishi, C. & Dyson, A. (2009). *Children, language, and literacy: Diverse learners in diverse times.* New York: Teachers College Press.

Genishi, C. & Goodwin, A.L. (Eds.). (2008). *Diversities in early childhood education: Rethinking and doing.* New York: Routledge.

Goodman, K. (1969). Analysis of oral reading miscues: Applied psycholinguistics. *Reading Research Quarterly*, 5(1), 9–30.

Guthrie, J.T. & Wigfield, A. (2000). Engagement and motivation in reading. In M.L. Kamil, P.B. Mosenthal, P.D. Pearson, & R. Barr (Eds.), *Handbook of reading research* (vol. III, pp. 403–22). New York: Erlbaum.

Heath, S. (2005). *Reading by grade 3: Reading first and no child left behind.* Retrieved April 21, 2009, from http://www.wrightslaw.com/nclb/reading.grade3.htm.

Hibbert, K. & Iannacci, L. (2005). From dissemination to discernment: The commodification of literacy instruction and the fostering of "good teacher consumerism." *The Reading Teacher*, 58(8), 716–27.

Kozol, J. (2005). *The shame of the nation: The restoration of apartheid schooling in America.* New York: Crown.

Krashen, S. (2002). Accelerated Reader: Does it work? If so, why? *School libraries in Canada*, 22(2), 1–7.

Lindfors, J. (1999). *Children's inquiry: Using language to make sense of the world.* New York: Teachers College Press.

——(2008). *Children's language: Connecting reading, writing, and talk.* New York: Teachers College Press.

Martin, B. (1967). *Brown bear, brown bear, what do you see?* New York: Henry Holt.

Nolen, S.B. & Nicholls, J.G. (1994). A place to begin (again) in research on student motivation: Teachers' beliefs. *Teaching & Teacher Education*, 10(1), 57–69.

Reading First, U.S. Department of Education. (2007). *Scientifically based reading instruction.* Retrieved November 24, 2007, from http://www.readingfirstsupport.us/default.asp?article_id=9.

Renaissance Learning, Inc. (2006). *Accelerated reader.* Retrieved March 21, 2006, from http://www.renlearn.com/ar/.

——(2007). *Accelerated Reader Enterprise.* Retrieved November 7, 2007, from http://www.renlearn.com/ar/.

Roeser, R.W., Midgley, C., & Urdan, T.C. (1996). Perceptions of the school psychological environment and early adolescents' psychological and behavioral functioning in school: The mediating role of goals and belonging. *Journal of Educational Psychology*, 88(3), 408–22.

Rosenheck, D., Caldwell, D., Calkins, J., & Perez, D.A. (1996). *Accelerated Reader impact on feelings about reading and library use*. Florida. (ERIC Document Reproduction Service No. ED399508.)

Shannon, P. (2001). A Marxist reading of reading education. *Cultural Logic*, 4(1), 1–11. Retrieved April 21, 2009, from http://clogic.eserver.org/4-1/shannon.html.

Sims Bishop, R. (2007). *Free within ourselves: The development of African American children's literature*. Portsmouth, NH: Heinemann.

Souto-Manning, M. (2010). Accelerating reading inequities in the early years. *Language Arts*, 88(2), 104–13.

Stevens, L.P. (2003). Reading first: A critical policy analysis. *The Reading Teacher*, 56(7), 662–68.

Stevenson, J.M. & Camarata, J.W. (2000). Imposters in whole language clothing: Undressing the Accelerating Reader program. *Talking Points*, 11(2), 8–11.

Sweet, A., Guthrie, J.T., & Ng, M. (1998). Teachers' perceptions and students' reading motivations. *Journal of Educational Psychology*, 90, 210–23.

Topping, K.J. & Paul, T.D. (1999). Computer-assisted assessment of practice at reading: A large scale survey using accelerated reader data. *Reading & Writing Quarterly*, 15, 213–31.

Turner, J.C. (1995). The influence of classroom contexts on young children's motivation for literacy. *Reading Research Quarterly*, 30, 410–41.

U.S. Department of Education. (2002). *No Child Left Behind*. Retrieved October 18, 2007, from http://www.ed.gov/admins/lead/account/nclbreference/reference.pdf.

Vasquez, V. (2010). *Getting beyond "I like the book": Creating spaces for critical literacy across the curriculum*. Newark, DE: IRA.

Vygotsky, L.S. (1978). *Mind in society: The development of higher mental processes*. Cambridge, MA: Harvard University Press.

White, E.B. (1952). *Charlotte's web*. New York: Harper & Row.

Part IV
Conclusion

To close the volume, we have selected two topics that span an examination of curriculum in different ways. In addition, we offer final conclusions.

In Chapter 14 Debora Wisneski and Stuart Reifel provide a discussion of play. Long an important part of the early childhood classroom across various curriculum models, current conceptualizations of curriculum and play present more conflicts. Wisneski and Reifel consider critiques of play and highlight possibilities for expanded understandings of play. They renew views of play by arguing for discourse that recognizes multiple forms of play in early childhood.

We acknowledged in the preface that our examination of curriculum in this volume was bounded. Yet, we also did not want to close the volume without pushing at those boundaries to indicate the wider understandings that must be negotiated. Katherine Delaney and Elizabeth Graue consider early childhood curriculum within "scientific, historical, social, political, and moral moments" in Chapter 15. In doing so they trace a history in which they claim understandings of curriculum have been rewritten, yet can still be reread. Their organizing concept is a palimpsest, which provides them a site to explore the meanings of the larger context for curriculum.

Finally, we close with a chapter that reviews major themes across these contributed chapters (Chapter 16). To do so, we utilize the volume's title, discussing how authors have provided opportunities for early childhood curriculum to be re-examined, rediscovered, and renewed.

14

THE PLACE OF PLAY IN EARLY CHILDHOOD CURRICULUM

Debora Basler Wisneski and Stuart Reifel

Play from the Start

Play is the highest expression of human development in childhood for it alone is the free expression of what is in a child's soul.

(Froebel, 1898/2005, p. 55)

Deep meaning lies often in childish play.

(Johann Friedrich von Schiller)

Children at play are not playing about. Their games should be seen as their most serious minded activity.

(Michel de Montaigne)

In play a child always behaves beyond his average age, above his daily behavior. In play it is as though he were a head taller than himself.

(Vygotsky, 1978, p. 102)

Play gives children a chance to practice what they are learning.

(Rogers, 1995, p. 90)

Play has been at the center of early childhood curriculum from the beginning of our history in early childhood education to present-day models—from Pestalozzi and Froebel's kindergartens to Montessori's method, and Rudolf Steiner's Waldorf schools to Reggio Emilia curriculum. As such, the descriptors of play in connection to early childhood education have been numerous—the play-based curriculum, play-oriented curriculum, play as pedagogy, play as curriculum, and play-centered programs. As Van Hoorn et al. stated:

> The idea of play as the center of the early childhood curriculum is grounded in work from four early childhood traditions: 1) early childhood practitioners, 2) researchers and theorists who have studied play, 3) researchers and theorists in the area of development and learning, and 4) educational historians.
>
> *(Van Hoorn et al., 2003, p. 4)*

In order to re-examine early childhood curriculum, we recognize the significant impact that children's play has had on our understanding of curriculum in the field.

At the same time, increasing pressures in terms of standardized child outcomes in the US and a resurgence of the school reform discourse indicate a devaluation of the play-based curriculum. Public school systems intentionally advertise their early childhood–preschool programs as "academically based" as opposed to "play based." School districts and private entrepreneurs across the country are opening "kindergarten boot camps," intense brief programs that drill children entering kindergarten on readiness skills such as singing the alphabet, counting, and cutting with scissors.

Miller and Almon (2009) alerted the public and the education community to concerns about the lack of play in early childhood education in their document *Crisis in the Kindergarten: Why Children Need Play in School*. Based on research regarding children's play and curriculum in kindergartens, the report highlighted the following:

- Teacher-directed activities, especially instruction in literacy and math skills, are taking up the lion's share of kindergarten classroom time.
- Standardized testing and preparation for tests are now a daily activity in most of the kindergartens studied.
- Free play, or "choice time," is usually limited to 30 minutes or less per day. In many classrooms there is no playtime at all.
- Most classrooms do not have enough materials for all children to engage in play at once; blocks, dramatic play materials, and sand and water for play and exploration are in particularly short supply.
- Teachers say that major obstacles to play in kindergarten are that the curriculum does not incorporate it, that there is not enough time, and that administrators do not value it.
- Most teachers say that play in kindergarten is important, although few teachers or administrators are able to articulate the relationship between play and learning.
- There are wide variations in what teachers and principals mean by "play."
- Many classroom activities that adults describe as play are in fact highly teacher-directed and involve little or no imagination or creativity on the part of children.

> *(Miller & Almon, 2009, p. 25)*

This report on the state of U.S. kindergartens is distressing when an overabundance of research has supported multiple benefits of play for the overall development of young children. In order to counteract such practices, educators, researchers, and pediatricians have begun a campaign to advocate for a place for play in early childhood programs. The campaign for play has recently reached the *New York Times*, in Stout's (2011) article "Effort to Restore Play Gains Momentum," and the *Chronicle of Higher Education*, in Bartlett's (2011) article "The Case for Play: How a Handful of Researchers Are Trying to Save Childhood." To frame this current struggle of play's place in the curriculum, in this chapter we will discuss what has traditionally been accepted within the dominant play-based curriculum paradigms drawing from early childhood practice, theory, and research. Also, we will explore many of the complications of using play as a form of curriculum as presented by teachers, theorists, and researchers, based on alternative ways of viewing play. Ultimately, in order to move us forward in this larger discussion, we hope to highlight possibilities to expand our understanding of play and our ways of using play as part of curriculum.

Current Practices of Play-Based Curriculum

There is a wide variety of play practice in contemporary early childhood programs, ranging from a total lack of play (no classroom play time or recess) to a more moderate amount of play, both indoors and out. While we can identify a few play-based programs with a significant part of the school day set aside for free play and projects, many who make use of play curricula are feeling pressure to reduce the time for play and substitute academics and test preparation. In this context of pressure for academic performance, it seems pertinent to revisit some of the research-based contributions of classroom play to young children's development and learning (Copple & Bredekamp, 2009; Frost et al., 2008).

The vast web of research on children's learning, development, and play reminds us of how play is linked not only to social and emotional development, cognition, creativity, language, and physical growth, but also to academics, including literacy, mathematics and physical science, and the social studies. These research connections and the lenses they provide us for viewing children in our programs are often forgotten, as issues like testing preoccupy us. And it is not easy for teachers to pay attention to multiple complex topics (such as play, or standardized assessment) simultaneously within intricate educational settings. So, we put out of our minds those ideas that we may believe to be important but that are not the topic of current practice or focus. We hope this chapter will remind readers of all the aspects of play that have been explored so fully in the past, with perhaps a few newer components that will remind us why we value play. With this we can look at play to see *all* the ways that children are learning and growing in our classrooms (Frost et al., 2008).

A review of early childhood programs and curricula reminds us that the variety of play included in classrooms reflects a wide range of beliefs about how play functions in the curriculum. Below we review several programs of play that represent a swath of the variety of ways play can be construed. Many of these programs derive from an array of overlapping theoretical lenses, including Piaget, Vygotsky, and Dewey. They bring differing emphases on how much children play, which play is emphasized, and in what ways the teacher is involved.

Some programs take the stance of trust-in-play, assuming that a range of important outcomes for the whole child are inherent in play processes. In other programs, the teacher and curriculum take a facilitate-play approach to enhance the developmental potential of social role play and make believe. Other programs reflect a learn-and-teach-through-play orientation, where the teacher becomes more involved in play to support non-play skills and concepts (Frost et al., 2008).

Trust-in-play programs bring their view of play from traditional, child development research and laboratory school practices. Free play allows children to engage with what is important to them, whether social, physical, emotional, or intellectual. In this view, the play process itself empowers children to take charge of their lives and their learning. Here, freely chosen play in early childhood is viewed as the best foundation not just for schooling, but for all of life. Teachers provide the tools (i.e. the toys) to support choice, and then interfere as little as possible so as not to disrupt the play process.

Teachers taking the facilitate-play approach believe that they can enhance some forms of play to promote positive outcomes. The developmental benefits of social role play, make believe, or games are supported by the teacher, with play props, field trips, board games, and teacher participation. One of earliest intervention studies relied on facilitated sociodramatic play to enhance intellectual, language, and other valued outcomes (Smilansky, 1968; Smilansky & Shefatya, 1990). In this vein, group games, including board games, have proven to be a kind of play where teachers can support social skills (such as turn taking, cooperation, and perspective taking) as well as logical-mathematical and physical knowledge (DeVries, 2002; DeVries et al., 2001; Kamii, 2003; Kamii & DeVries, 1980). The Tools of the Mind (Bodrova & Leong, 2006) curriculum has shown how teacher scaffolding can lead to more mature play, self-regulation, peer scaffolding, and oral language and literacy enhancement. In all of these approaches, children are supported to play in particular ways that research suggests contribute to learning.

We can also understand some classroom practice in terms of learn-and-teach-through-play. Many programs encourage more teacher involvement in play to support non-play skills and concepts. Bank Street has always respected the whole child by providing a wealth of traditional play materials such as block, clay, paint, and dramatic play costumes, but its program also focuses the teacher on how children solve problems as they play. The Creative Curriculum has children in play centers, while the teacher draws out creative responses (Dodge et al., 2002). The HighScope program has a long history of providing play centers where children make choices, using the "plan–do–review" process to guide their preferred play. Literacy play can be supported by teachers by means of having children play with literacy objects (e.g. a phone book by the play house telephone) and having children function with print in their play (e.g. pretending to read the menu when playing restaurant) (Roskos & Neuman, 1998, 2003). Play of all sorts provides a context where particular skills or concepts can be identified by the teacher, then supported by teacher involvement in the play. The use of intentional play in the classroom has been shown to contribute to long-term improvements in school and related life performance (Schweinhart & Weikart, 1996).

We can see the many ways that teachers can plan for and engage children in classroom play. Some programs and teachers value a hands-off approach; they set up the room and give the children great latitude and responsibility for their play choices. Other programs and teachers emphasize particular play materials and practices that have been shown to be associated with developmental and learning outcomes. Yet other programs and teachers plan their play with particular purposes, such as problem solving or literacy engagement.

Notably, our view of teacher involvement in play has evolved over the years, building from the trust-in-play perspective that defined practice in the early laboratory schools. Additionally, the insights that we gain from observing, questioning, and discussing the meanings of play *with* children have broadened our understandings of how play can be a tool for teaching young children (Reifel, 2007; Reifel et al., 2004). While we can trust children to play about issues that are important to them, the teacher can learn to contribute to children's thinking by highlighting concepts and ideas that arise in their play; additionally, during play the teacher can introduce concepts and ideas that have come up in other interactions or events throughout the day.

Beyond the Progressive Rhetoric of Play

Miller and Almon (2009) identify at least 12 different types of play in early childhood: large motor play, small motor play, mastery play, rules-based play, construction play, make believe play, symbolic play, language play, playing with the arts, sensory play, rough and tumble play, and risk taking play. Thus, when, as educators, we speak of play in curriculum, we must attempt to be clear about what types of play we are considering. All play is not alike. And while all play is not alike, our ways of viewing play are not alike, either.

Sutton-Smith (1997) provides a framework to consider different types of play. In his piece *The Ambiguity of Play*, he reviews play through a variety of disciplines beyond education, including anthropology, biology, psychology, literary studies, and sociology. From his analysis of research in these areas he found there to be seven general "rhetorics" of play. Sutton-Smith defines a rhetoric as an adopted belief system or set of values or ideologies that certain fields seem to adopt. According to Sutton-Smith, four of the rhetorics are grounded in beliefs from the Ancient Greeks (Fate, Power, Identity, and Frivolity), and three come from post-Enlightenment beliefs (Progress, Imaginary, and Self).

For the most part, the field of early childhood education has largely viewed play through one rhetoric—the rhetoric of Progress, operating from the notion that play is beneficial for children's growth and development. While we do not disagree with this rhetoric, we also argue that early childhood play curriculum will be limited if we continue to primarily view play only through this lens. New and alternative ways of examining play can provide insight into aspects of play that are not typically represented in traditional early childhood curriculum play models. (Two of these in particular are rough and tumble play or risk taking play, and points of conflict within play events often seen in classrooms, such as fighting and arguments.) By looking at play beyond progressive developmental domains educators will develop a more complex understanding of children's play in ways that may otherwise be disregarded, misunderstood, or prevented when play is considered only via one lens. The following sections address issues about play that complicate its use in the classroom, as well as highlighting alternative ways of viewing play that have not been traditionally a part of play as curriculum. While the examples are not extensive—nor are they all completely outside of the rhetoric of Progress—we do hope they spark an interest in the reader to consider play in a more expansive manner.

The Interpretative Turn in Play: Making Meaning

In order to understand more about interpretations of play in the classroom, researchers and educators are beginning to find ways to open up our study of play with lenses that call for multiple interpretations. To illustrate we begin with a story from Reifel et al.:

> "Why do all your stories have to do with fighting?" I asked a group of my kindergarten boys in the spring of the year. "It seems you are always chasing and killing and fighting."
>
> One child named Sam gives me an incredulous look, as if to wonder if I could really be so stupid. He explains slowly for me, "we're not fighting. We are *saving* in our stories." The other children nod their heads in agreement.
>
> (Reifel et al., 2004, p. 215)

According to our experiences playing with children and based upon the research of Bennett et. al. (1997), we have seen that there can be a disconnect between the teacher's intentions and interpretations of play and children's intentions and interpretations of the play. In the example above, the teacher (who actually was Wisneski) intended for children's dramatic play to support their literacy learning and interpreted the play as having violent intentions. After discussion with the children involved, she discovered the children were more interested in playing out their ideas of gender roles. (After more discussion the boys explained their saving was in preparation for when they were older men.)

In this example we could employ the use of a particular interpretivist lens—hermeneutics—to help us deconstruct our understanding of the moment, and then reconstruct the meaning of the play. Hermeneutics is a philosophically based process of interpreting texts using a chosen perspective, reflecting upon the perspective, and reconstructing a perspective taking into account a person's culture (VanderVen, 2004). In the case of play, play is the "text" that theorists and educators can interpret and re-interpret. As VanderVen explains:

> A hermeneutic approach could be brought to the reflection by removing the right–wrong aspect [of children's play], and simply requesting comment on the child's understanding.
>
> *(VanderVen, 2004, p. 202)*

In this case the teacher's interpretation was limited and she perceived the play in a negative manner, which may have led to a request to cease the play, thus cutting off the potential for a new learning opportunity. Asking for the child's interpretation allowed her to re-interpret the motives of the play, laying open a space for her to explore with the children, for example, gender in play.

Questions to consider from this perspective might be: What if the hermeneutic approach could become a part of the reflective teacher's process of retrospection? What if teachers were reading texts with an attempt to make more local knowledge and investigate the meaning making of the child? What types of curricular decisions would teachers make when using hermeneutical text analysis as part of their practice? If this is a part of teaching young children, how will teacher preparation programs assist teachers in becoming readers and investigators of play texts with children?

Beyond the Script: Play as Improv, Performance, and Rhizome

Another issue regarding children's play in the classroom is that child's play rarely follows the logical anticipated path that adults often expect. A common critique of educators' understandings of play is that our conceptualizations of play are often too rigid and our representations of play too scripted. However, there are researchers and educators who approach play as volatile, unpredictable, and more fluid. Sawyer (1997) has used psycholinguistic theory and his knowledge of jazz improvisation to analyze children's conversations in pretend play. He demonstrates how children are constantly signaling to one another about what they are playing and about their relationships. Children's pretend signals are similar to jazz improv in that there are some social rules that can be changed as situations arise. Lobman (2006) and Lobman and Lundquist (2007) have extended the play-as-improvisation idea further by drawing upon theater and Vygotskian theory to explore ways teachers can interact with children in play in a more responsive way. While building on the idea of play as unpredictable, Lobman's work allows adults to find a place in the play. In essence, the lens of improvisation opens up teaching and playing as inventing relationships and learning.

Another theoretical lens that allows us to conceptualize play as curriculum in a more expansive and unsettled way is through Deleuzo-Guattarian concepts, such as the rhizome. In Sellers's (2010) research on understanding children's process and perspective of play as a mode of curriculum, the child's play is described as "rhizomatic," "imaginary," and as "milieus," so that play can be seen with no true beginning or end, with unexpected connections, multiple directions, and avoiding assigning one meaning to an experience. Sellers describes (and literally maps out) some of the children's play as follows:

> For example, the milieu(s) of games being played (out) within the snippets of my research data used here (e)merge from/with/in several games that are happening alongside each other, games that are both separated and connected, games that in differing moments are either and/or both of the exteriority and the intermediary. The milieu(s) is/are constituted of three girls playing a Goldilocks game, which segues into a strong girls' game (involving more girls) through which they morph into butterfly strong girls. Also of the milieu(s) are similarly (e)merging games of a group of boys, (a) game(s) that slip and slide through Charlie's chocolate factory and a muddy monster game with a constantly changing Willy Wonka~monster~bear assumed by Kane.
>
> *(Sellers, 2010, p. 565)*

Through rhizo-mapping, teachers may be able to tend to the children's performances of play in the moment, follow the children's lead in understanding the play, and be less inclined to normalize children's behaviors.

Play as Identity and Community

Play, for some teachers and researchers, has been a space for figuring out who we (children and adults) are, as individuals and collectively. This often requires a process of examination and deep discussion with children about the stories which they play out, the other children with whom they play, and the process in which the play unfolds (Paley, 1993, 2010). Social issues regarding equity, friendship, community, and fairness often arise in our studies of children's play when using a social constructionist lens (Corsaro, 2003; Lash, 2008; Wisneski, forthcoming). Such a lens allows teachers to consider the process and context in which children are trying to make sense of their own identities and how they relate to others.

Postmodern-feminist theories have also allowed new ways of looking at identity formation, particularly viewing play as identity performance in which children use their sense of agency and power to embody multiple identities. Femininity, masculinity, and heteronormativity are challenged when researchers and educators have used these lenses to re-interpret our understanding of gender identity in children's play in a more fluid way (Blaise, 2005; Howard, 2010; MacNaughton, 2000).

Growing out from adults' fear that violent play will lead to violent children (Carlsson-Paige & Levin, 2005), Edmiston (2008) has examined how mythical play (pretend involving good and evil characters and themes) is an aesthetic experience in which children can explore with adults ethical dimensions of their identities. As such, then, play can become an ethical pedagogy in which children and adults can co-author their ethical selves in an approach that requires open listening and deep dialogue.

What these various perspectives of play provide for educators is the potential to address the many dilemmas that arise through play in the classroom and issues that are often not part of the dialogue of play in relation to curriculum. For many of the researchers and educators who study play in this manner, these issues should not be outside of the curriculum, but rather these issues *are* the curriculum. These lenses on play begin to break down the dichotomy of children's imaginations versus adults' pedagogical plans, and children's active bodies versus the adult desire to control.

Critiques of Play with/in Curriculum

Play and curriculum does not come without its critics. While play can be a valid form of experience in the classroom, there are those who contend we must clarify our definitions of play and attempt a different discourse of play that includes inquiry (Youngquist & Pataray-Ching, 2004). Still, others suggest that the ways in which play is controlled, regulated, and assessed are not conducive to honoring children's participation in their own learning or honoring the deep potential of knowing the world in play. Chappell (2010) states, "As curriculum and instruction have become open to the use of play—and children's material culture more generally—as a forum for learning, intersections have emerged between schooling and culture at large" (p. 1). Chappell recognizes that the adult world of consumer marketing, social injustices, and adult control shapes children's play and that these influences need to be recognized.

So, too, does the power of the child in relation to adults. As Ailwood states:

> The ideas of children's competence, children's participation and understanding the complexities of play also enable shifts in children's relationships with adults ... power relationships between adults and children in schools depend also on children's freedoms and resistance. Play is a key site where these are negotiated ... in continuing to question and problematize play, we can reveal relationships of power between children and adults, and between children and children.
>
> *(Ailwood, 2010, p. 29)*

Ignoring how power and children's agency in play in the classroom influence how we interpret play and include play as part of learning seems unfortunate from this perspective. Essentially these critiques of play as part of curriculum are calling on educators of young children not to take play for granted or assume all is knowable through and about play. Rogers (2010) suggests that play not be "viewed simply as a vehicle for delivering the curriculum, under the guise of 'play-based learning'" (p. 15). Rather, play should be viewed as the context and negotiated, co-constructed, relational space "to explore identities and desires, and consider questions of voice and power in the classroom" (p. 15). This requires educators to attempt to view play more from the child's perspective and to be more accepting of play that is sometimes viewed as "inappropriate" in the classroom.

Continuing to "Play" with Play

We believe play will always have place in the early childhood curriculum in some fashion as long as educators honor the way children explore the world and express themselves through this medium. In this chapter we hoped to outline and examine myriad ways in which play has been understood and examined in order to demonstrate the possibilities of its place in children's lives and the possibilities educators have in thinking about play. We hope educators and researchers will continue to "play" with the idea of play in early childhood programs. After reflecting upon play as part of curriculum we offer the following questions about ways in which the field of early childhood can support play in the classroom:

1 We hope educators will continue to recognize the multiple forms of play within a day that can be part of curriculum, including recess and outdoor play or scientific inquiry through play and identity performances. We hope educators will recognize the philosophical explorations of children in the context of societal issues like social justice, peace, and community. We hope educators will be willing to explore the world through children's play even when children's play is not familiar or comfortable.
2 While we recognize the strong connections early childhood researchers and educators have made between play development and learning the content of the disciplines (i.e. Drew et al., 2008; Fleer, 2008; Singer et al., 2006), we hope to see other connections of play and playful exploration *within* disciplines, such as science, art, literature, and mathematics. (For example, see Root-Bernstein & Root-Bernstein, 1999.)
3 We hope early childhood researchers and educators can continue to advocate for play by contributing to the discourse of play in the public arena in order to disrupt misconceptions about children's play as it relates to curriculum. One example is by challenging the dichotomy often made between "play-based" curriculum vs. "cognitively" or "academically" based curriculum.
4 We hope more teacher education programs will make a concerted effort to invite preservice and inservice teachers to *study and reflect upon* play through many lenses and as part of curriculum. We were disheartened to find that there are reports of early childhood programs that do not address play or specific curriculum models in educating preschool teachers (Lobman et al., n.d.). We hope more teacher education programs will offer a concerted effort to invite preservice and inservice teachers to study and reflect upon play through many lenses and as part of curriculum (Sherwood & Reifel, 2010).

5   We hope that the field of early childhood education will not limit our vision of play to something controllable and regulated within the curriculum but rather be able to embrace play as a space for exploring contentious issues, examining identities, discovering new insights into the study of the world, and much more than what we can even imagine. We believe this requires that broader theories and methods in research become a part of the discourse of play as curriculum.

Most of all, we hope the field of early childhood education will be open to play—with children in our classrooms and, as professionals, with one another.

References

Ailwood, J. (2010). It's about power: Researching play, pedagogy, and participation in the early years of school. In Rogers, S. (Ed.), *Rethinking play and pedagogy in early childhood education: Concepts, contexts, and cultures* (pp. 19–31). New York: Routledge.

Bartlett, T. (2011). The case for play: How a handful of researchers are trying to save childhood. *Chronicle of Higher Education*, February 20. Retrieved from http://chronicle.com/article/The-Case-for-Play/126382/.

Bennett, N., Wood, L., & Rogers, S. (1998). *Teaching through play: Teachers' thinking and classroom practice*. Philadelphia, PA: Open University Press.

Blaise, M. (2005). *Playing it straight: Uncovering gender discourses in the early childhood classroom.* New York: Routledge.

Bodrova, E. & Leong, D. (2006). *Tools of the mind: The Vygotskian approach to early childhood education.* Upper Saddle River, NJ: Merrill/Prentice Hall.

Carlsson-Paige, N. & Levin, D.E. (2005). *The war play dilemma: Balancing needs and values in the early childhood classroom.* New York: Teachers College Press.

Chappell, D. (Ed.). (2010). *Children under construction: Critical essays on play as curriculum.* New York: Peter Lang.

Copple, C. & Bredekamp, S. (2009) *Developmentally appropriate practice in early childhood programs serving children from birth through age 8* (3rd ed.). Washington, DC: National Association for the Education of Young Children.

Corsaro, W.A. (2003). *"We're friends, right?" Inside kids' culture.* Washington, DC: Joseph Henry Press.

DeVries, R. (2002). *Developing constructivist early childhood curriculum: Practical principles and activities.* New York: Teachers College Press.

DeVries, R., Zan, B., Hildebrandt, C., Edmiaston, R., & Sales, C. (2001). *Developing a constructivist early childhood curriculum.* New York: Teachers College Press.

Dodge, D.T., Coker, L.J., & Heroman, C. (2002). *The Creative Curriculum for preschool.* Florence, KY: Cengage Learning.

Drew, W.F., Christie, J., Johnson, J.E., Meckley, A.M, & Nell, M.L. (2008). Constructive play: A value-added strategy for meeting early learning standards. *Young Children*, 63(4), 38–44.

Edmiston, B. (2008). *Forming ethical identities in early childhood play.* New York: Routledge.

Fleer, M. (2008). Understanding the dialectical relations between everyday concepts and scientific concepts within play-based programs. *Research in Science Education*, 39(2), 281–306.

Froebel, F. (1898/2005). *The education of man.* Mineola, NY: Dover Publications, Inc.

Frost, J.L., Wortham, S.C., and Reifel, S. (2008). *Play and child development.* Upper Saddle River, NJ: Pearson.

Howard, R. (2010). What are little (gender "normal" heterosexual) kids made of? Performing and subverting the status quo in the dramatic play area. In D. Chappell (Ed.),

Children under construction: Critical essays on play as curriculum (pp. 107–26). New York: Peter Lang.

Kamii, C. (2003). *Young children reinvent arithmetic* (2nd ed.). New York: Teachers College Press.

Kamii, C. & DeVries, R. (1980). *Group games in early education: Implications of Piaget's theory.* Washington, DC: National Association for the Education of Young Children.

Lash, M. (2008). Classroom community and peer culture in kindergarten. *Early Childhood Education Journal*, 36, 33–38.

Lobman, C. (2006). Improvisation: An analytical tool for examining teacher–child interactions in the early childhood classroom. *Early Childhood Research Quarterly*, 21(4), 455–70.

Lobman, C. & Lundquist, M. (2007). *Unscripted learning: Using improv activities across the K-8 curriculum.* New York: Teachers College Press.

Lobman, C., Ryan, S., McLaughlin, J., & Ackerman, D.J. (n.d.) *Educating preschool teachers: Mapping the teacher preparation and professional development system in New Jersey.* New York: Foundation for Child Development.

MacNaughton, G. (2000). *Rethinking gender in early childhood education.* London: Paul Chapman Publishing.

Miller, E. & Almon, J. (2009). *Crisis in the kindergarten: Why children need play in school.* College Park, MD: Alliance for Childhood.

Paley, V. (1993). *You can't say you can't play.* Cambridge, MA: Harvard University Press.

——(2010). *The boy on the beach: Building community through play.* Chicago, IL: Chicago University Press.

Reifel, S. (2007). Hermeneutic text analysis of play: Exploring meaningful early childhood classroom events. In J.A. Hatch (Ed.), *Early childhood qualitative research* (pp. 25–42). New York: Routledge.

Reifel, S., Hoke, P., Pape, D., & Wisneski, D. (2004). From context to texts: DAP, hermeneutics, and reading classroom play. In S. Reifel & M. Brown (Eds.), *Social contexts of early education, and reconceptualizing play (II): Advances in early education and day care* (vol. 13, pp. 207–18). New York: JAI/Elsevier.

Rogers, F. (1995). *You are special: Words of wisdom for all ages from a beloved neighbor.* New York: Penguin Books.

Rogers, S. (Ed.). (2010). *Rethinking play and pedagogy in early childhood education: Concepts, contexts, and cultures.* New York: Routledge.

Root-Bernstein, R. & Root-Bernstein, M. (1999). *Sparks of genius: The 13 thinking tools of the world's most creative people.* New York: Houghton-Mifflin.

Roskos, K. & Neuman, S. (1998). Descriptive observations of adults' facilitation of literacy in young children's play. *Early Childhood Research Quarterly*, 8, 77–98.

——(2003). Environment and its influences for early literacy teaching and learning. In S. Neuman, & D. Dickinson (Eds.), *Handbook of early literacy* (vol. 1, pp. 281–294). New York: Guilford Press.

Sawyer, R.K. (1997). *Pretend play as improvisation: Conversation in the preschool classroom.* Mahwah, NJ: Lawrence Erlbaum Associates.

Schweinhart, L.J. & Weikart, D.P. (1997). The High/Scope Preschool Curriculum Comparison Study through age 23. *Early Childhood Research Quarterly*, 12, 117–143.

Sellers, M. (2010) Re(con)ceiving young children's curricular performativity. *International Journal of Qualitative Studies in Education*, 23(5), 557–77.

Sherwood, S. & Reifel, S. (2010). The multiple meanings of play: Exploring preservice teachers' beliefs about a central element of early childhood education. *Journal of Early Childhood Teacher Education*, 31, 322–43.

Singer, D., Golinkoff, R.M., & Hirsh-Pasek, K. (Eds.). (2006). *Play = Learning: How play motivates and enhances children's cognitive and social-emotional growth.* New York: Oxford University Press.

Smilansky, S. (1968). *The effects of sociodramatic play on disadvantaged preschool children.* New York: Wiley.

Smilansky, S. & Shefatya, L. (1990). *Facilitating play: A medium for promoting cognitive, socioemotional and academic development in young children.* Gaithersburg, MD: Psychosocial and Educational Publications.

Stout, H. (2011). Effort to restore play gains momentum. *New York Times,* January 6. Retrieved from http://www.nytimes.com/2011/01/06/garden/06play.html?_r=1&scp=1&sq=play%20children&st=cse.

Sutton-Smith, B. (1997). *The ambiguity of play.* Cambridge, MA: Harvard University Press.

Van Hoorn, J., Nourot, P.M., Scales, B., & Alward, K.R. (2003). *Play at the center of the curriculum.* Upper Saddle River, NJ: Merrill/Prentice Hall.

VanderVen, K. (2004). Beyond fun and games towards a meaningful theory of play: Can a hermeneutic perspective contribute? In S. Reifel & M. Brown (Eds.), *Social contexts of early education, and reconceptualizing play (II): Advances in early education and day care* (vol. 13, pp. 165–206). New York: JAI/Elsevier.

Vygostky, L.S. (1978). *Mind in society: The development of higher psychological processes.* Cambridge, MA: Harvard University Press.

Wisneski, D.B. (forthcoming). Complicating the role of play in building classroom community. In C. Lobman & B. O'Neill (Eds.), *Play as performance: Play & culture studies* (vol. 11). New York: University Press of America.

Youngquist, J. & Pataray-Ching, J. (2004). Revisiting "play": Analyzing and articulating acts of inquiry. *Early Childhood Education Journal,* 31(3), 171–78.

15

EARLY CHILDHOOD CURRICULUM AS PALIMPSEST

Katherine Delaney and Elizabeth Graue

Introduction

What are the origins of early childhood curriculum? The foundations of early childhood practice have been written and rewrittten through contributions from the teaching and learning experiences of generations of teachers of young children. Whether guided by this collective foundation, developmentally appropriate practices, or local standards, early childhood curriculum today is increasingly detailed in terms of our knowledge as a professional community and our measures of children. However, in light of all that we know, it is striking that the curricular choices that we make as early childhood educators today seem to be more tightly aligned to standards and assessments than ever before. Districts and schools use this focus to justify curriculum and classroom environments that feels less like pre-K or kindergarten and more like first or second grade. Although professional organizations like the National Association for the Education of Young Children (NAEYC) argue our work should reflect the knowledge base of early education and measures of individual children's learning and development, we find ourselves tied to elementary school standards and testing (Bredekamp & Copple, 2009). Is this quantification of childhood something that is new to our practice?

This focus on evidence—where educators are urged to use observation and analysis to support their practice—has roots in the mid-19th century with the advent of the kindergarten movement. Focus on data and sciences has ebbed and flowed over time, with practitioners relying on developmental scales, age norms, and content-based standards and assessments to varying degrees across the years. This ebb and flow of curricular justification is what interests us. The push and pull of social, political, and institutional forces shape the early childhood curriculum, writing and rewriting how we engage with, teach, and learn from children.

We believe that early childhood curriculum is like a palimpsest. A *palimpsest* is a writing surface on which a story or a moment in history has been written more than once. As the ancients reused parchment or vellum, they scraped away earlier words or images to make room for new texts. However, words on the palimpsest are never completely removed. Instead, they reappear over time, seeping up through later writings. As with a palimpsest, the institution of early childhood has been erased and rewritten countless times throughout history. So what today appears to us to be a new view of evidence-based practice, standards, and testing is in fact linked to past conceptions that have been scraped away, but not completely cleared from our collective memories. They have remained etched on the palimpsest of early childhood education.

Our goal is to carefully read this palimpsest, interpreting early childhood practices across time, space, and context. In doing so, we hope to better understand how these layers have been enacted within early childhood curriculum and still influence our work today. Early childhood curriculum reflects scientific, historical, social, political, and moral moments in time written into our practice. By examining the early childhood palimpsest and the writings of earlier curriculum we can gauge how conceptions of children, families, schooling, and education influence our work today. This will also help us to better understand the choices that we make today in our practice, theorizing, and understanding of children and childhood.

Looking Back across the Palimpsest

We'll begin by looking at the emergence of formalized settings for teaching young children. In the United States, this largely began in the mid- to late 19th century. Even this is tricky, though, since what is meant by "formalized," "teaching," and "young children" varies by theorist and institution. We have chosen to compare the conceptions and meanings of kindergarten across time by viewing several distinct moments—looking first at early childhood curriculum in the 19th century, then at Progressive educational reform and the Child Study movement in the early 20th century, the 1960s movement away from a play-based curriculum, the shift of focus towards standards in the 1980s and 1990s, and the current version in today's schools. These moments in time were chosen very purposefully, to examine fragments of kindergarten's story.

This chapter is an examination of how kindergarten has always been seen as a space between, reflecting the push and pull of the broader system of education. By choosing these moments of change, we examine how what has been written over time has shaped what meanings we carry of both the kindergarten and early childhood curriculum.

Kindergarten

Our current image of kindergarten is as a transition into formal schooling, the bridge between home and school. Tearful mothers and proud papas leave their children at the kindergarten door on the first day, anxious for their children to develop a love of learning and the ability to eat everything in their lunchbox. A look inside a kindergarten classroom finds low tables, brightly colored bulletin boards, and an environment distinctly designed to foster children's play. But on closer examination, the text of the kindergarten is not so simple, and this familiar context has undergone a quiet rewriting. The playfulness of the classroom is written over by the intentionality of academic learning—the formerly child-centered practice has become teacher-directed curriculum.

Learning in this classroom is driven by specific content knowledge goals and standards. The spaces formerly devoted to block building and dancing are populated now with writing materials, math manipulatives, and leveled reading books. The kindergarten schedule is anchored by teacher-led activities—guided reading, a math block, and science lessons. Only then do we begin to see what is missing—the housekeeping corner, the sensory table, the easels, and teachers engaging in imaginative play with their students. What we thought was kindergarten, a place to develop the social, artistic, and creative child, has given way to a different kind of educational space. But that earlier kindergarten is still there, slightly faded and written over with our new foci.

Kindergarten: The Earliest Writings

When the industrial revolution of the early 1800s began to draw rural families and new immigrants into cities for work, the demand for care for young children outside of the home exploded. Because formalized public school education did not begin until age six, charitable organizations known as Infant Schools began to care for children from infancy through to school age. However, teachers at Infant Schools found themselves in a bind. Charged with caring for these young children, the teachers needed a curriculum to guide their practices—however, none existed since children under six were considered to be too young to benefit from educational experiences. In response, the teachers developed a new curriculum as they learned from and responded to the children in their care (Beatty, 1995). Focused on replicating the lived experiences of children as the basis for their curriculum, the teachers engaged the children in learning new skills, thereby creating a curriculum where none had been before (Bloch, 1987; Beatty, 1995). Child-sized tools and materials (including brooms, brushes, hammers, and saws), as well as opportunities for sewing, music, and cooking, were central to the emerging curriculum (Beatty, 1995). While the curriculum focused on everyday tasks, teachers also provided instruction in reading, writing, and mathematics to those children who were ready to learn these skills (Bloch, 1987).

As Infant Schools grew and their curriculum became more developed, stories of learning in Infant Schools peppered the mainstream press. Educators emphasized the role of Infant Schools in facilitating the development of children (Beatty, 1995). Hearing this, many middle class families responded by opening their own private, tuition-based Infant Schools. With momentum added by middle class families, the idea of providing earlier school experiences for young children began to seem less unusual and surprising.

Many educational theorists and leaders, however, were not convinced that young children ought to experience school settings. Horace Mann warned that early instruction could harm the developing minds of young children, predisposing them to learning and emotional difficulties later in life (Bloch, 1987). Whereas families were advocating for earlier schooling experiences for their young children, reformers of the period believed strongly that children should be cared for in their homes by their mothers (Apple, 2006). In the face of expert advice, middle class families stopped sending their young children to Infant Schools and returned their focus to life within the family home (Bloch, 1987; Beatty, 1995).

With the collapse of the middle class Infant School movement, the children of working class and poor families were recast by societal and education leaders as *needing* the early schooling that their wealthier peers did not. In the case of these children, early schooling experiences were not seen as a means to greater learning, but rather as a way to save them from the poverty of their home lives (Bloch, 1987). These experiences were largely provided by newly emerging organizations known as Settlement Houses.

Located in urban centers like Chicago, New York, and Milwaukee, Settlement Houses were run by well-educated, single, white middle class women who wanted to help "Americanize" the large influxes of immigrants who entered the United States in the 19th and early 20th centuries. Settlement House teachers cared for the very young children of poor and working class immigrants while their mothers worked, and also aimed to "train" immigrant mothers in American standards of cooking, cleaning, and, particularly, childrearing (Apple, 2006). The responsive curriculum that had emerged in the Infant Schools in many ways carried over into the curricular practices in Settlement Houses. This responsive approach to the development, interests, and needs of young children greatly influenced the practices of these early childhood practitioners (Beatty, 1995). As this early form of early childhood education was being realized, however, new social changes were occurring in the United States that rewrote the emerging curriculum again.

Kindergarten: The Children's Garden

Beginning in the 1850s waves of German immigrants arrived in the United States. As they settled in the US, they also began setting up kindergartens (literally, "children's gardens") for their young children. Based on the philosophies and curriculum of Friedrich Froebel that they had brought with them from Germany, these kindergartens were run largely by mothers, often trained by Froebel himself. The kindergartens used a curriculum that Froebel based on his own scientific research about children and child development (Beatty, 2011).

Whereas middle class Infant Schools had been criticized for providing academic learning experiences at too young an age, Froebel's kindergartens had an entirely different focus. Froebel's curriculum focused on *aiding development*—a development that he had mapped through careful observation and his self-proclaimed scientific methods. Focusing on the development of children through specific activities, materials, and play, rather than academic subject matter, Froebel side-stepped arguments about the proper place of academic instruction for very young children.

The Froebelian kindergarten was characterized by a tightly scripted curriculum that used specific materials (*gifts*) and activities (*occupations*) (Allen, 1986; Beatty, 1995). Many of the gifts and occupations, including wooden puzzles and beads, blocks, marble runs, flannel boards and finger plays, and songs, are items still common to early childhood classrooms today. However, their goals were not playful, but tightly linked to the focus on the development of each child (Beatty, 2011). Knowledge of the pace and order of the 20 gifts and occupations required considerable teacher training and extensive knowledge and observation of the children and their development (Allen, 1986, 1988).

While Froebel viewed play as an essential part of growth and learning for young children, much like the gifts and occupations, the purpose of play was to further the development of the child. Froebel was skeptical about the benefits of spontaneous or free play, and preferred children to play with provided materials or with a teacher (Allen, 1988; Beatty, 1995). Teachers engaged in play with children in order to build warm and loving relationships with them, to gain better under-standing of their development and readiness, and to chart their proper development (Beatty, 2011). Play was purposeful, not playful.

By the 1870s, kindergartens had sprung up across the United States, as had a library of English language books for guiding the practices of teachers (Beatty, 1995). The Froebelian kindergarten movement was so compelling that even the Settlement Houses began to modify their schools to more closely align with the practices of the children's garden. As a result, Froebelian kindergartens were the most common curriculum in privately run, largely middle class schools, some public schools, and in Settlement House classrooms for the next 30 years (Allen, 1988). For the first time in the United States, an early childhood institution transcended class and social boundaries and began to organize around fundamental goals and theories of the learning of young children.

These children's gardens, with their scientifically based curriculum, strong following, and persuasive, charismatic leader, were well established as the foremost early childhood curriculum in the United States for the next 20 years. The writing of the Froebelian kindergarten has left indelible marks on the ways in which we continue to conceptualize early childhood curriculum, the role of teachers, observations, play, the environment, and the importance of materials within the classroom.

Kindergarten: A Progressive Rewriting

By the late 1890s, critiques of Froebel's children's garden were becoming increasingly prevalent. Both Progressive educators and scientists in developmental psychology and Child Study questioned the scripted nature of Froebel's curriculum and its benefits for young children. Just as the Froebelian kindergarten had rewritten early childhood as a "children's garden," these new participants in the field of early childhood began their own rewriting of what was best for the learning and development of young children. These new writings were part of a larger political and social conversation in the United States about the goals of public schooling and the growing belief that public schools were central to developing strong and lasting democratic nations (Lascarides & Hinitz, 2000).

For educators like John Dewey, kindergarten was an important place to begin this reform. For the Child Study movement, scientific understandings of young children meant that teachers could provide the most appropriate experiences for children at each age (Beatty, 1995). Educators and psychologists connected expectations for early childhood curriculum to expectations for society as a whole, deeply influencing their writing of the kindergarten curriculum.

Congruences in perspectives and in historical timing bind together these two fields in once again rewriting our understandings of the kindergarten. Just as Dewey opened the University of Chicago Lab School and began to design programs to engage children in kindergarten learning, Hall completed the first systematic study in the United States of the development of young children (Beatty, 1995; Lascarides & Hinitz, 2000). Basing his research in the predominantly Froebelian kindergartens of Massachusetts, Hall feared that the Froebelian kindergarten was undermining the natural development of young children, pushing children to focus on tasks that were beyond their developmental levels. As such, Hall feared that the kindergarten curriculum was in fact doing more harm than good (Hulbert, 2003).

According to Hall, the Froebelian kindergarten was too closely tied to gifts and occupations, which in turn prevented children from engaging with the world around them. To Hall, this was central to fostering proper development (Beatty, 1995). For example, Hall was concerned that the fine motor skills required for the paper weaving and intricate puzzles seen as central to the Froebelian curriculum were in fact too small and too focused for the hands of four-, five-, and six-year-olds (Beatty, 1995). Instead, Hall suggested that objects should be larger, less intricate and more suited to the daily experiences of the child. In addition, Hall advocated for activities to help children look outward and engage with one another, rather than focusing on task completion in solitude.

From the Child Study perspective, the kindergarten curriculum was meant to build upon the lived experiences of children, using what children viewed as important and relevant to their lives to engage them in meaningful and experiential learning. Advocated by Hall and others, this scientifically based perspective had an enormous influence on the development of kindergarten curriculum by researchers and teachers (Cuban, 1992). Armed with the support of the Child Study movement, Progressive school reformers rewrote the kindergarten as a very different garden.

In a radical departure from strict Froebelian curriculum, Dewey's kindergarten took an entirely experimental approach. Working with a small group of parents, who provided both moral and financial support, teachers at the Lab School "play [ed] games related to the [children's] homes and family members and ma[de] practical objects that they could use" (Beatty, 1995, p. 86). Dewey and the teachers at the Lab School aimed for a more modern approach to kindergarten that was more responsive to and knowledgeable about children and their development.

The classroom schedule for the Lab School reflected this, making time for housekeeping and cooking, arts and crafts, and songs and finger plays (Lascarides & Hinitz, 2000). Patty Hill Smith, a teacher trained by Dewey, promoted the role of unit block play for helping children recreate and engage with their world through sense making and imaginative play (Beatty, 1995). Children were also given time to engage with the natural world around them. The role of learning through engagement and experience was paramount in the modern kindergarten written during the Progressive period.

While the time of the Lab School kindergarten was relatively short lived, the writings and work of Dewey and Smith, as well as other Progressive era teachers and researchers, formed the strong curricular base on which the child-centered kindergarten curriculum was practiced into the 1960s. The work of the Progressives and Child Study scientists helped to redefine and isolate children's garden into a special year denoted as the transitional step between home and primary school. As the public kindergarten movement grew and became fully recognized as a part of primary schooling in the early 20th century, the ideals of the Progressive era were tempered by school-focused expectations. With the rewriting of the Froebelian kindergarten, however, the focus shifted from scripted learning of the gifts and occupations to a more organic approach to the child and environment (Russell, 2011). Interestingly, many of the gifts of the earlier Froebelian period remained, repurposed to the new Progressive era context and practices.

Until the 1960s, kindergarten continued to focus on the social-emotional development of young children and to respond with practical experiences designed as appropriate for five-year-olds. Kindergarten teachers were educated in programs separate from their elementary peers, focused on curriculum based on knowledge of child development and the tools that the environment could provide in supporting this development (Beatty, 1995). As a result, the kindergarten largely remained a place where young children could come to know themselves and others through play and interaction. The adopted elements of Infant Schools, the Settlement Houses, and Froebelian practices helped to shelter the newest writings of kindergarten from the academic focus of the primary school years.

The only major change during the period from the early 1900s to the late 1950s was the evolving length of the kindergarten day. The length of day shifted from part to full day then back again, as women entered the workforce during World War II and then retreated home as men returned to postwar jobs. The baby boom created a tidal wave of students that could not be accommodated through full day programs. These schedule changes were framed in terms of children's needs, although the social context and the needs of adults were often the driving force.

Conceptions of child development had shifted from Gesell's maturationism through Skinner's behaviorism to Piaget's constructivism. However, the kindergarten remained a garden where children were encouraged to play, to socialize, and to learn to get along. A 1957 article in the *Chicago Tribune* highlighted the educational value of kindergarten despite its focus on play:

> But the value of kindergarten ... lies not so much in intellectual accomplishment as in social development. Your child becomes accustomed to working in a group, conforming to school rules, accepting criticism and suggestions, expressing himself, and solving problems. He learns to repress certain impulses and express others. He learns how quarrels may be quietly resolved.
>
> *(Pompian, 1957, p. C35)*

This continued focus on the socio-emotional benefits of the kindergarten and its nature as a transitional space between home and primary school, however, was coming to an end.

Rewriting Again: Kindergarten as Springboard

As the Cold War translated into an educational arms race, many of these earlier practices were rewritten in favor of a curriculum that focused on readiness for first grade or outflanking the Soviets—whichever came first. An example of this evolution is *Time* magazine's consideration of the "outdated kindergarten" in 1960. An interview with a former public high school teacher turned kindergarten teacher revealed that "today's fives are tired of play; they are eager and ready to be doing serious work" (*Time*, 1960). The "serious work" this teacher imagined was learning to read, write, and reason mathematically. If children *could* do this kind of work, shouldn't the kindergarten curriculum help them do it?

The *Time* magazine article represents larger conversations about the uses, goals, and outcomes of kindergarten that emerged in the 1960s. While still seen as a transitional year between home and school, where children learned through play, kindergarten was marked by the notion of readiness for first grade, and kindergarten was rewritten as a launching pad for future success. Kindergarten became a critical moment in a child's educational career. Otherwise, parents and teachers might just as well consider kindergarten an "unimportant or expendable" year in the child's life (*Time*, 1960).

As kindergarten became an academic springboard for future success, two trends in the preschool years shifted kindergarten's baseline and, over time, its purpose. First, the War on Poverty produced compensatory programs for preschool children to ameliorate economically based inequality. One of these, Head Start, was conceptualized as a comprehensive child development program designed to address physical, social, educational, and emotional development. Initially designed as a six-week summer program staffed by community volunteers, the purpose of Head Start morphed as theories and popular belief evolved over the types of experiences needed to overcome the problem of poverty. Head Start began as a social action program in which parents were explicitly recruited into teaching positions. Over time, however, the role of the Head Start teacher was professionalized, requiring teacher credentialing or certification. Head Start curriculum focused increasingly on early literacy, with student outcomes used as a measure of program success. The notion that kindergarten was too late to provide successful interventions propelled investments into Head Start and later public pre-K programs. For many children and their families the official transition into education came before kindergarten.

At the same time that social welfare programs supported early childhood initiatives like Head Start, more women joined the workforce, with a resulting rise in the number of children in childcare. Between 1975 and 2008, the proportion of women with children under the age of six who were employed outside the home grew from 38% to 64% (http://www.bls.gov/opub/ted/2010/ted_20100507_data. htm). This increase inserted a new transition for many children, with childcare (and not kindergarten) becoming the first out of home educational context for many children and families.

As more children came to kindergarten having experienced group educational settings, the traditional kindergarten focused on play seemed less and less relevant. Slowly, a different content, and therefore a different curriculum, established itself. First it was shapes and colors, then letters and numbers. The academization of kindergarten took off at warp speed with the advent of the standards movement, which was promoted as a tool for aligning education expectations and practices (Bredekamp & Rosegrant, 2002). In addition, it was argued that standards would make more equitable the expectations for all children (Bowman, 2006).

Kindergarten: The Most Recent Writings

Kindergarten was traditionally positioned as a transitional space apart, with different practices and curriculum from the rest of the K-12 system. However, as standards have given way to accountability, the kindergarten curriculum has become more closely aligned with the rest of the educational organization (Hatch, 2002). With the advent of No Child Left Behind in 2001, kindergarten's transitional role came to an end. Today, teacher knowledge of developmentally appropriate practices bumps up against external mandates, changing expectations of families, and pressures to prepare kindergartners academically rather than socially and emotionally (Goldstein, 2007; Graue, 2001; Hatch, 2002).

Whereas kindergarten teachers were formerly free to design programs with broad developmental goals and teach in ways that responded to children's interests, they are now required to work toward grade level standards designed to ensure that all children would read on grade level by grade three (Goldstein, 2008). And if grade level expectations do not exist for kindergarten, the solution is to simply scale down the skills and standards expected in first grade and apply these to kindergarten students. The specialized knowledge and skills of well-trained kindergarten teachers were exchanged for these trajectories, outcomes, and standards (Goldstein, 2007).

Two forces ensured the transition of kindergarten into the elementary program. The first, standards, defined the threshold skills required at each grade in highly specified terms. Most states had both early childhood standards, designed around developmental areas, and elementary standards, organized by academic content. In a striking example of kindergarten's new home, kindergartens typically used the elementary standards to guide their practice. Second, the kindergarten curriculum was set to a metric of child data. Careful work to meet the standards required equally careful work in documenting child growth. All kindergarten work was designed to be intentional, related to the curricular frameworks and standards set out by district staff.

Two additional and rather counter-intuitive trends also shaped the kindergarten curriculum. Slowly and pervasively the age at which children entered kindergarten changed so that it became a program for five- and six-year-olds rather than four- and five-year-olds. The kindergarten entrance cutoff, which 25 years ago was predominantly December or January, moved to a September cutoff as states addressed concerns about child readiness. In a context where children had more out of home experiences prior to kindergarten, it seems curious that policymakers would require children to start kindergarten at an older age. But wanting to protect children from inappropriate academic demands, districts went with the idea that older was better. Thinking ecologically, with kindergarten as the ecosystem, it could be said that the "graying" of the kindergarten was contributing to the very problem it was to solve. As kindergartners get older, more complex expectations become the norm, so that we need older kindergartners, and so on and so on.

What did this do to the kindergarten curriculum? The increased attention to elementary content—literacy, mathematics, science, and social studies—meant that activities outside these domains received less and less attention (Hatch, 2002). Free play time gave way to literacy centers; outside recess disappeared and became snack and a book. The notion of open-ended curriculum that followed children's interests through in-depth study faded, and scripted investigations took their place. Teachers became increasingly reliant on guides developed by content experts who developed activities and assessments derived from standards and benchmarks. Equipment and material that supported the imagination, the development of sensory, aesthetic, or social skills became curious artifacts from the golden age when children had time to play (Goldstein, 2008).

These changes signal that kindergarten is not so much a children's garden as the first step in an elementary assembly line. Kindergartens have come about as the result of complex social, historical, political, and economic forces. The kindergarten curriculum has been responsive to children but we have to ask *which* children? Is it the child of the immigrant, who we must socialize and Americanize? Is it the child of the middle class, who is assumed to come from a rich, nurturing home environment? Or is it the child whose scores will be used to judge the programs and staff? Is the curriculum actually a sorting device that creates the need for interventions for children who do not fit the specifications?

Conclusions

Curriculum is a reflection of our political, historical, and cultural contexts, embodying struggles over social practices and in turn rewriting the palimpsest of early childhood. As we look at the kindergarten curriculum of today, what traces of earlier writing still exist? Its status as a cultural icon of a major life transition endures, reflected in the tears of kindergarten parents and the media coverage of new-to-school students. Artifacts of the Infant Schools, Settlement House, Froebel and the Progressive era are seen in the design of traditional kindergarten materials like unit blocks and parquetry blocks, peg boards and finger plays, child-sized housekeeping materials, and the child-centered layout of the classroom. Recognition of the specific needs of kindergartners is seen in the training of kindergarten teachers, but that too is fading as the kindergarten is integrated into the overall elementary program. The drive to get children to grade level expertise by grade three pulls expectations and activity away from kindergarten's past, toward a hybrid that is much more like first grade. How does this make kindergarten like Janus (the Roman god of beginnings and endings), who looks simultaneously to the past and the future? What do we gain and what do we lose in this evolution?

For kindergarten to be a relevant institution, it should evolve. But evolution of institutions, much like that of ecologies, must be carefully managed so that elements remain in balance. We worry that we will lose something very important if we erase the notion of a child-centered kindergarten curriculum, responsive to multiple dimensions of development. While evolution is a part of life, in order for the early childhood community to maintain its connection to what we know and what we learn about children, we must be thoughtful about change. Our aim in this chapter was to read the early childhood palimpsest, examining moments, practices, and knowledge that we value across space, time, and context. The characters and plots have recurring themes authored by theorists and psychologists, reformers and educators. In current inscriptions of the early childhood curriculum many of these writings—so important in our institutional past—have been scraped away and written over. But we can still read them, especially if we look very closely. And look closely we must. Otherwise, we fear that the very essence of the early childhood community will be lost entirely, and what will be left is a standardized script. And shouldn't the story be about children?

References

Allen, A.T. (1986). Gardens of children, gardens of God: Kindergartens and day-care centers in nineteenth-century Germany. *Journal of Social History*, 19, 433–50.

——(1988). "Let us live with our children": Kindergarten movements in Germany and the United States, 1840–1914. *History of Education Quarterly*, 28(1), 23–48.

Apple, R.D. (2006). *Perfect motherhood: Science and childrearing in America.* New Brunswick, NJ: Rutgers University Press.

Beatty, B. (1995). *Preschool education in America: The culture of young children from the colonial era to the present.* New Haven, CT: Yale University Press.

——(2011). The dilemma of scripted instruction: Comparing teacher autonomy, fidelity, and resistance in the Froebelian kindergarten, Montessori, Direct Instruction, and Success for All. *Teachers College Record*, 113(3), 395–430. Retrieved from http://www.tcrecord.org/content.asp?contentid=16048.

Bloch, M. (1987). Becoming scientific and professional: An historical perspective on the aims and effects of early education. In T. Popkewitz (Ed.), *The formation of school subjects: The struggle for creating an American institution* (pp. 25–62). New York: Falmer Press.

Bowman, B.T. (2006). Standards at the heart of educational equality. *Young Children,* 61(5), 1–8.

Bredekamp, S. & Copple, C. (2009). *Developmentally appropriate practice in early childhood programs serving children from birth through age 8* (3rd ed.). Washington, DC: National Association for the Education of Young Children.

Bredekamp, S. & Rosegrant, T. (2002). Reaching potentials through national standards: Panacea or pipe dream? In S. Bredekamp and T. Rosegrant (Eds.), *Reaching potentials: Transforming early childhood curriculum and assessment* (vol. 2). Washington, DC: National Association for the Education of Young Children.

Cuban, L. (1992). Why some reforms last: The case of the kindergarten. *American Journal of Education*, 100, 166–94.

Goldstein, L.S. (2007). Beyond the DAP versus standards dilemma: Examining the unforgiving complexity of kindergarten teaching in the United States. *Early Childhood Research Quarterly*, 22, 39–54.

——(2008). Teaching the standards is developmentally appropriate practice: Strategies for incorporating the sociopolitical dimension of DAP in early childhood teaching. *Early Childhood Education Journal*, 36, 253–60.

Graue, M.E. (2001). What's going on in the children's garden? Kindergarten today. *Young Children*, 56(3), 67–73.

Hatch, J.A. (2002). Accountability shove-down: Resisting the standards movement in early childhood education. *Phi Delta Kappan*, 83, 457–63.

Henry, W.A., III. (1990). Making the grade in today's schools. *Time*, April 9, 135, 28–31.

Hulbert, A. (2003). *Raising America: Experts, parents, and a century of advice about children.* New York: Alfred A. Knopf.

Lascarides, V.C. & Hinitz, B.S.F. (2000). *History of early childhood education.* London: Falmer Press.

Pompian, L. (1957). At Age 100—The kindergarten is under fire. *Chicago Daily Tribune,* May 5, p. C35.

Russell, J.L. (2011). From child's garden to academic press: The role of shifting institutional logics in redefining kindergarten education. *American Educational Research Journal*, 48, 236–67.

Time. (1960). Education: The outdated kindergarten. *Time*, April 18. Retrieved from http://www.time.com/time/printout/0,8816,874054,00.html.

16

STRENGTHENING CURRICULUM IN EARLY CHILDHOOD

Nancy File, Debora Basler Wisneski, and Jennifer J. Mueller

Introduction

Looking back at this volume in an attempt to provide conclusions is a daunting but exciting task. We have covered a lot of ground from start to finish, revealing new information, thinking about what has been taken for granted, and finding ourselves contemplating the future based upon authors' suggestions and questions. In the end, one stance that resonates with us is that curriculum represents an "impossible fiction," a concept used by Walkerdine (1992) to critique teacher roles, curriculum, play, school, and power within a progressive pedagogy.

Where is the "impossible" for us, and where is the "fiction"? We find that most often the curriculum presented to teachers is predetermined. If we know enough about child development, enough about important content, enough about expected outcomes, then we can assume to plan from and toward an idealized curriculum. We believe we can, indeed, aspire to fully meet children's needs. This fictionalized story has resulted in a plethora of published curricula, all marketed as aligning with any of the potential systems of standards found from state to state and auspice to auspice. We have any number of "packages" available representing the curriculum for a group of children. This fictionalized story has also led to the teacher being positioned as the knower and the child as the known—as if human experience and identities can be controlled and fashioned into an ideal image, ignoring the complexity, uniqueness, and agency within each teacher's, child's, and community's context, and without imagining other ways of being.

Is this ideal possible or even desirable? We believe not. Any classroom teacher knows how quickly the classroom becomes a messy and unique context. Children bring their own backgrounds, their funds of knowledge, and, importantly, the questions that drive their quest to make sense of the world. Furthermore, is this form of curriculum sufficient? Is identifying the ends (in the form of standards, goals, and/or objectives that describe what children will know) and the means (in the form of activities and materials) all that curriculum is about? Ultimately, how much is knowable about the teaching and learning process, and thus predictable and controllable? The empiricists believe the task is within reach. From critical perspectives the stories are many and complex, ultimately resulting in a knowledge that is bounded and partial.

In this volume we have read thoughtful critiques that reflect upon the impossible fiction of our topic. Below we provide a summary of major ideas, followed by questions for the future.

Re-Examining, Rediscovering, and Renewing Our Understanding of Curriculum

Using the subtitle of this volume, we revisit the work below, identifying themes that have emerged across the contributions of different authors. While many distinctive directions are represented across the chapters, we also found intersections and linkages.

The authors who have written about curriculum approaches have helped us to re-examine what we may have known about, or felt we knew about, with fresh eyes. In Chapter 9, Horm, Goble, and Branscomb provided us a deeper under-standing of change over time in how infants and toddlers have been conceptualized by curriculum developers, a re-examination made possible by their comparative approach. In considering the ways in which curriculum approaches focus on diver-sity among children, we found ourselves thinking more deeply about HighScope and the Creative Curriculum with Michael-Luna and Heimer (Chapter 10). We found ourselves distressed when imagining Souto-Manning's task of engaging children as readers in a system in which they were labeled, directed, and managed outside of the teacher's own professional judgment (Chapter 13).

Yet, we also found reason to be hopeful in reading about Reggio Emilia and *Te Whāriki*. The profound respect for both children and teachers described by Stremmel (Chapter 11) and Ritchie and Buzzelli (Chapter 12) is inspiring. Many have attempted to base curriculum on Reggio practice. In some cases, this is approached as imitation for an ideal, referred to by Grieshaber (2008) as a "haste with which many early childhood practitioners have sought to 'Reggio' their day or their programs" (p. 509). But Stremmel has approached the task taking to heart the importance of context in influencing curriculum. In the case of *Te Whāriki*, translation to the United States has not been so obvious. Yet, we find there is much to learn from the New Zealanders' work in attempting to fashion and implement a bicultural curriculum approach that requires teacher reflexivity.

We note also a re-examination of our field's history. In Chapter 1, Wisneski located stories not often told among our own and used them to look differently at the work of curriculum development. In Chapter 15, Delaney and Graue presented a history that may not be entirely unfamiliar, yet by organizing it around the concept of rewriting via the palimpsest, they have invited us to re-examine what we believe we know and re-envision its meaning to our work. In a review of research, in Chapter 2, File offered a re-examination of how we have attempted to build knowledge about curriculum, questioning where we might most effectively move toward understanding teaching and learning.

Other authors have pointed us in the direction of rediscovering curriculum in our field. Those who have offered explanations and critiques of theory, File, Mueller, and Blaise and Ryan, have reminded us of fields of inquiry that may be old acquaintances yet can be met anew. In each case, the authors have led us to construct new understandings of the work done to lay the foundation for curriculum. File raised questions in Chapter 3 aimed at a (re)discovery of how child development might inform curriculum work. In Chapter 5, Mueller offered a review of literature from curriculum studies and curriculum theory that has been largely undiscovered/undiscussed in early childhood. And Blaise and Ryan pointed out new directions for the continued contributions from critical theory in Chapter 7. As a piece, they remind us to consider multi-faceted approaches to our work.

These contributions were further illuminated by the work of Hatch, Helm, and Cahill and Gibson, who shifted from the theoretical underpinnings of curriculum to discuss how thought moves into action. The intricacies of that process and the evolution of the struggle were poignantly illustrated by Hatch in Chapter 4. Helm offered an explanation of how one theory from decades ago has been rediscovered in the work she and others have done to develop project approaches to learning (Chapter 6). Finally, in Chapter 8 Cahill and Gibson contributed examples from their own work and their work with teachers in which teaching—the action—has been rediscovered via the lens of critical theory—the thought.

In Chapter 14, Wisneski and Reifel helped us to rediscover play, something that has been part and parcel of the early childhood curriculum conversation since our beginnings. The place of play has come in and out of favor within schooling as our historical and political contexts have changed. Just as we were buoyed by the possibilities for curriculum presented by Stremmel and Ritchie and Buzzelli, we found the possibilities described by Wisneski and Reifel a place for renewing our own understanding of the place of play in early childhood curriculum.

In the end, we aimed for this volume to be about renewal. We asked the contributors and ourselves to dig more deeply, to offer critique and pose questions. These are the types of dialogues that we believe can renew our meaning of curriculum. Given all that we have pause to now reconsider, we must ask, "Where do we go from here?" If the "impossible fiction" is truly impossible, then to what are we left to aspire? We hope that by raising the questions of this volume we have spurred readers to examine the taken-for-granted assumptions and ascription to dominant culture hegemony in their own beliefs about teaching and learning, in their own teaching, and in curriculum processes they engage in. The continued push to view curriculum as a living, shifting, process-oriented entity, we hope, is a call to us all to explore and re-envision our own curricular enactments, performances, and engagements with teachers, students, and children—to truly take on the responsibility of making curriculum empowering for all.

An evocation that has emerged throughout the chapters in this volume is the notion of how we go about supporting teachers and teachers-to-be to take on these more complex, involved, and ambiguous conceptions of curriculum. How do we do this whilst they struggle in the day-to-day realities of classrooms that insist upon fidelity to curriculum, standards, developmental milestones, and an assumption of knowledge as set and attainable? If the more contextualized, nuanced, post-structural, post-modern ideas that take on the empowering aspects of curriculum are to be realized more readily in classrooms, we argue that the crux of this lies in our ability to support educators to take on and to enact these visions.

While we have not delved much into teacher education in this volume, the "how do we do this?" question certainly begs attention to preparing and supporting those on the front lines trying to make sense of all that we ask them to de- and re-construct. Most of our early childhood teachers have been long socialized into the identity of being the "good" student. From there they have graduated into being the "good" early childhood teacher, who in this political moment is characterized by adhering to a curriculum and set of classroom enactments prescribed by an authority. A piece of what we do with them in our own teaching is to help them re-envision themselves and their roles as educators, which must entail a commitment to advocacy for children. And we believe we need to support them toward renewal of the fact that that advocacy will come in forms that they are not expecting and may not even be able to see initially, but that are essential for children nonetheless. We need to support them to see that they have a knowledge base that can guide them to be decision-makers and questioners in their classrooms and beyond. We need to help them embrace the ambiguity and uncertainty of their profession, coming to see it as an asset and space for contestation and agency.

This will involve those of us who live in the space of teacher education to interrogate our own curriculum decision-making and what that means for how we engage the students and teachers with whom we work. Could we put forward a book about curriculum without acknowledging that we ourselves create and enact curriculum? If we want our students to press the system to make curriculum more democratic for the children in their stead, then we must also look to ourselves and the systems within which we operate. It is no wonder our students view knowledge as compartmentalized and categorizable, when they take a separate "methods" course for each school content area, or consider separate domains for children's development, while we do little to help them integrate and understand relationships across disciplines and domains. We do little to move them to understanding the connectedness and situatedness of meaning making if we do not acknowledge their own positions' connectedness and situatedness within curriculum. It would seem that early childhood, given our homes across several disciplinary spaces (which continue to become increasingly diverse as the reconceptualist movement introduces new lenses and visions), might actually be the perfect space to continue to explore and apply multiplicity and diversity of perspective, in essence, to proliferate.

In envisioning the future we borrow from curriculum theorist Malewski to help us think about how the field can push forward. He notes:

> Proliferation does not require that we see the field develop in a mode of debate and synthesis where one cluster of theories overtakes another on the way toward "one right way" approaches. Rather it means to maintain a commitment to a field that celebrates the growth of its theories and stories—and to be seized by its vigor and intensity—and to assert our human inventiveness so as to personalize our theorizing regardless of how unsettling and unwieldy.
>
> *(Malewski, 2010, p. 23)*

In embracing this idea of proliferation perhaps we may give up our fictionalized dreams of the ideal teacher, the ideal child, and the ideal curriculum that constrain our imaginations of childhood and learning. Rather, may we create a space for conversation and performance of curriculum that includes multiple perspectives and possibilities for a multitude of teachers and *all* children to explore their own ways of becoming, engaging, and learning together.

References

Grieshaber, S. (2008). Interrupting stereotypes: Teaching and the education of young children. *Early Education and Development*, 19, 505–18.

Malewski, E. (2010). Introduction: Proliferating curriculum. In E. Malewski (Ed.), *Curriculum studies handbook: The next moment* (pp. 1–39). New York: Routledge.

Walkerdine, V. (1992). Progressive pedagogy and political struggle. In C. Luke and J. Gore (Eds.), *Feminisms and critical pedagogy* (pp.15–24). New York: Routledge.

INDEX